Meet Me At the Fair

100 Views of the 1904 World's Fair
St. Louis, Missouri

Original Stereoscopic Photographs by
T. W. Ingersoll

Michael W. Lemberger
Leigh Michaels

PBL Limited
Ottumwa, Iowa

MEET ME AT THE FAIR

100 Views of the 1904 World's Fair
St. Louis, Missouri

Original Stereoscopic Photographs by
T. W. Ingersoll copyright 1904

This edition published 2014

10 9 8 7 6 5 4 3 2 1

ISBN-10: 1-892689-16-2
ISBN -13: 978-1-892689-16-0

Printed in the United States of America

Rights Editor
PBL Limited
P.O. Box 935
Ottumwa IA 52501-0935
www.pbllimited.com

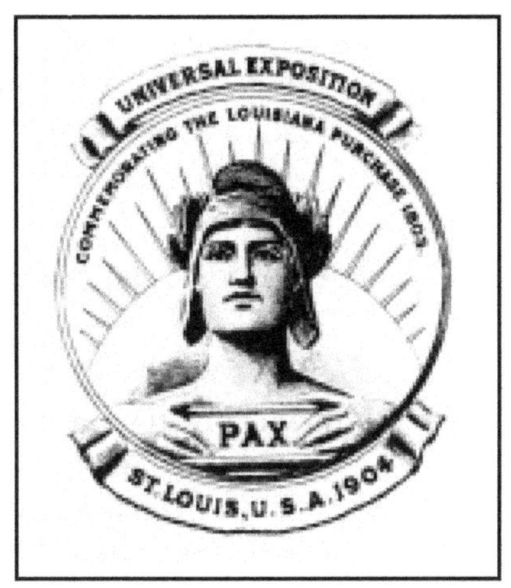

The Fair

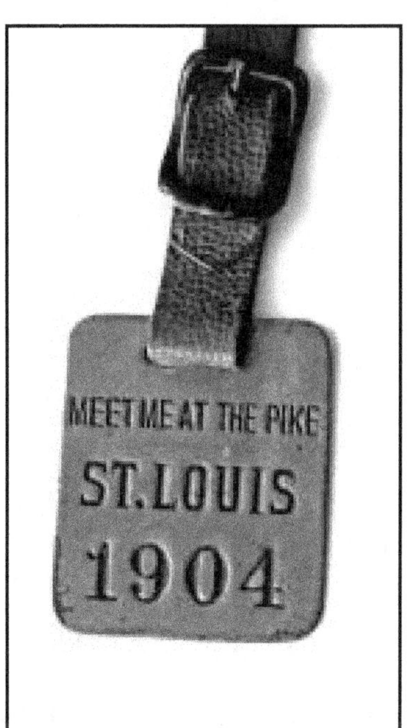

One of the most important events in the history of the new United States occurred in the early 1800s when U.S. President Thomas Jefferson negotiated the purchase of the Louisiana Territory from France, doubling the size of the country.

In December 1801, ownership of Lower Louisiana was transferred to the United States, and on March 10, 1804, the rest of the territory was formally turned over to the new owners.

As early as 1889, civic leaders of St. Louis had begun to agitate for some official commemoration of the one hundredth anniversary of the Louisiana Purchase. St Louis, a territorial capital in 1804 and a leading city of the West in 1904, seemed the logical location for such a commemoration.

The Louisiana Purchase Exposition Company was organized by May of 1901, and 93 directors were elected from stockholders. Funding of the fair – a total budget of $15,000,000 – was to be one-third federal money, one-third municipal bonds, and one-third raised through public subscription and contributions.

In June 1901 the decision was made to locate the fair at the western end of the existing Forest Park. However, it soon became obvious that the original 657 acres of the park would not be enough land, and so the fair's promoters leased Washington University's new campus, just to the west of the park, to make a site of 1,270 acres.

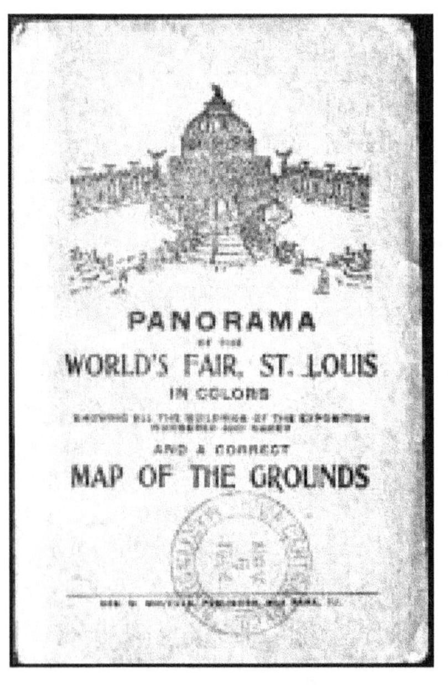

The St. Louis World's Fair – officially the Louisiana Purchase Exposition – was the largest fair held on American soil. In fact it was nearly as large as the four previous fairs added together. The Centennial Exposition in 1876 in Philadelphia, the World's Columbian in 1893 in Chicago, the Trans Mississippi at Omaha, and the Pan American at Buffalo together covered 1319 acres.

The work of building the fair began at high noon on Sept 3, 1901. On Dec. 20, the 100th anniversary of Lower Louisiana's transfer to United States, the formal groundbreaking was held, with a bonfire built over the chosen spot to melt the snow and thaw the ground enough for the fair president, David Francis, to lift a token shovelful of earth.

The fair was originally intended to open April 30, 1903, the 100th anniversary of the Louisiana Purchase Treaty. Because of the scope of planning and the time required, the opening date was put off for a year to allow more foreign countries time to develop and build exhibits.

On opening day, April 30, 1904, more than 200,000 people assembled for opening ceremonies. Ten thousand flags flew across the grounds, and from the White House in Washington, D.C., President Theodore Roosevelt turned on the electricity which would power the fair.

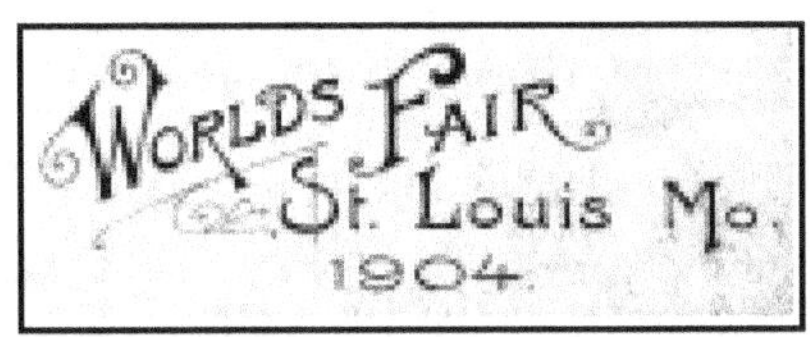

The 1904 Olympic Games were held in combination with the Fair, taking place on the campus of Washington University at the western end of the fairgrounds. Also the International Congresses, where the world's foremost leaders in every branch of human knowledge were invited to attend and share their developments, were a part of the Exposition.

Firsts at the fair included iced tea, ice cream cones, and the first concrete stadium in the United States.

There were 5 million square feet of exhibit space in the palaces, with outdoor exhibits occupying 6 million more square feet. There were 75 miles of roads and walks in the grounds. A map of the United States showed each state filled in with its prevailing crop, with cinder paths as the state boundaries. The Pike, the official amusement street of the fair, offered 448 concessions.

The observation wheel, 260 feet high, with 36 cars which could each hold 60 passengers, was moved to St. Louis from Chicago where it had been part of the Columbian Exposition in 1893, and The Liberty Bell was brought from Philadelphia to the fair.

By the time the fair closed Dec 1, 1904, twenty million people had visited.

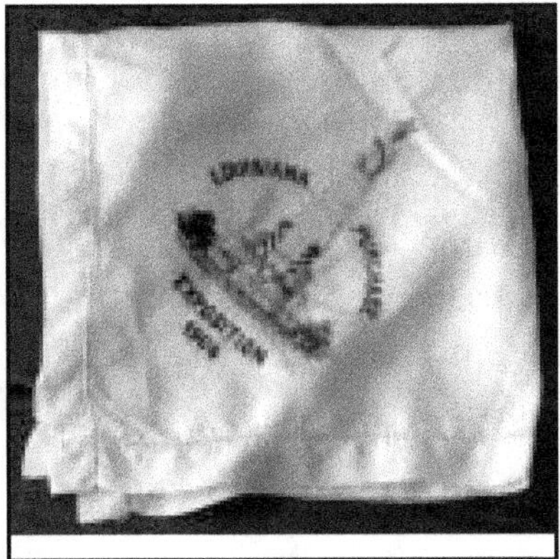

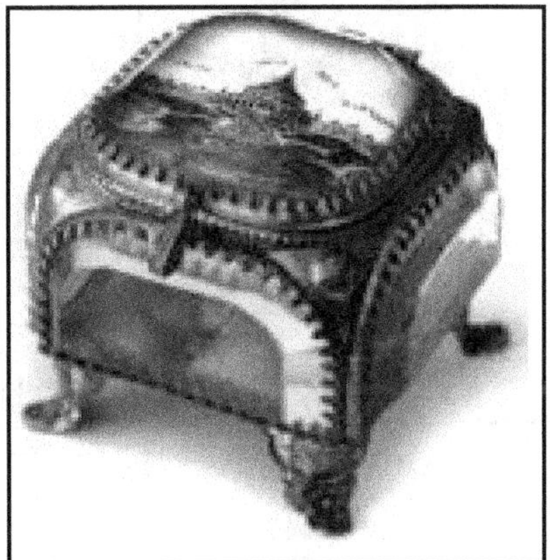

What's left from the fair? Not much; nearly all of the buildings planned for the St. Louis World's Fair were to be temporary. One exception, the central part of the Palace of Art, was intended from the beginning to become a city art museum. It still crowns Art Hill, overlooking the remains of the Grand Basin. One other survivor of the fair is still to be seen in Forest Park; the enormous aviary or "mammoth bird cage" is now part of the St. Louis Zoo. The Missouri Building, though intended to be permanent, burned shortly before the end of the fair; a pavilion was built on the site just after the fair and remains to this day. The statue of St. Louis, originally

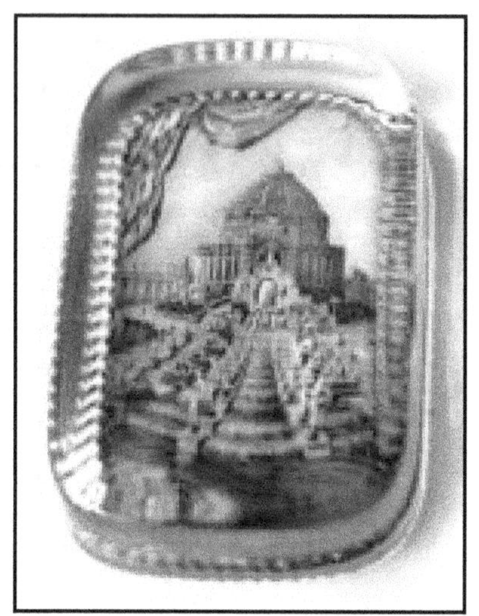

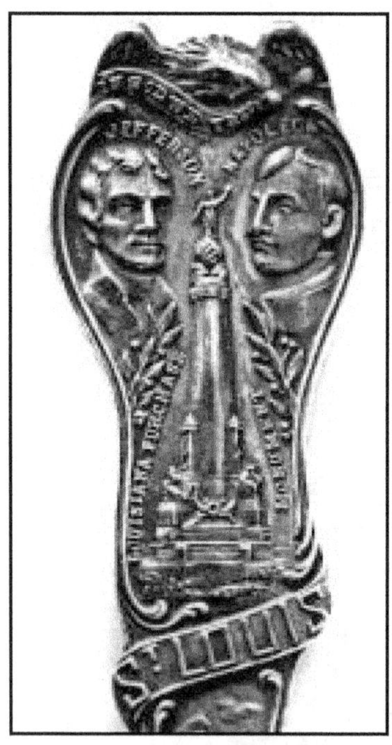

produced in staff (a mixture of plaster and fiber which could be molded, cast, and sawed), was recast in bronze and moved to the crest of Art Hill, where it remains. Fire hydrants installed for the fair offer an intriguing glimpse of the original street layout. The remaining buildings and palaces, most built of wood and staff, were removed.

By Sept 1908 the buildings were all gone and the park was restored to its original function. A few years later, the Jefferson Memorial Building was erected at the site of the main entrance to the exposition grounds, where it houses the Missouri Historical Society.

The Photographs

The 100 photographic views in this series were taken in 1904 by T. W. Ingersoll of St. Paul, Minnesota, and published as stereoscopic cards.

Truman Ward Ingersoll (born 1862, died 1922) was a well known and well traveled photographer who produced both stereoscopic and regular photography from about 1890 until well past the turn of the twentieth century. His office was at 27 East Third Street, St. Paul, Minnesota, where he was listed as a landscape photographer who offered printing for amateur photographers and was also a Kodak sales agent. Later his address is listed as 40 East Third Street in St. Paul.

By shortly after 1900, he was producing stereoscopic cards under his own imprint. He photographed many uniquely American events and scenes – not only fairs but national parks, the White House, battleships, sports events, and hunters with their prize trophies. He also published collections of stereoscopic views from the Middle East and other areas of world interest, and series of humorous views.

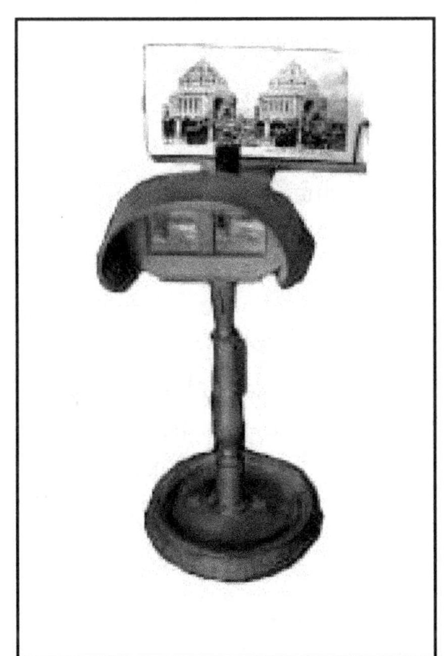

Stereoscopic views were taken with a special camera which had two lenses placed about two and a half inches apart, the same distance that separates a human's eyes. Each click of the shutter produced two simultaneous but slightly different photographs. The two nearly-identical photographs which form a stereo view were mounted on a stiff card about 7 inches wide and 3 ½ inches tall. When viewed with a special binocular viewer, the two photos blend together and appear to be a single three-dimensional image.

Stereoscopic views were extremely popular in the latter part of the nineteenth century, both for education and for entertainment. Mass production of a stereo viewer starting in about 1850 made the cards practical and pleasurable to view. The art form remained popular until the 1920s when the popularity of the cinema and halftone illustrations in periodicals sent stereoscopes into retirement.

Stereoscopic views were photographed in black and white. The cards were most often reproduced with a halftone publishing process, with many editions (including the originals of these cards) being released in colorized versions.

Though complete sets are relatively rare, stereoscopic cards can still be found at reasonable prices at antique stores and online stores and auctions. The more unusual the view, the more valuable the card is. Photo cards (rather than those reproduced by a half-tone process) are more valuable.

Though each original stereoscopic card showed two very similar views, we have reproduced just one photograph of each pair, since it requires a special viewer to get the three-dimensional effect of the cards and such an effect could not be easily reproduced in a book form.

We have presented the photos in the order set up originally by the photographer and publisher. For whatever reason, not all the photos of a particular area of the fair were published in order – for instance, cards 39 to 42 show the Tyrolean Village, but the Village also appears in photos 82 and 98. Photos 43 to 45 show the Philippine Village, which reappears in photo 73, 86, and 97, but the theme of the Philippine Village is first introduced in photo 16.

Some sets of stereoscopic cards included extensive captions printed on the backs. Though the set of 100 cards from which this book was produced did not include captions, we were able to locate thirty-nine of the same views in other T. W. Ingersoll sets which did include captions.

Those descriptive paragraphs are included here and credited as "*original 1904 captions.*" In a few cases we have corrected obvious typographical errors in the captions, but largely we have reproduced the publisher's original words, complete with unusual punctuation, creative language usage, and gushing enthusiasm. We have also included, without further comment, an occasional statement which today will be viewed with horror as politically incorrect.

Other captions have been assembled from books of the period or general sources about the Fair. These have been credited with the book title. In a few cases we were not able to locate either original captions or further information about the subjects.

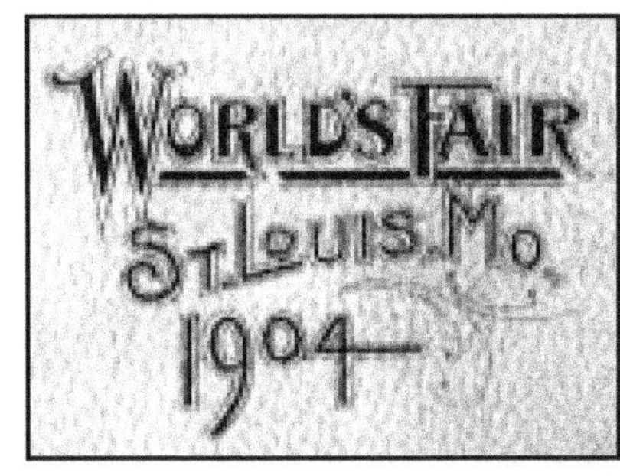

List of Illustrations

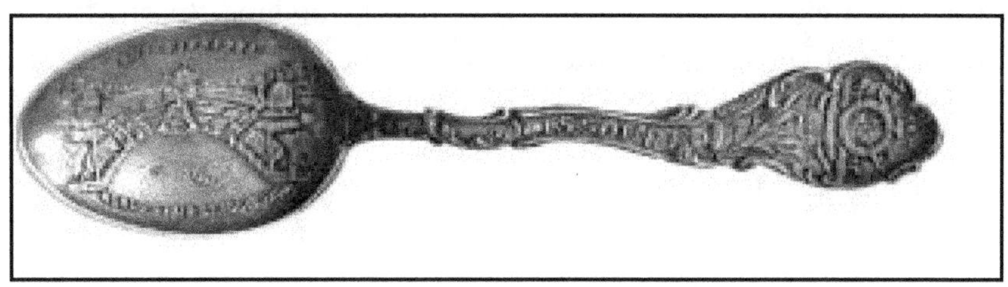

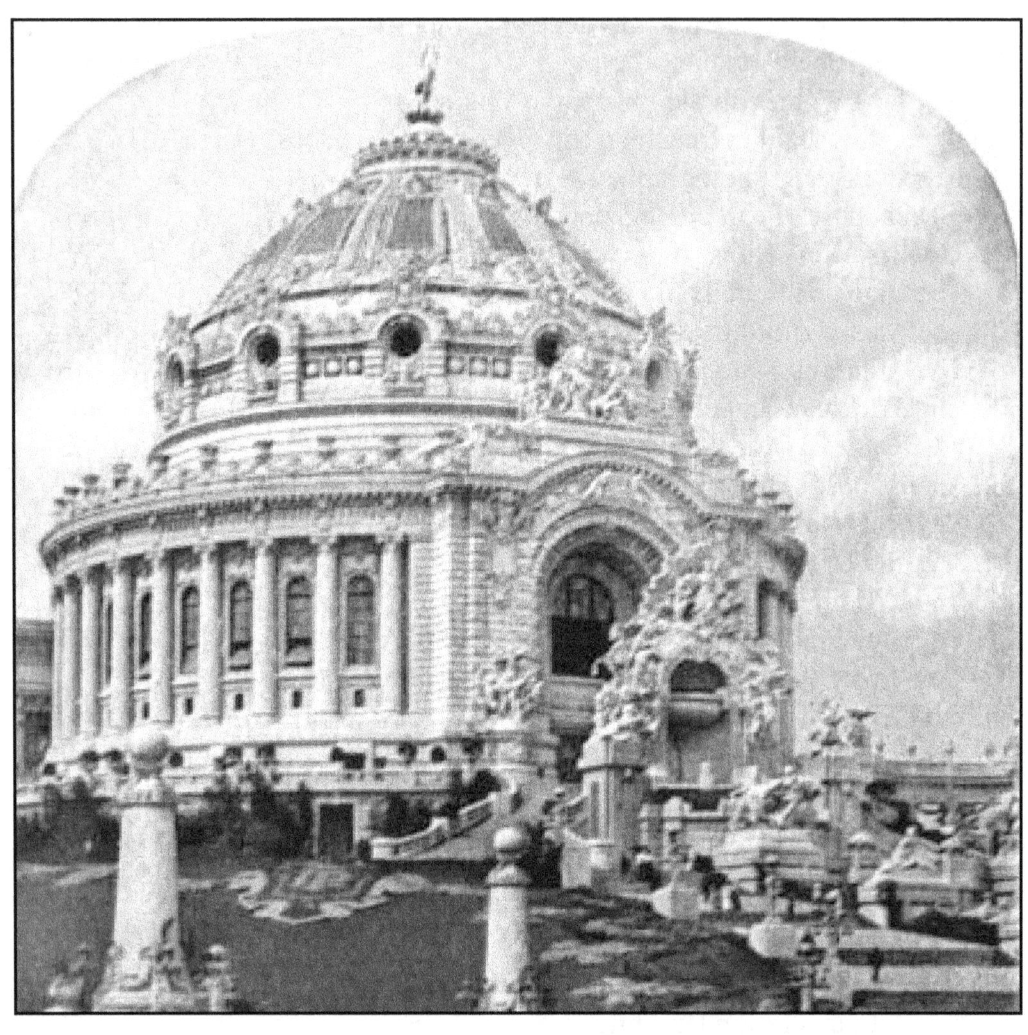

No. 1. Festival Hall

Festival Hall, the centerpiece of the fair, rose 200 feet above the crown of Art Hill, anchoring the Colonnade of States, which showcased the fourteen states and territories which had been formed from the Louisiana Purchase at the time of the fair. Festival Hall was the site of orchestra concerts and organ recitals throughout the Exposition, with a seating capacity of 3,500 and the largest pipe organ in the world.

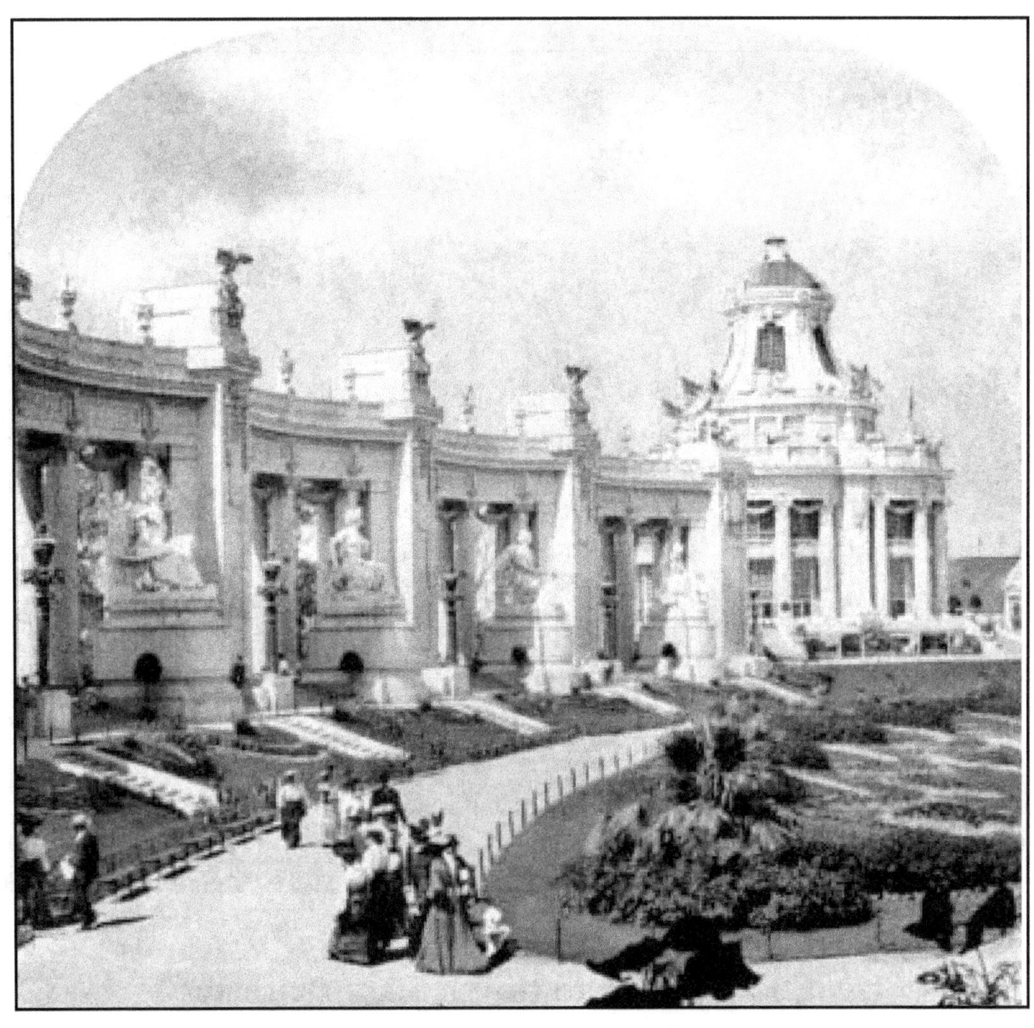

No. 2. The Terrace of States

Extending east and west from Festival Hall, the Colonnades were each divided into seven sections, and each section was devoted to the heroic, symbolic figure of one of the fourteen states and territories that have been carved out of the land embraced in the Louisiana Purchase. Over each statue, on the lintel of the Colonnade was carved the name of the state and the year when it acquired statehood. Our picture shows the western portion of this beautifully conceived and artistically wrought idealization of the western commonwealths. *(original 1904 caption)*

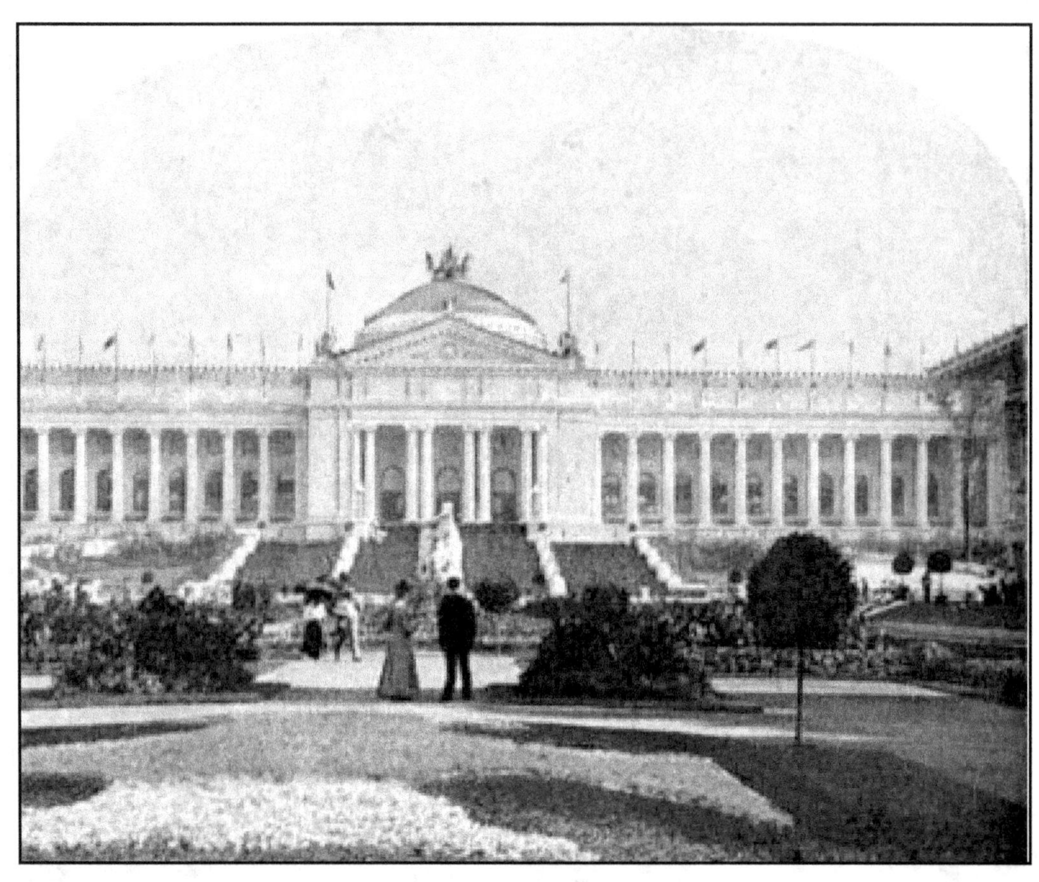

No. 3. Entrance to Government Building

The Government of the United States has generously participated in all the important expositions in the country, and its building at the Louisiana Purchase Exposition was the largest ever erected by Federal authority. It was situated upon a wide terrace in the eastern part of the grounds high above the level of the exposition palaces proper. It was 800 feet long and 200 feet deep. Entering the central portal, the visitor was confronted by half a battleship with full armament and equipment. The War Department had a large display of modern arms. The Smithsonian Institute occupied the northwestern corner, and the Post office the northeastern corner. *(original 1904 caption)*

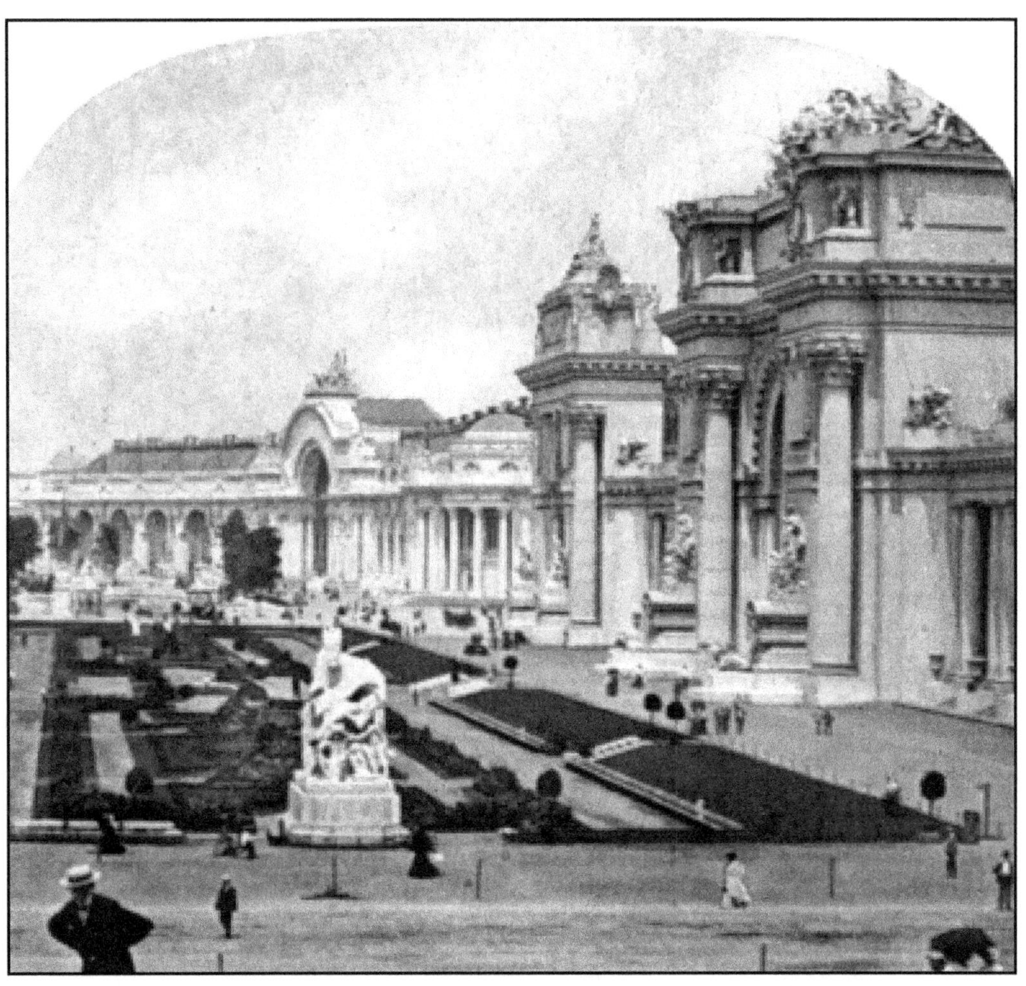

No. 4. Sunken Gardens, Palace of Liberal Arts

Of the many choice examples of landscape gardening at the Exposition, none is more pleasing than the Sunken Garden, a richly planted parterre lying between the Palace of Mines and Metallurgy and the Palace of Liberal Arts. ... A graceful slope of fine turf forms the frame for the beautiful picture. At midsummer cannas and other gorgeous flowers are judiciously distributed. Tropical foliage shows forth, new dispositions are made of the bay trees, and a transformation is worked in the whole prospect by the army of gardeners who are always at work at the Fair. There are seats for hundreds of visitors around the parterre, and the exhibit palaces afford shade in the heat of the day, so that the Sunken Garden is one of the most delightful resting places at the Exposition. *(Universal Exposition)*

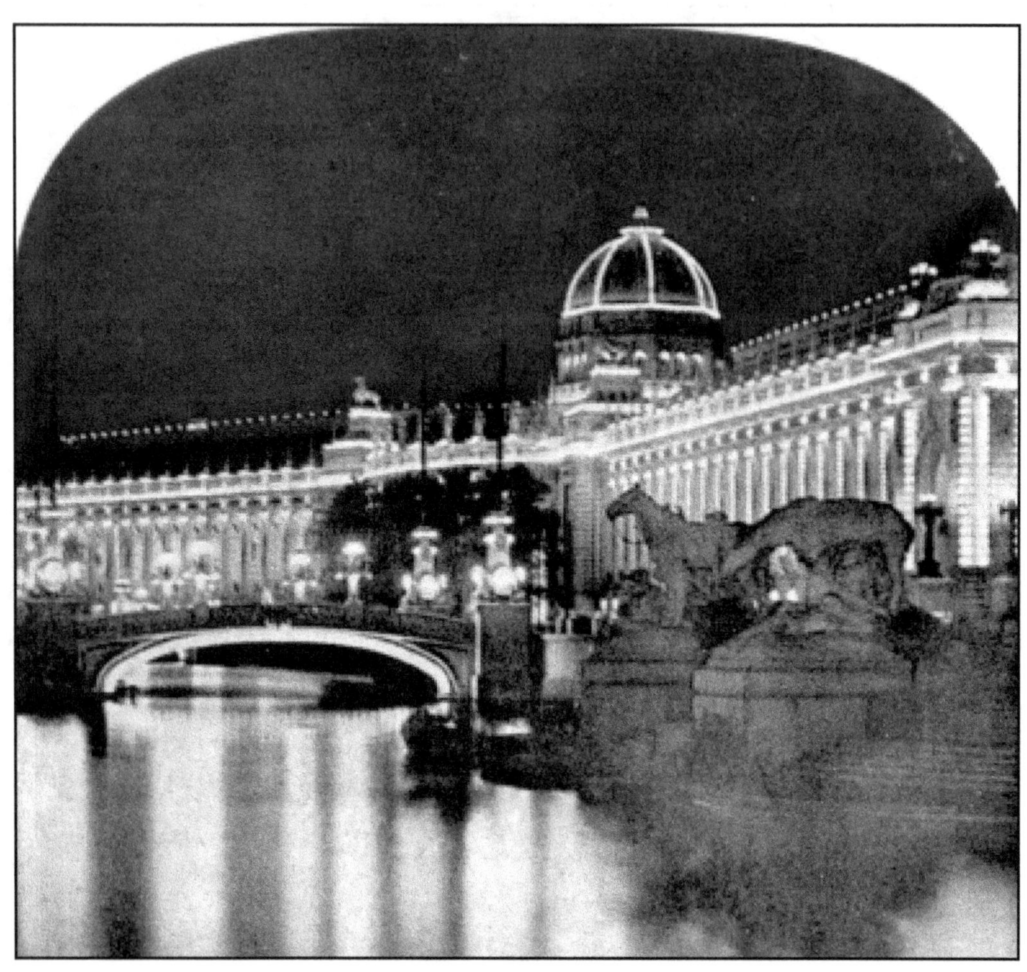

No. 5. Palace of Varied Industries at Night

Directly north from the beautiful Palace of Electricity stood the Palace of Varied Industries. The former was designed with a view to electric light effects at night. Not only its architecture but also its sculptural ornamentations were planned and massed in such a way that an exceedingly rich and varied picture resulted when the electric current was turned on and the thousands of bulbs glowed with festive radiance. The effect was enchanting... And in order to learn that the sober, classical lines of Grecian architecture do not suffer from the electric light, one needed only to turn to the Palace of Varied Industries, whose plain, stately columns and dome stood out brilliantly and beautifully in the modern light. *(original 1904 caption)*

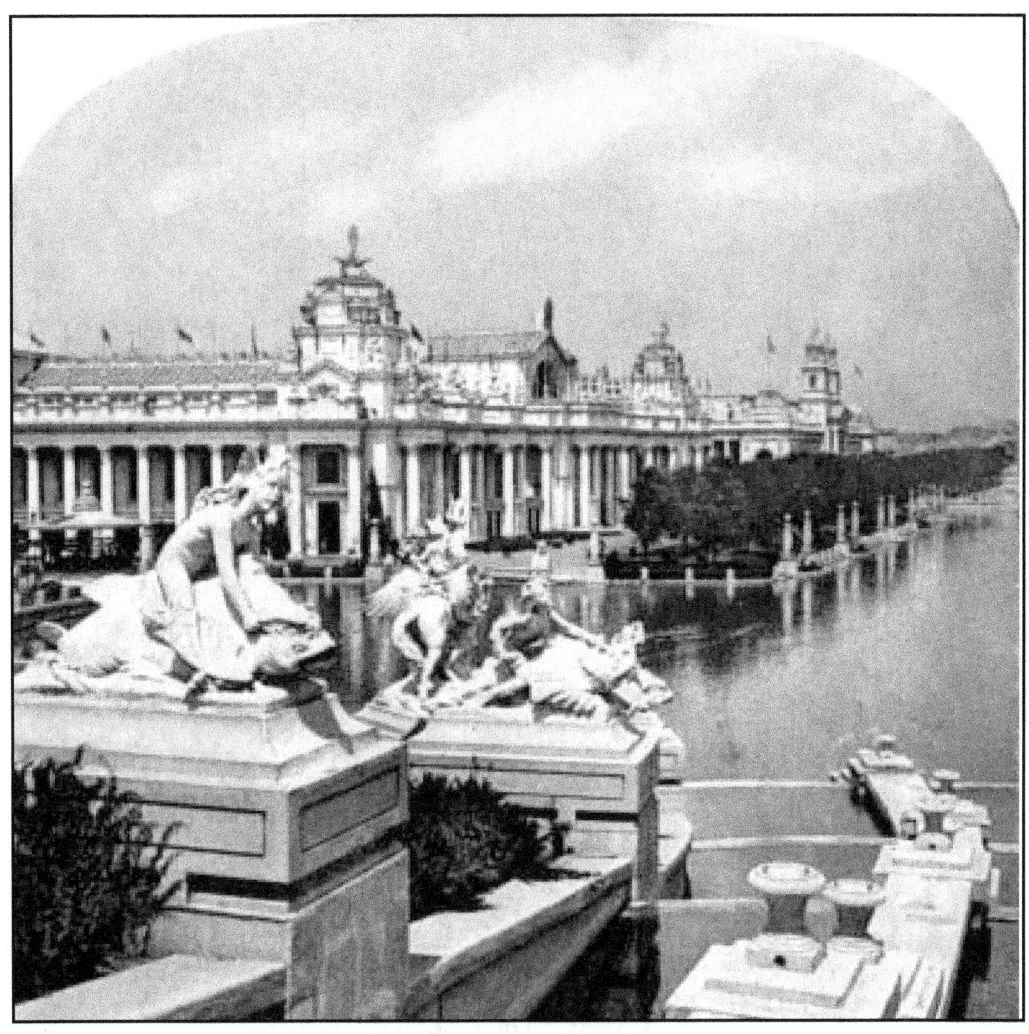

No. 6. Palace of Electricity

The remarkable advance in electrical engineering and the new discoveries in the sciences during the last ten years made the exhibition in the Palace of Electricity one of the most interesting among all the wonders at the Exposition. The treatment of diseases by the employment of electricity, of the X-ray apparatus and the Finsen light were demonstrated. The wonderful strides electro-chemistry has made were shown, also the progress in electric lighting and the adaptation of electric power to a thousand problems of human activity. The view of this palace from the Cascades, across the green lawns, fine trees, statuary and the water, was one of the most enchanting on the exposition grounds. *(original 1904 caption)*

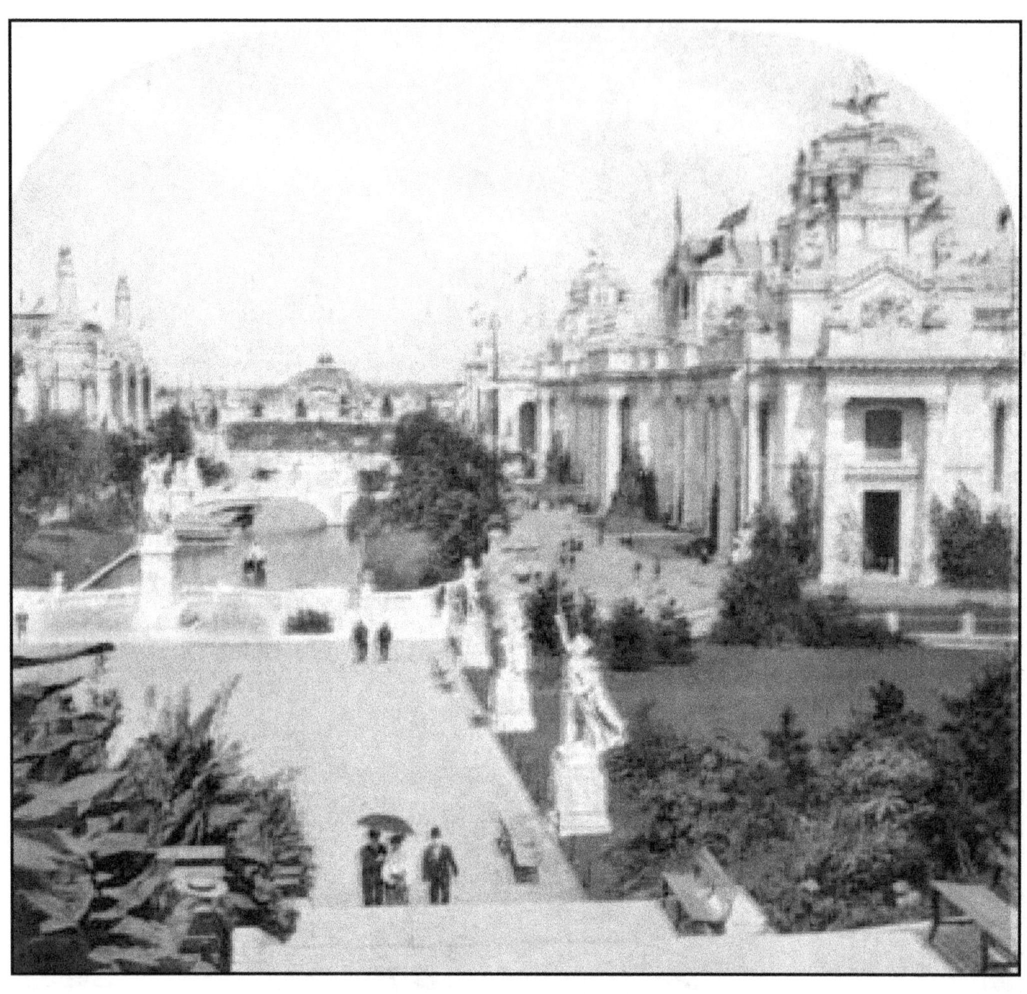

No. 7. Palace of Electricity

Including the court, the building covers eight acres and the cost was $400,000. The groups of lofty columns about the entrances and their classic details give the building a dignity worthy of its central position in the "main picture" of the Exposition. The remarkable advance in electrical engineering and the new discoveries of the science during the last ten years made possible the most comprehensive exhibit ever assembled. Definite progress has been made during recent years in the use of electricity in the treatment of diseases. How it is thus used is illustrated with X-ray apparatus and the famous Finsen light. ... Small but powerful electric locomotives for mining purposes make an interesting exhibit. ... (*Universal Exposition*)

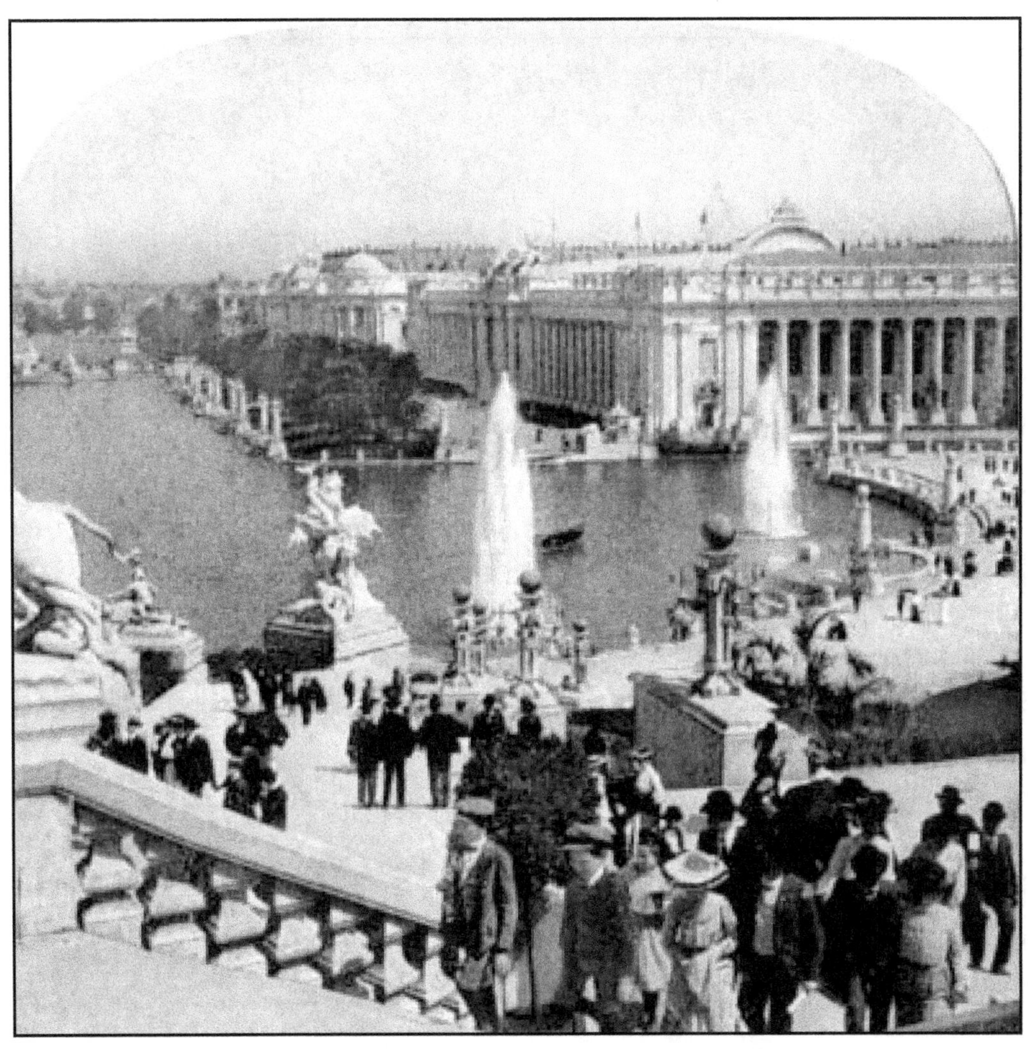

No. 8. Palaces of Education and Manufacture

On an island created by the digging of the lagoons stood in purely classical, Grecian architecture the Palace of Education. The building covered eight acres and cost $400,000. The educational exhibits represented everything from the kindergarten to the highest university courses. Technical and agricultural schools, commercial and industrial training, all had their places. There was a complete exhibit of physical and chemical laboratory work. All the leading colleges had exhibits. There were schools showing the methods for teaching the deaf, dumb and blind, the work of polytechnic schools and institutes of art, and a model lecture hall. *(original 1904 caption)*

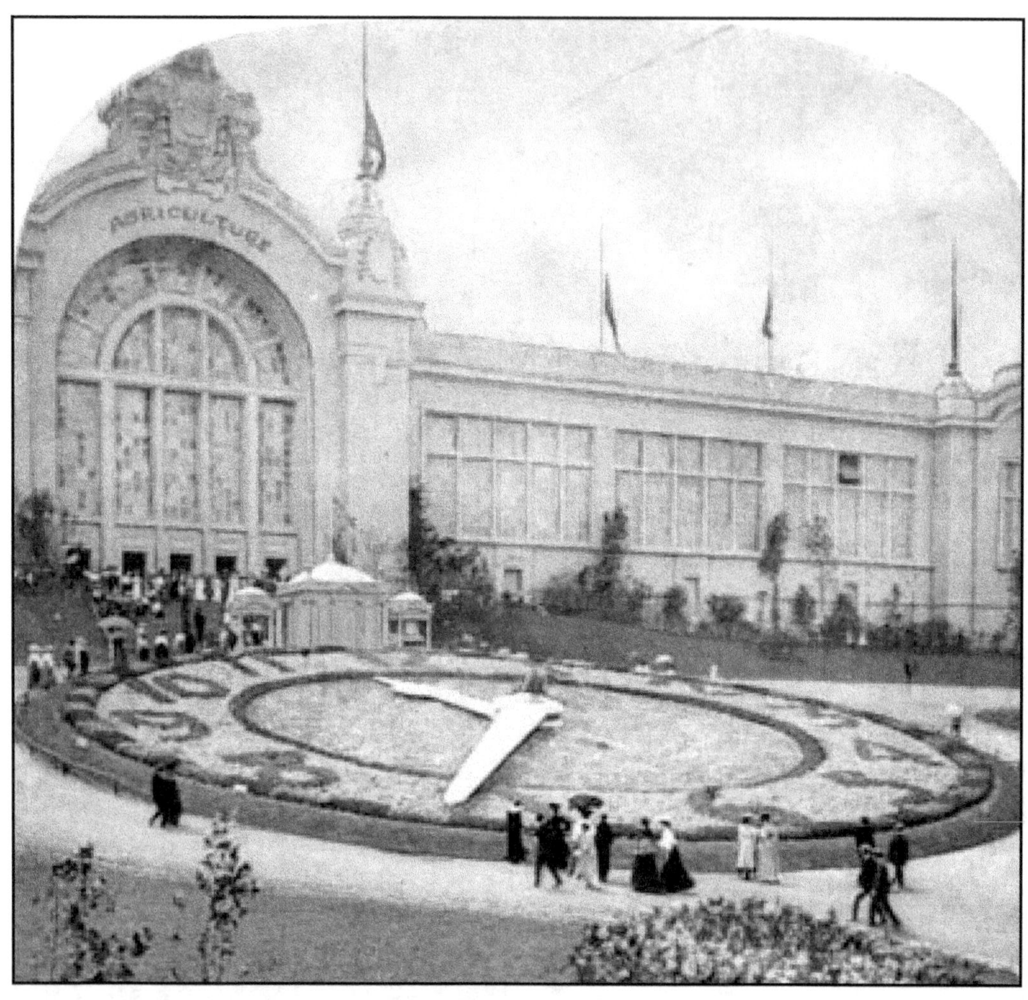

No. 9. Floral Clock, Palace of Agriculture

One of the novelties of the Exposition was the Floral Clock. Its great dial, 112 feet in diameter, was laid out in flowers and plants of bright foliage, and as it was located on a slope, in front of the Palace of Agriculture, it was visible from great distances. Its minute hand, 74 feet long and weighing 2,700 pounds, moved five feet every minute. The machinery to drive this clock was a small clock work which every minute set in motion a compressed air piston that in its turn moved the hands of the Floral Clock. The hours and half hours were struck on a bell weighing 5,000 pounds. The same small clock also reversed every hour an hour-glass which held 100 pounds of sand, and it turned a terrestrial globe once in twenty-four hours. *(original 1904 caption)*

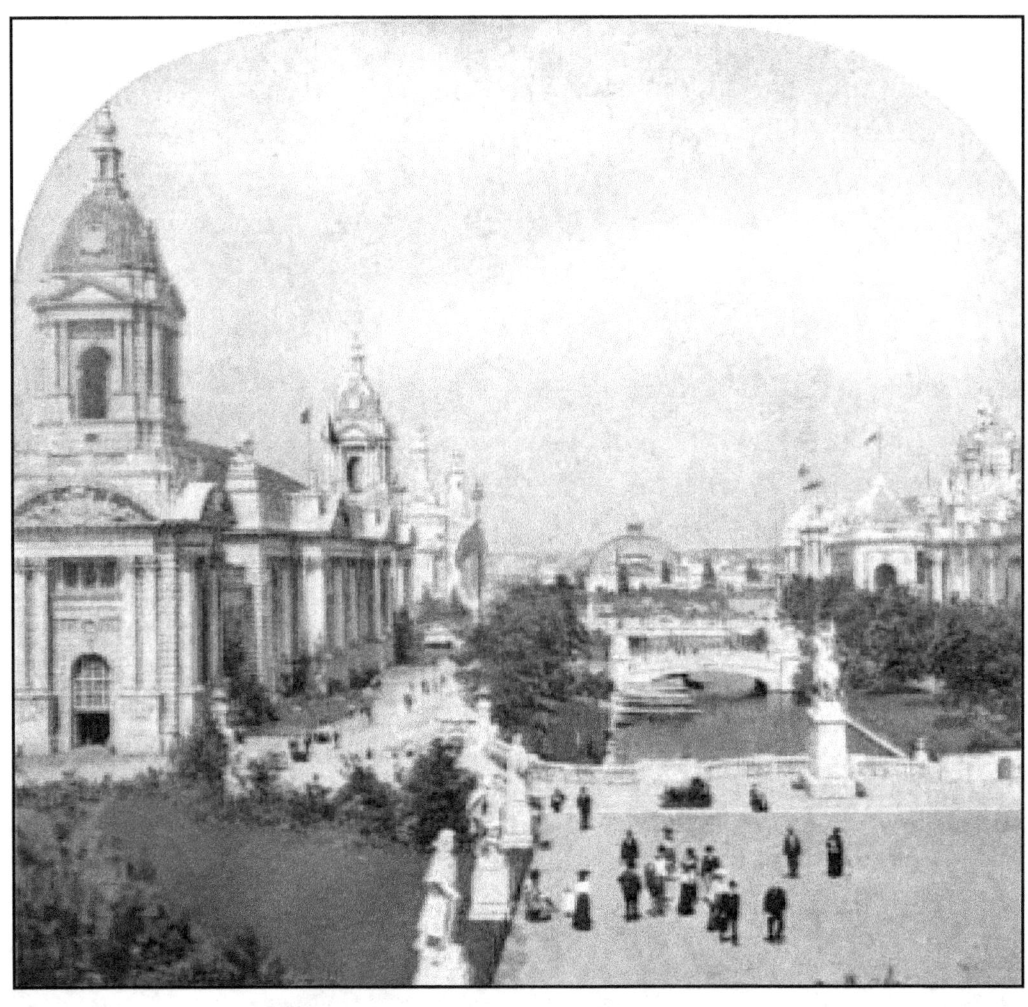

No. 10. Palace of Machinery and Lagoon

If an artist had had to define the style of the Palace of Machinery, he would have designated it as German renaissance. At each corner there stood a massive bell tower, and the principal entrance was flanked by two towers of the height of 265 feet. The size of the building was 1,000 by 500 feet. In the western end of the palace was the power plant of the Exposition, where an aggregate energy of 45,000 horse power were developed. The largest of the engines exhibited was the Allis-Chalmers vertical and horizontal refrigerating engine of 5,000 horse power, while the most powerful was the Curtis steam turbine, capable of producing 12,000 horse power. At the Philadelphia Centennial Exposition the great Corliss engine showed only 300 horse power. *(original 1904 caption)*

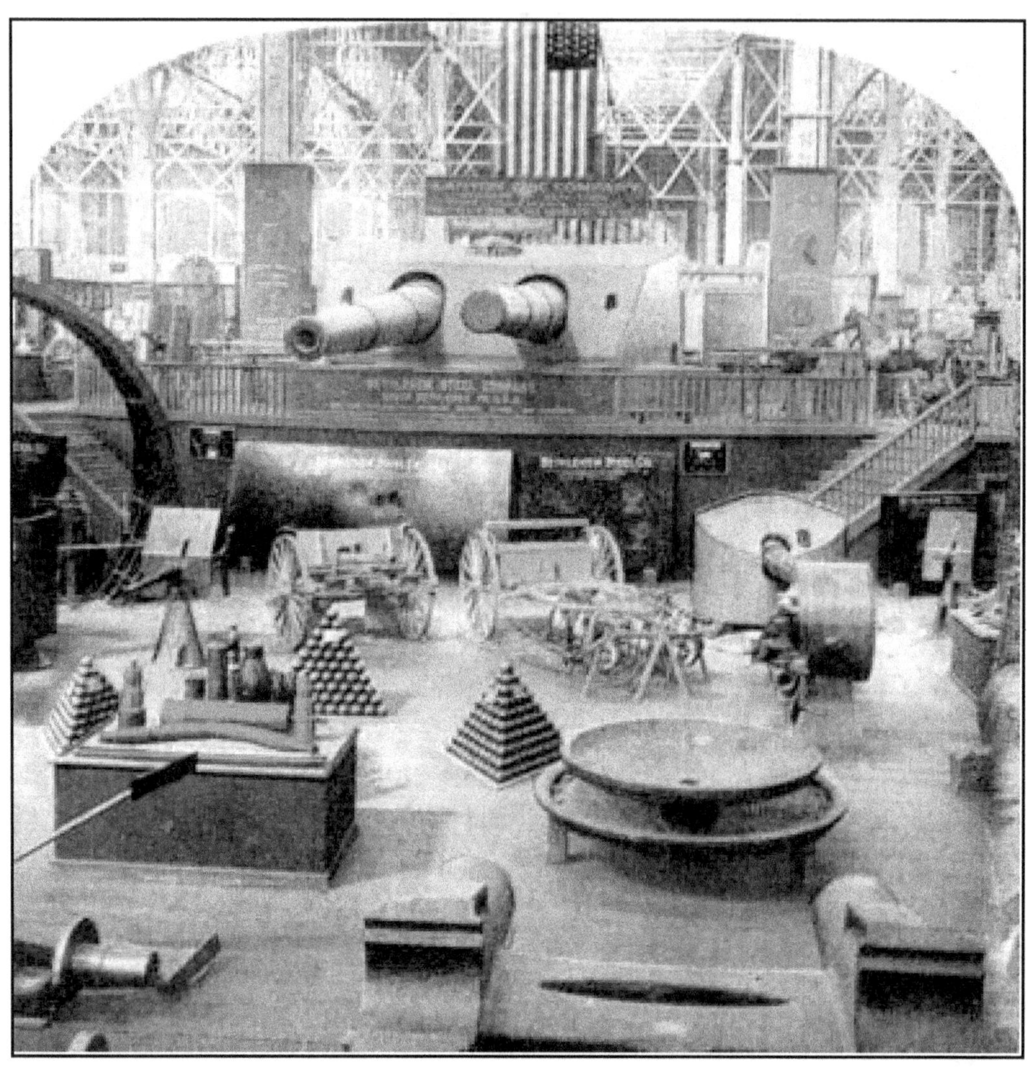

No. 11. Bethlehem Steel Co.'s Exhibit

The Bethlehem Steel Company centers on the military and naval products it produces, including field artillery pieces and naval deck guns. In the center top is a full-scale working model of a battleship turret with twelve-inch guns.

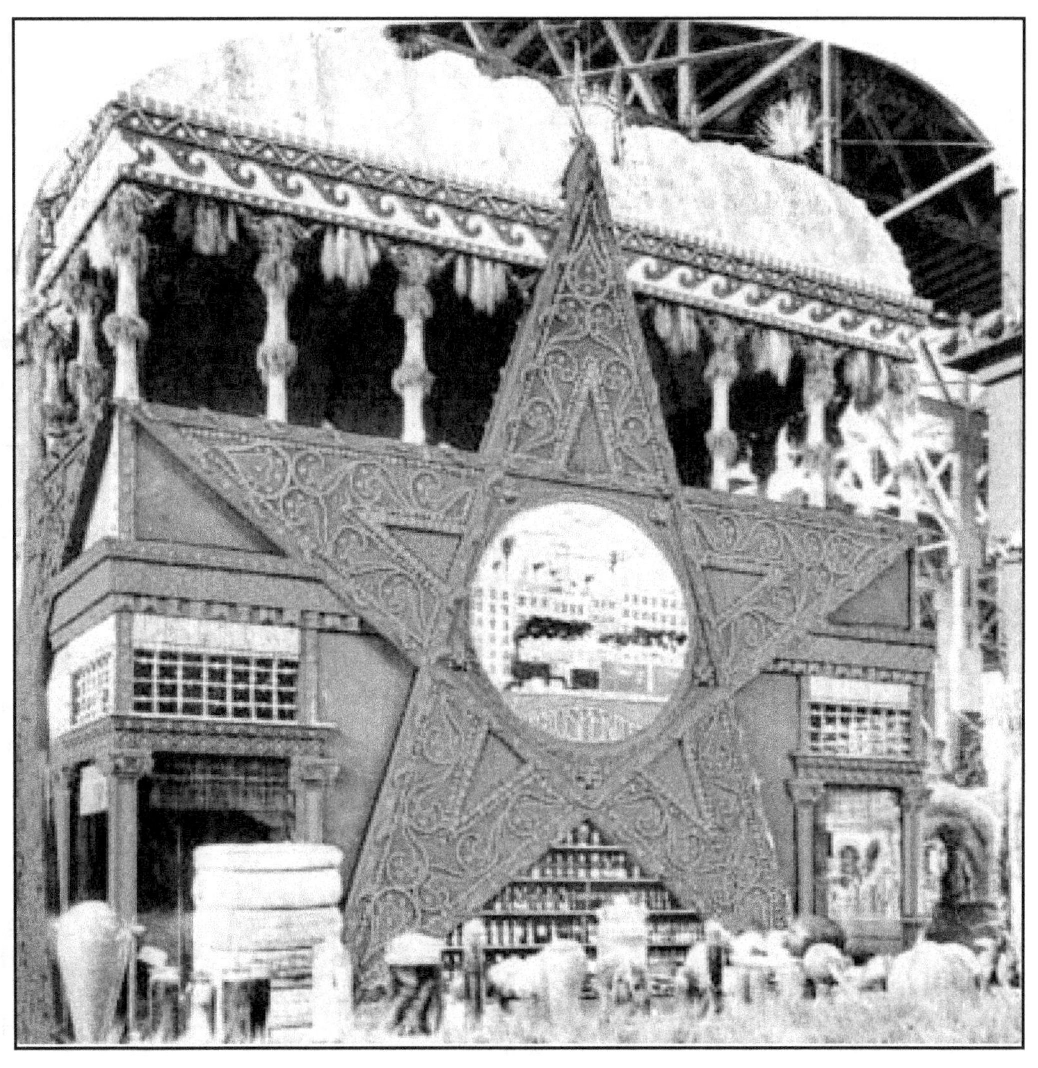

No. 12. "Lone Star" of Texas, Made of Grains

The state of Texas reproduces its Lone Star emblem in native grains and grasses in an exhibit in the Palace of Agriculture.

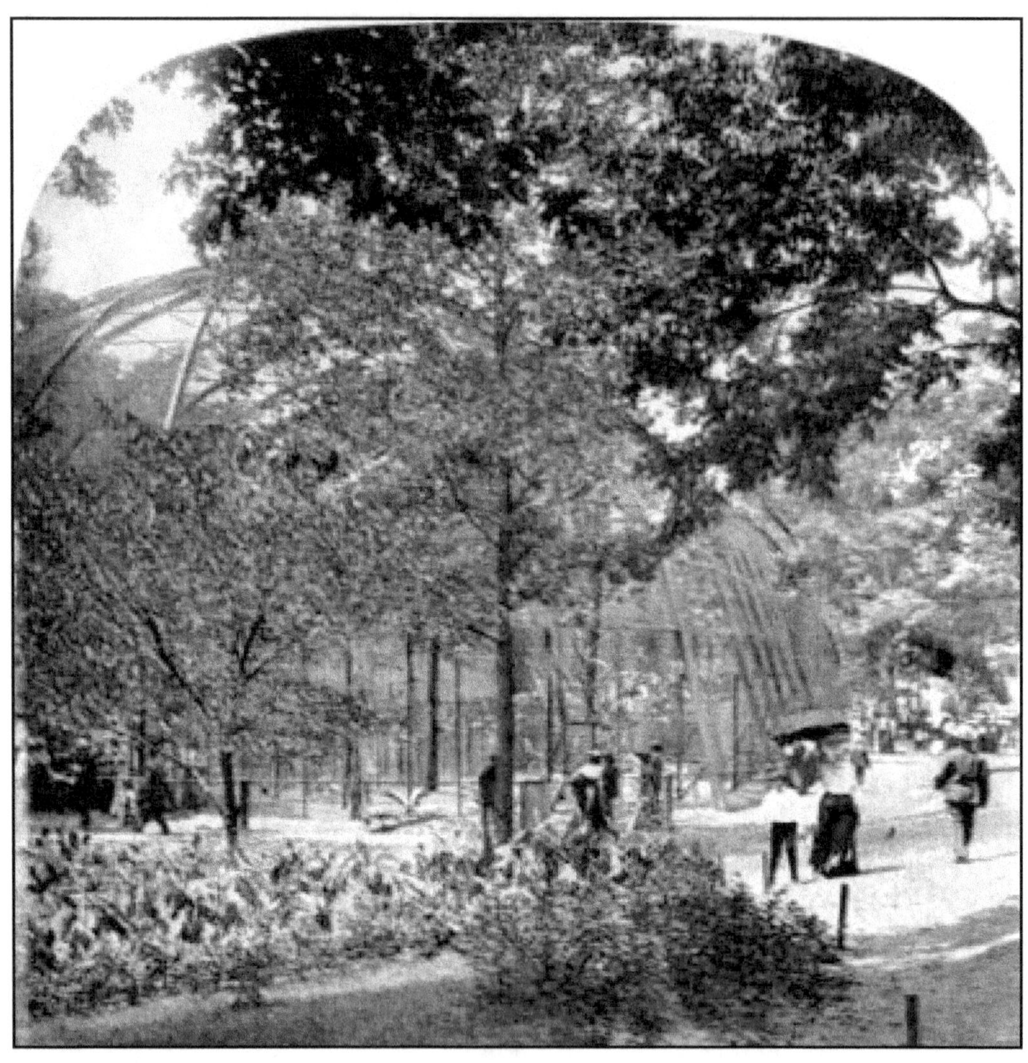

NO. 13. THE MAMMOTH BIRD CAGE

The bird cage, a walk-through aviary, was the United States Bird Exhibit sponsored by the Smithsonian Institute. It later became part of the St. Louis Zoo and remains in Forest Park.

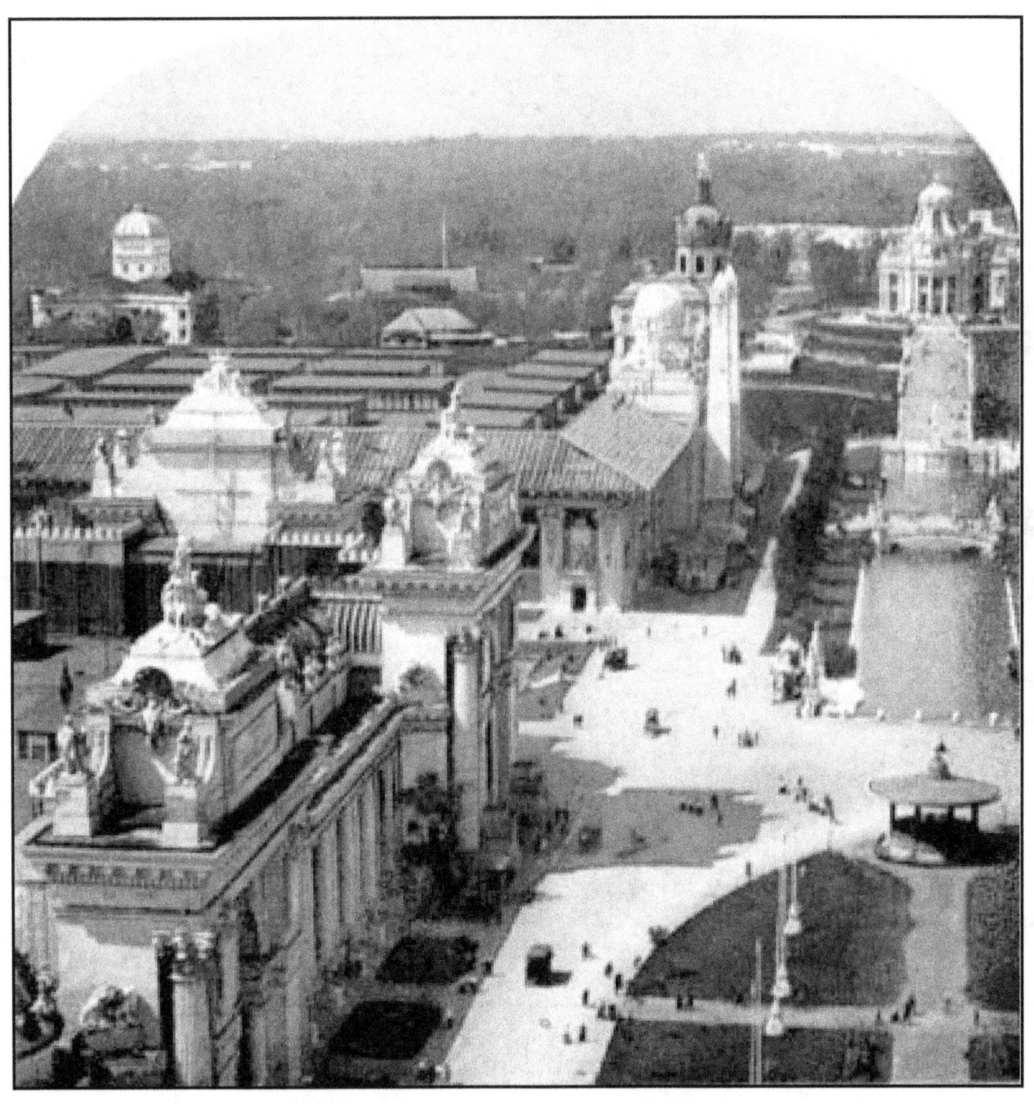

No. 14. Birds'-eye View from Buffalo Tower

Buffalo Tower was also known as the Wireless Telegraph Tower. Located at the parade entrance, near the Lindell entrance to the fairgrounds, it overlooked the Palace of Liberal Arts and Palace of Mines to the left. The lagoon at right leads up to the restaurant at the end of the eastern colonnade of states.

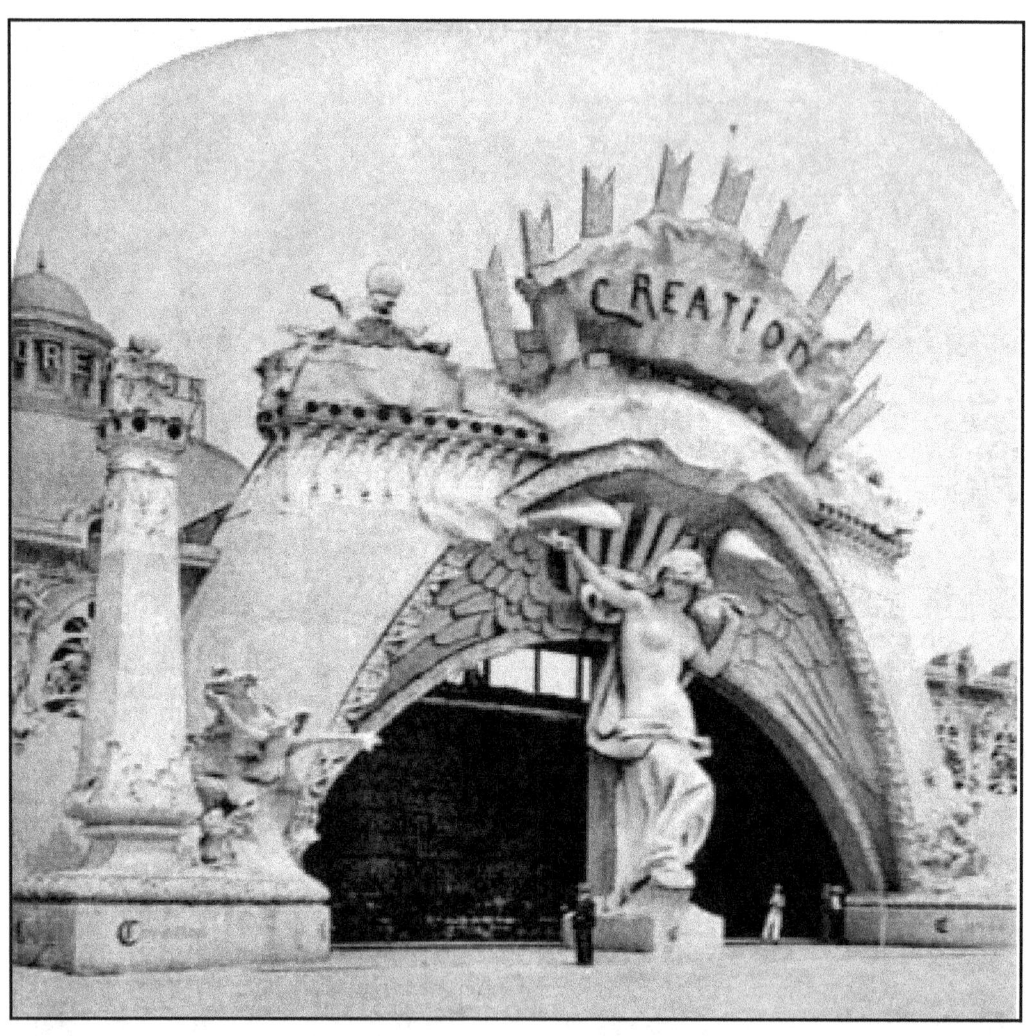

No. 15. Entrance to "Creation" on the Pike

Among the amusement features on the Pike was one that appealed alike to the idle curious and the exact student. On the basis of investigations by scientists and geologists, a history of the development of the earth, showing the sixty centuries that are believed to have elapsed since man made his appearance on this globe, was compiled and carried out in a realistic representation. The visitor was carried past these views in a boat ride through a canal. The mighty forces that shaped our earth, terrible upheavals of mountain ranges and table lands, slow erosion by wind and water, immense work done by glaciers in the glacial period and silent activity of the coral building, tiny denizens of the deep sea were here alike and vividly portrayed. *(original 1904 caption)*

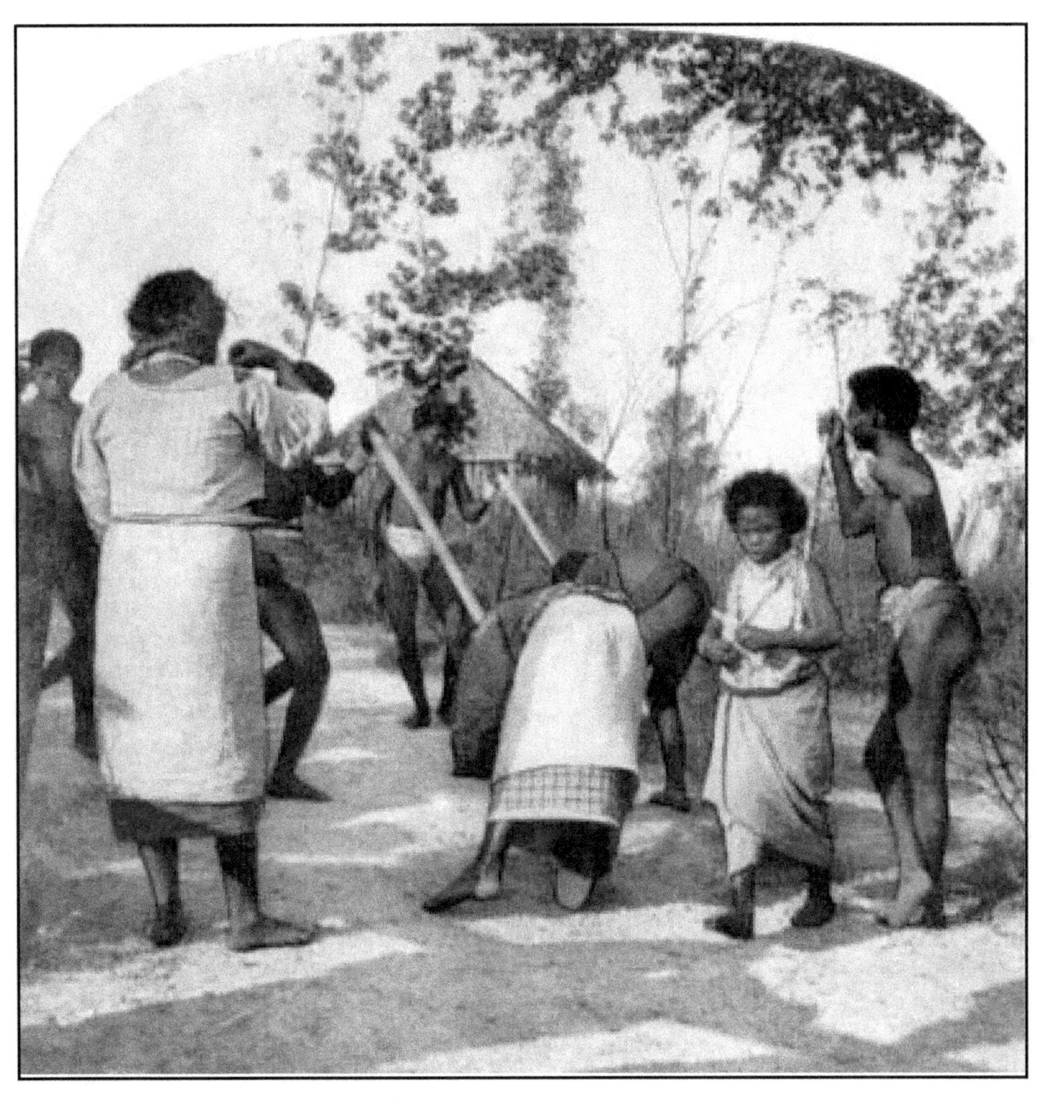

No. 16. Natives Planting Rice, Philippine Village

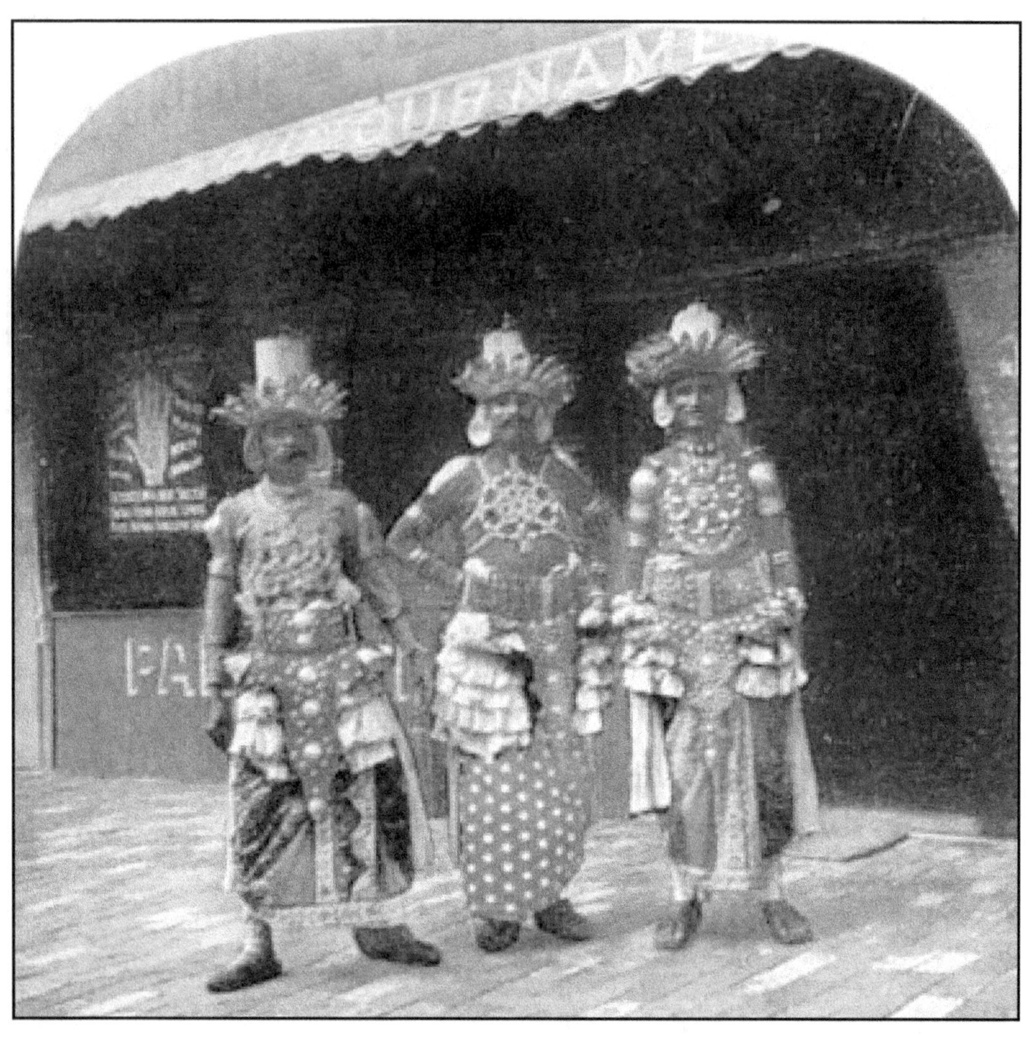

No. 17. Three Magicians in the "Court of Asia"

"Mysterious Asia" offers visitors a glimpse of the Orient. With sections devoted to Persia, India, Ceylon, and other Oriental countries, it encourages visitors to wander through exotic streets and purchase souvenirs. Here three magicians pose for the camera.

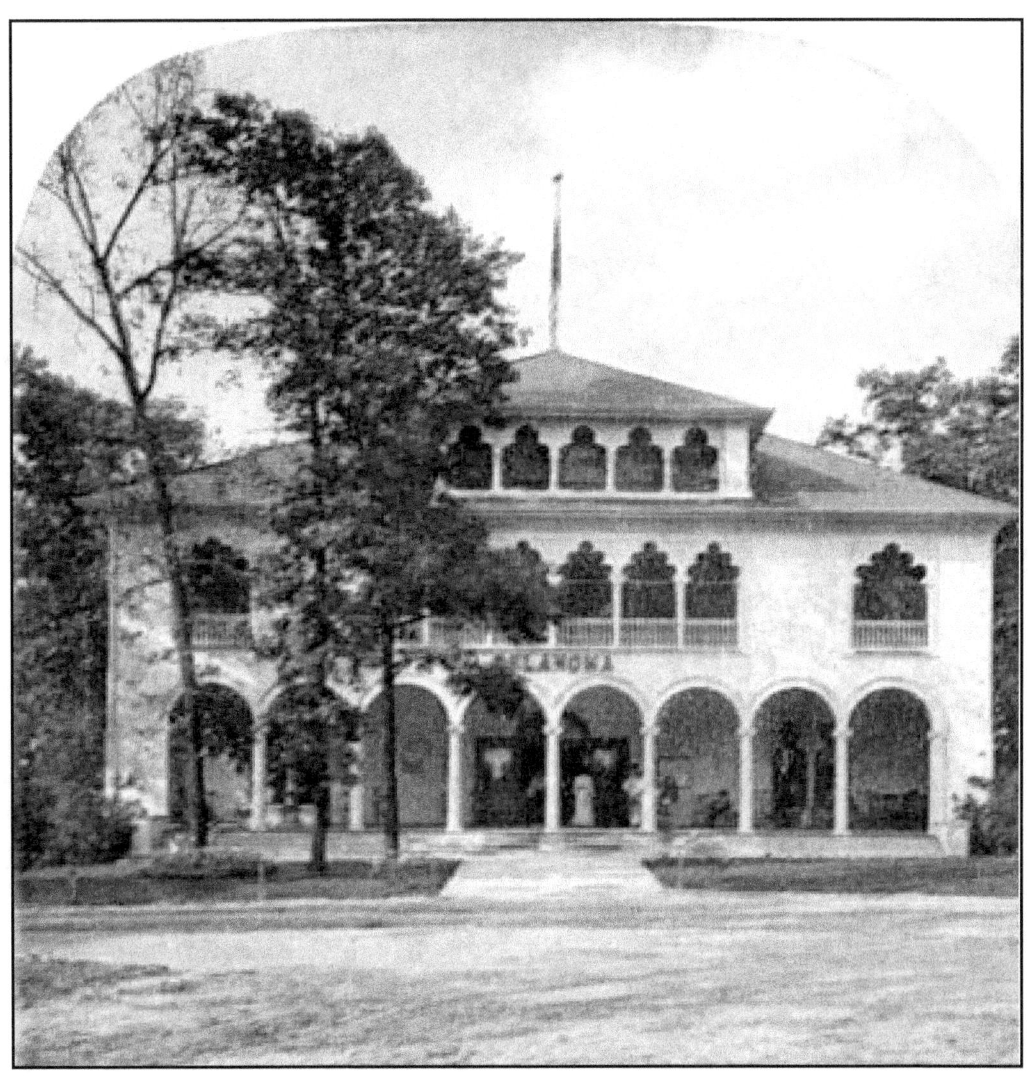

No. 18. Oklahoma State Building

The Oklahoma appropriation was $100,000, the building costing $16,000. It is the Moorish type of architecture. (*Universal Exposition*)

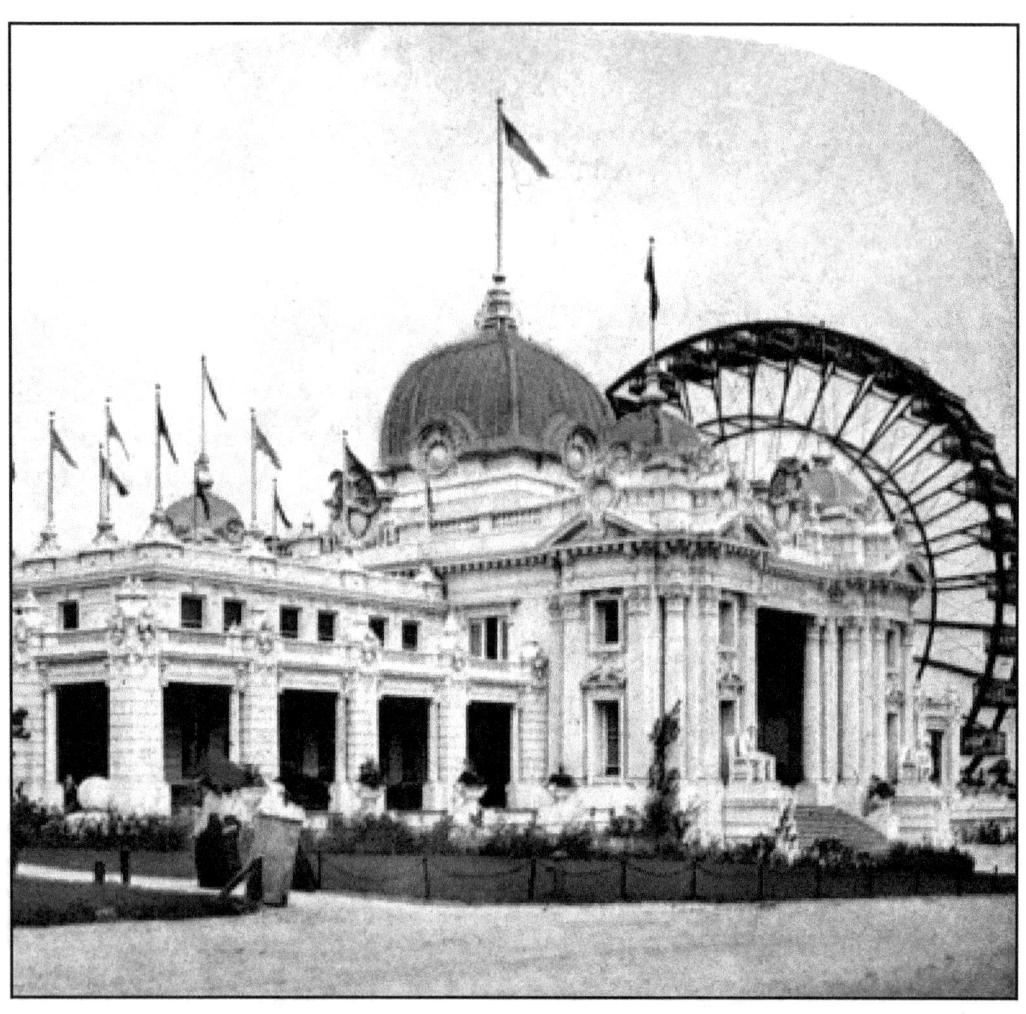

No. 19. Illinois State Building

The State of Illinois appropriated $250,000 for its representation at the World's Fair and the State Building represents an outlay of $75,000. It occupies a site on high ground southwest of the Palace of Machinery near the California Building. The Observation Wheel lies just beyond the Illinois Building. (*Universal Exposition*)

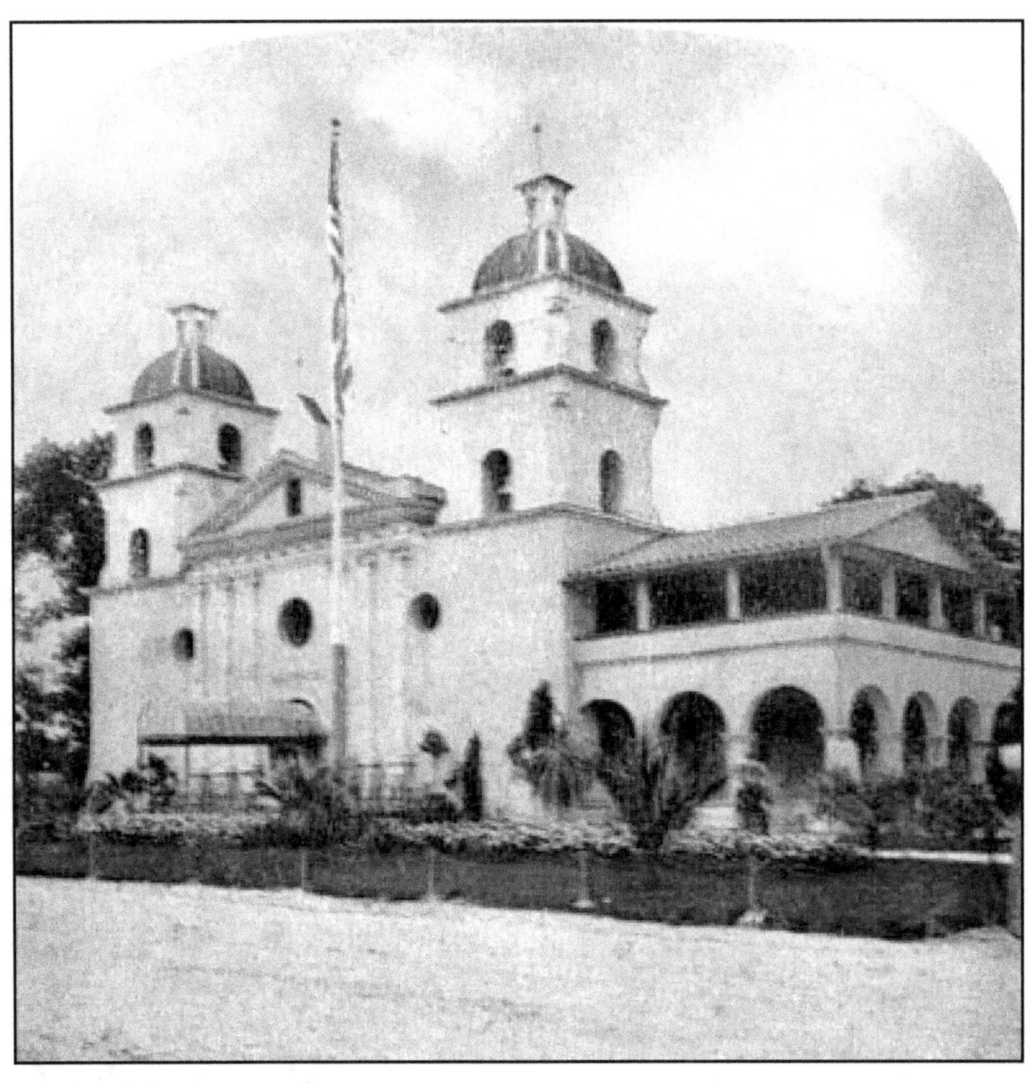

No. 20. California's Old Mission Building

The California Building is an exact reproduction of the LaRabida Mission at Santa Barbara and stands almost in the center of the Exposition grounds. The interior is handsomely furnished with furniture made of California woods, and all the decorations are suggestive of the state. (*Universal Exposition*)

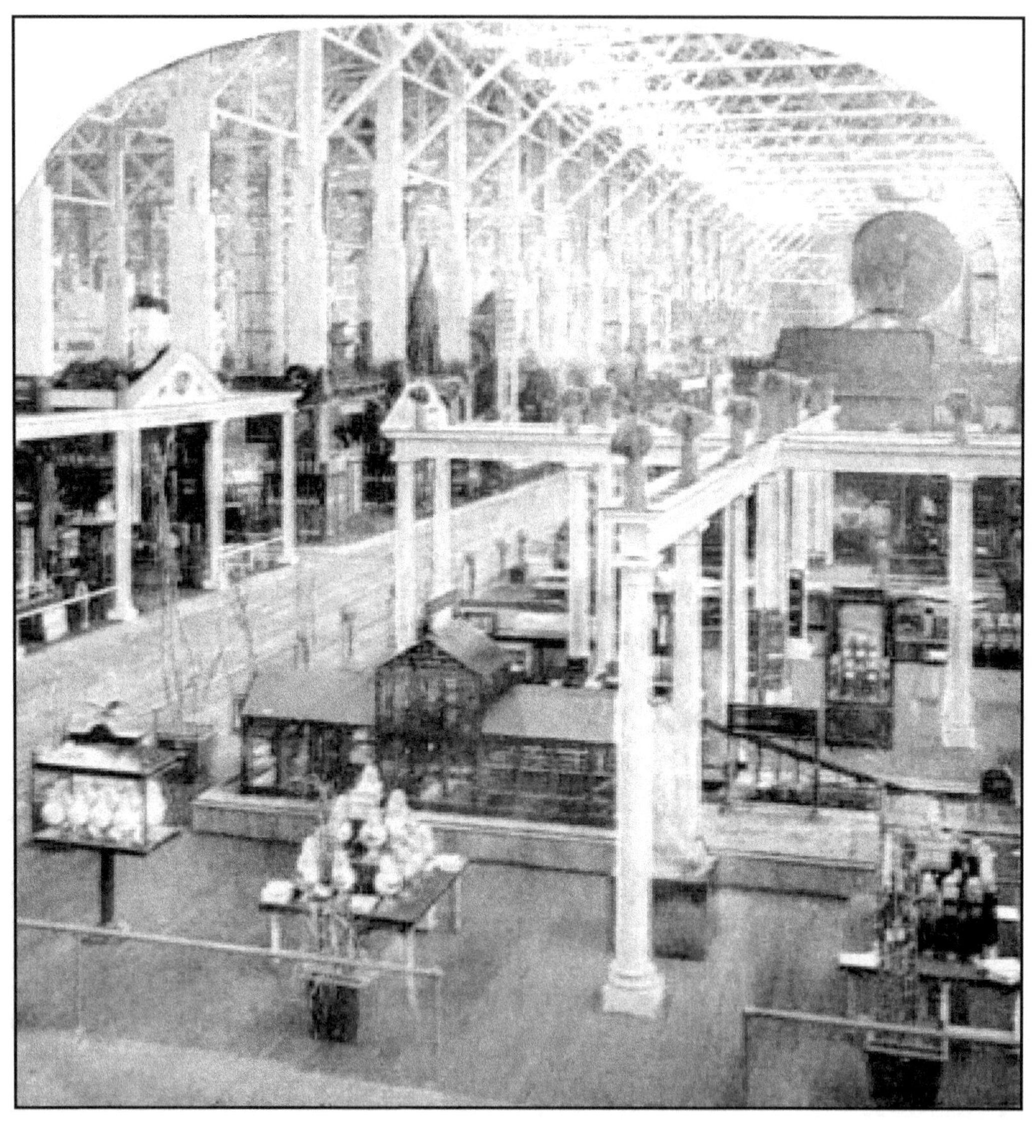

No. 21. Louisiana's State Exhibit

Though Louisiana had a building at the fair (a reproduction of the Cabildo where the transfer of the Louisiana Purchase was actually carried out in 1803) this view is of the state's exhibit in one of the large palaces.

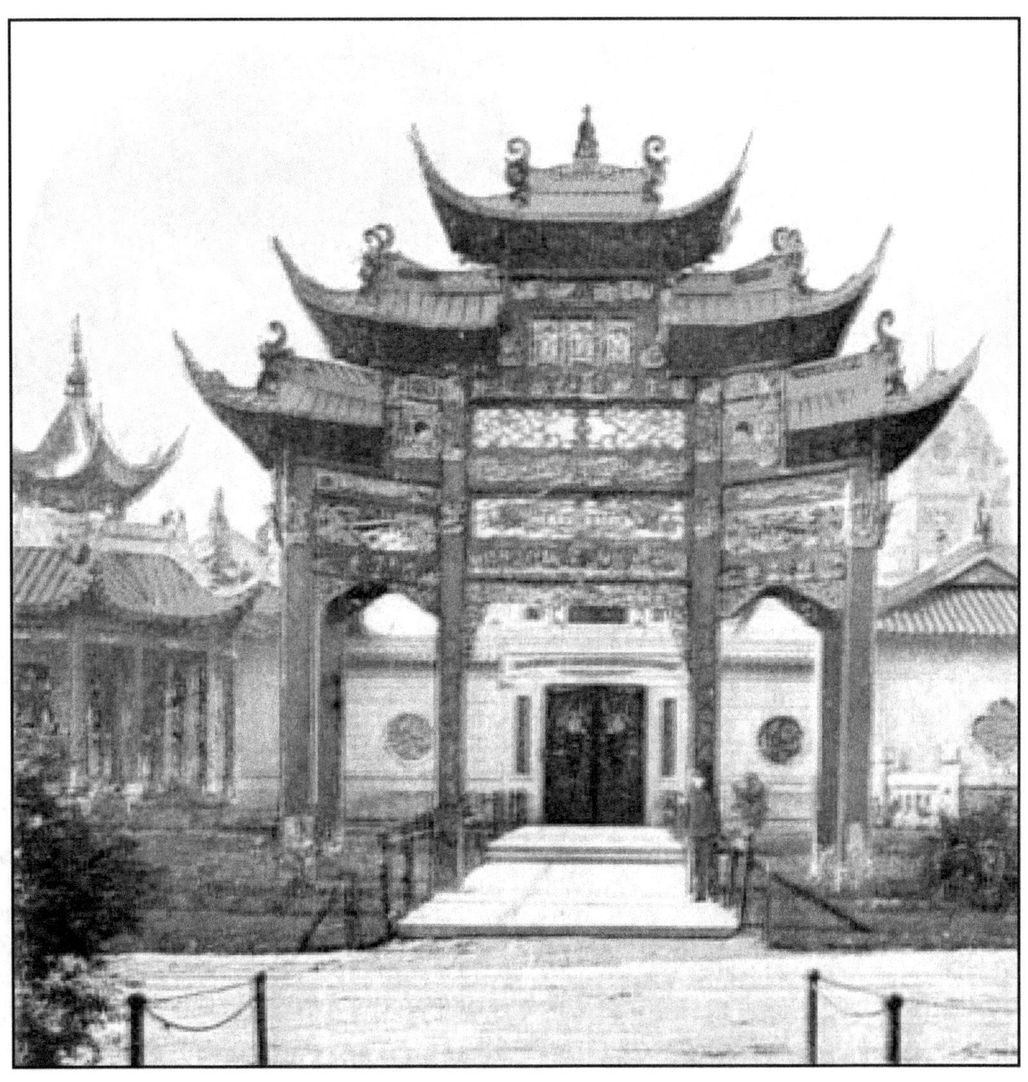

No. 22. Royal Gateway to China's Exhibit

This elaborate gateway, rich in color effects and with quaint triple roofs upturned at the corners, led to the Chinese Pavilion, a reproduction of the country seat of Prince Pu Lun, the imperial Commissioner to the Exposition. The main building was erected on three sides of a court. The doors were covered with wood carved to resemble wrought metal, and the wall was incrusted with ivory in the most delicate workmanship. The court had all the effect of a garden, enhanced by a goldfish pool in the center, set in a mass of Chinese roses, lilies and peonies. *(original 1904 caption)*

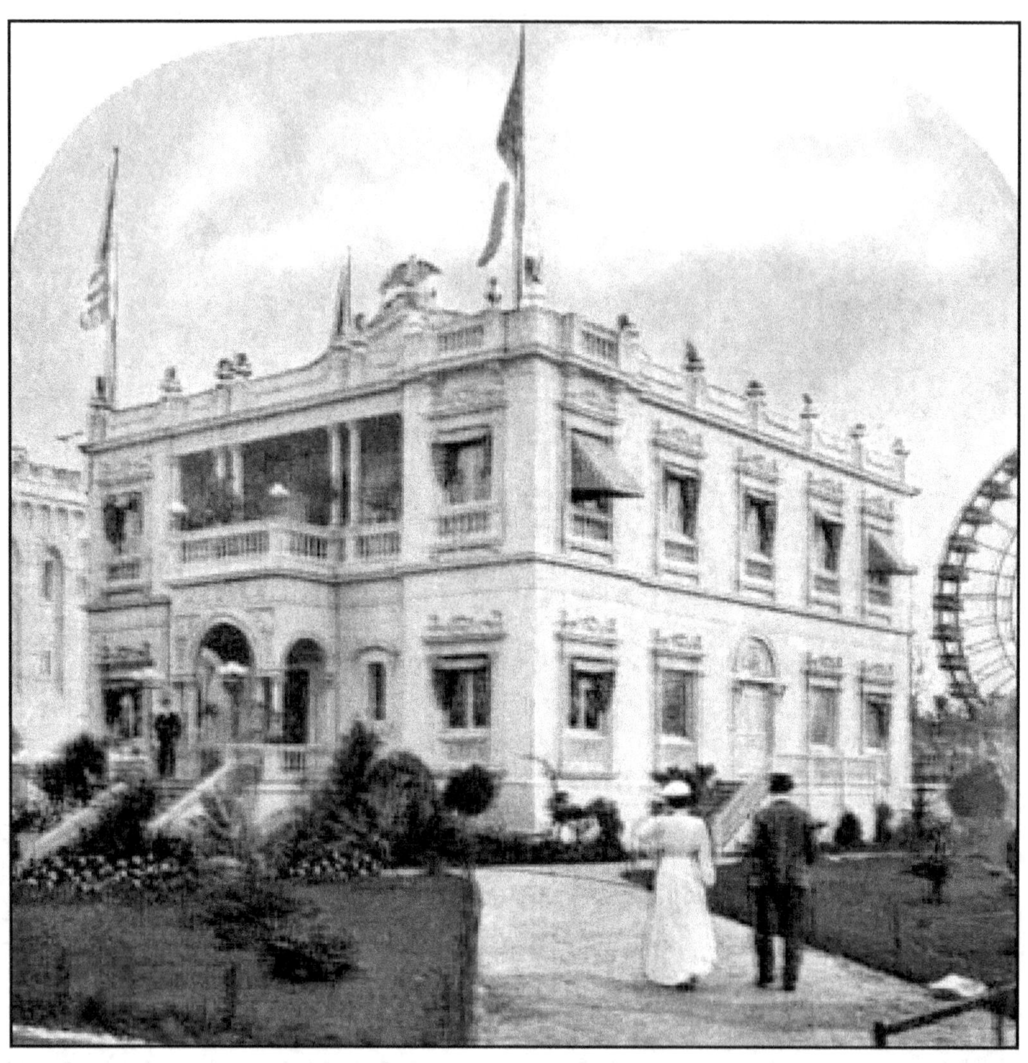

No. 23. The Mexican Government's Pavilion

Mexico was an earnest supporter of the World's Fair from the inception of the enterprise and President Porfirio Diaz has shown great personal interest in the representation of the republic. The Mexican building, which stands between the British building and the French Trianon on Administration way, is a center of hospitality. The Mexican Building contains a large public reception room below with a central patio. Offices of the commission open from the balcony. (*Universal Exposition*)

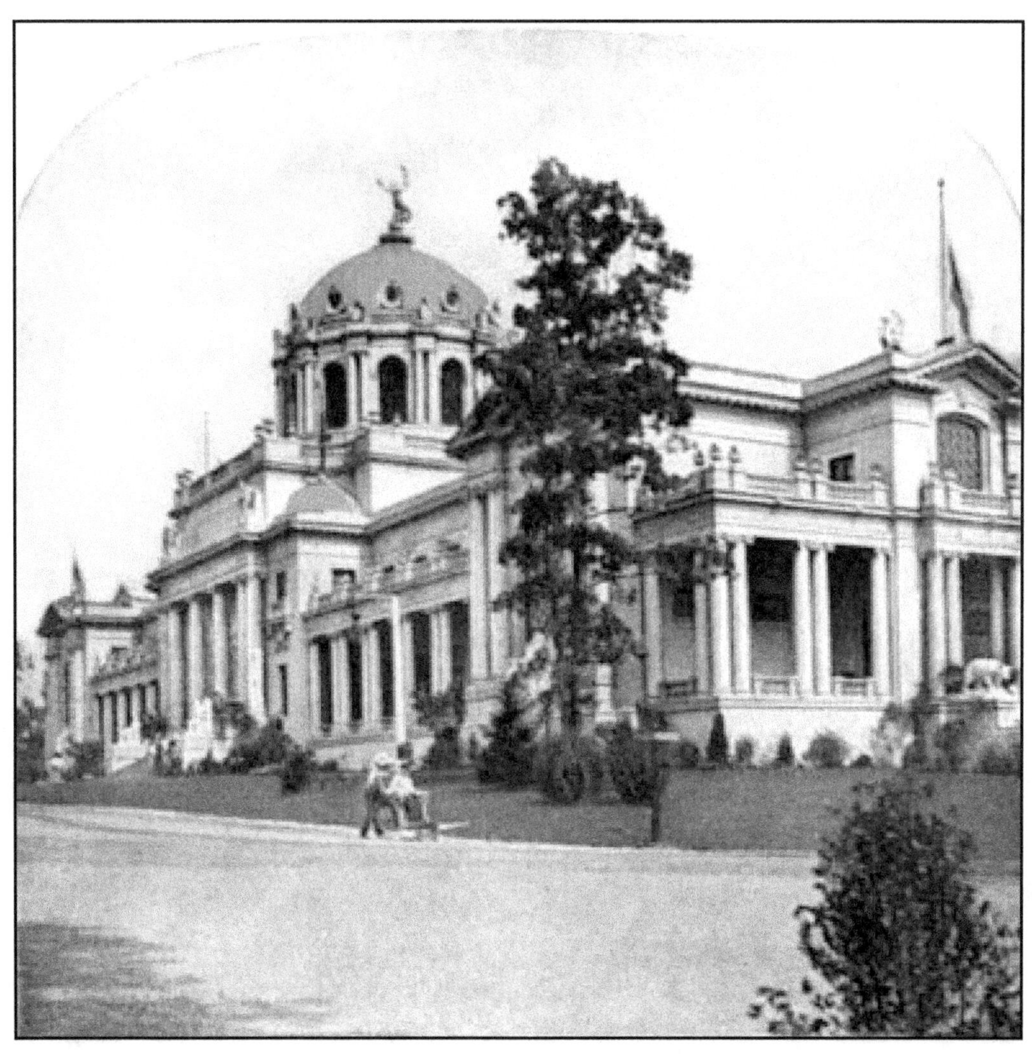

NO. 24. THE MISSOURI STATE BUILDING

The Missouri State Building is 312 by 160 feet in area, and cost $125,000. To the predominating Roman type of architecture have been added some purely American features. The dome is a perfect hemisphere, gilded and crowned with the magnificent statue of Winged Victory. A rotunda 76 feet square is the principal interior feature, adjoining an auditorium and reception room seating 1,500 persons. The mantel in this room cost $1,000, and in the center of the rotunda is an electric fountain gushing ice water, installed at a cost of $2,000. The building is equipped with a cooling system for use in hot weather. (*Universal Exposition*)

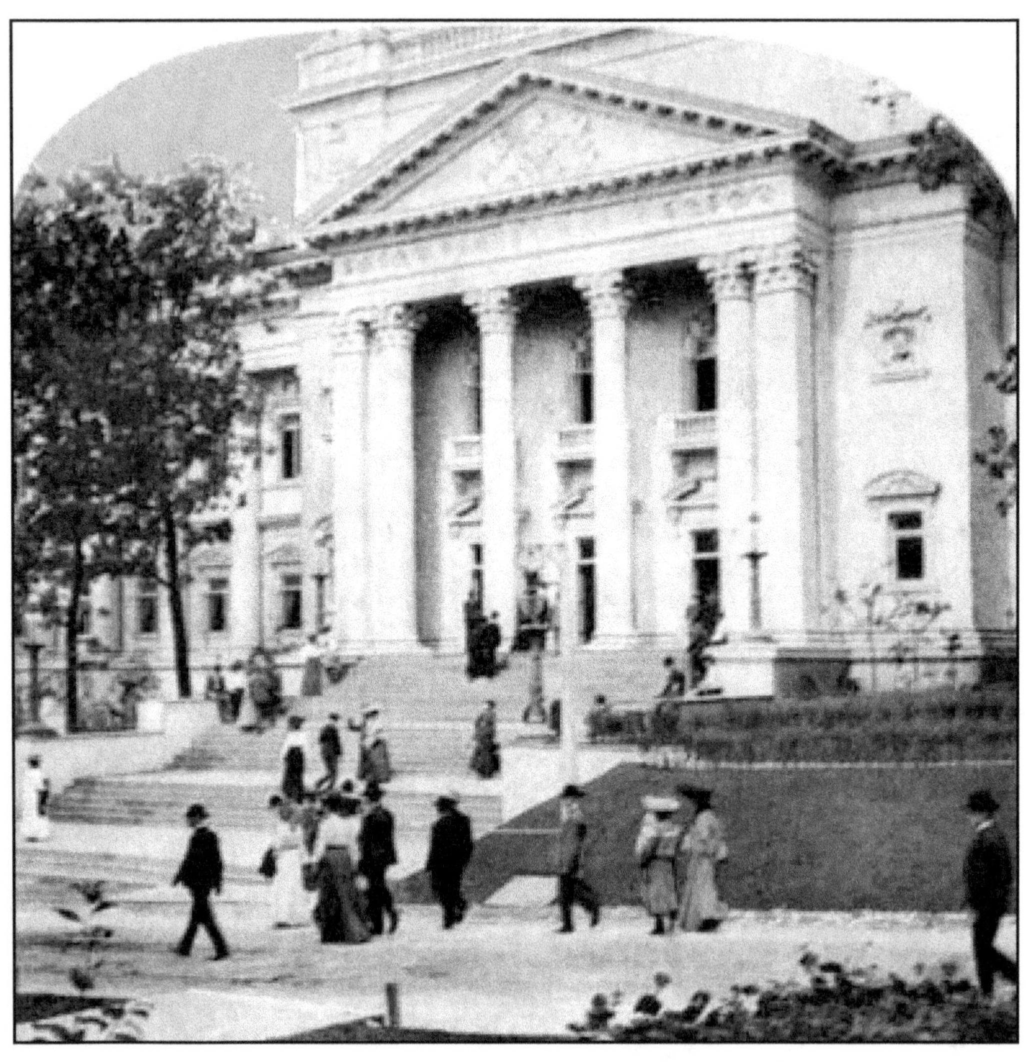

No. 25. Pennsylvania State Building

From her appropriation of $300,000 Pennsylvania has erected one of the largest and finest state buildings at the Exposition. The Liberty Bell is the chief attraction here. (*Universal Exposition*)

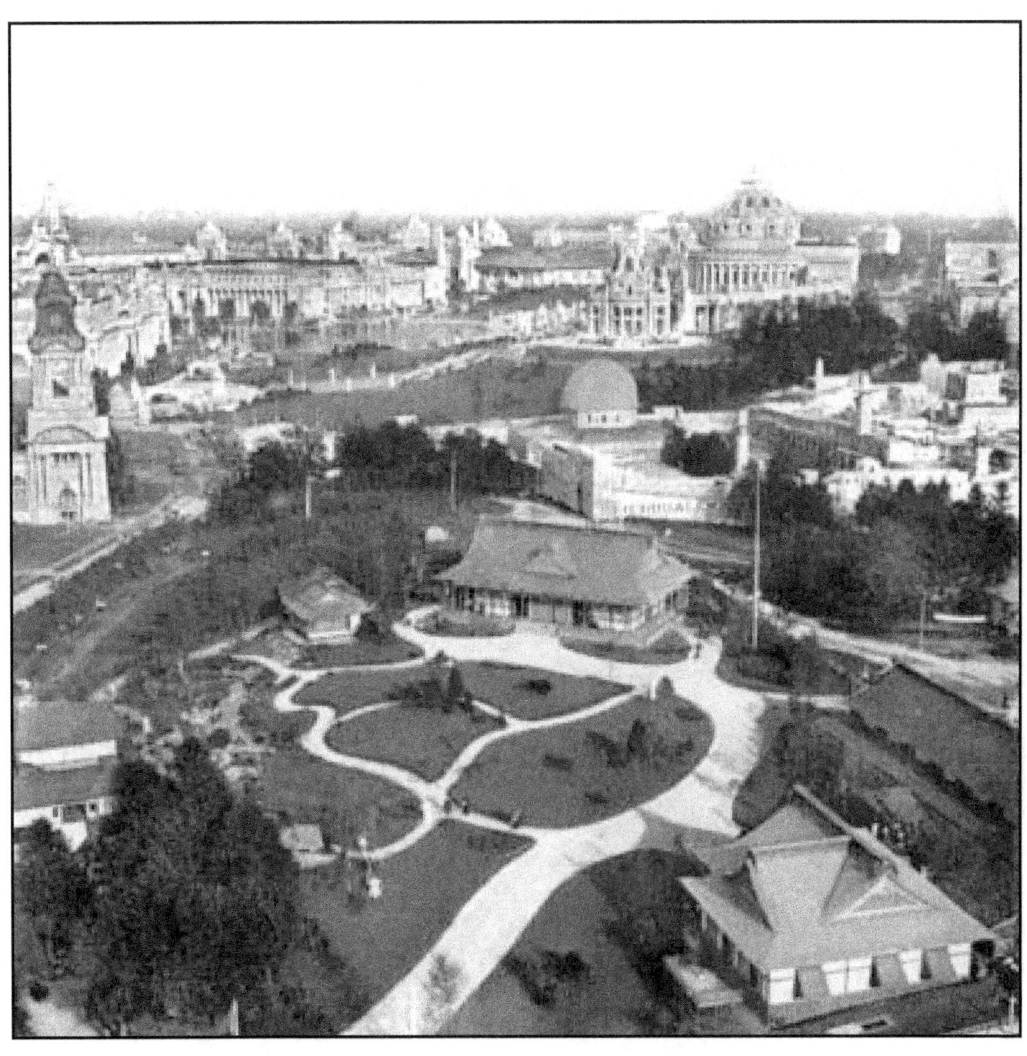

No. 26. Bird's-eye View from Observation Wheel

In the foreground are the Japanese Gardens, behind them the white walls of Jerusalem and the round dome of the Mosque of Omar, and Festival Hall with the west restaurant pavilion. To the left is the blue water of the Grand Basin, mirroring the beautiful colonnades of the Palace of Education. The tower at the left is part of the Palace of Machinery. The green lawns of the Japanese Gardens with their winding paths and red roofs, set off by an endless array of ivory-white buildings of classic architecture with towering domes, will never be forgotten by those who were privileged to see them. *(original 1904 caption)*

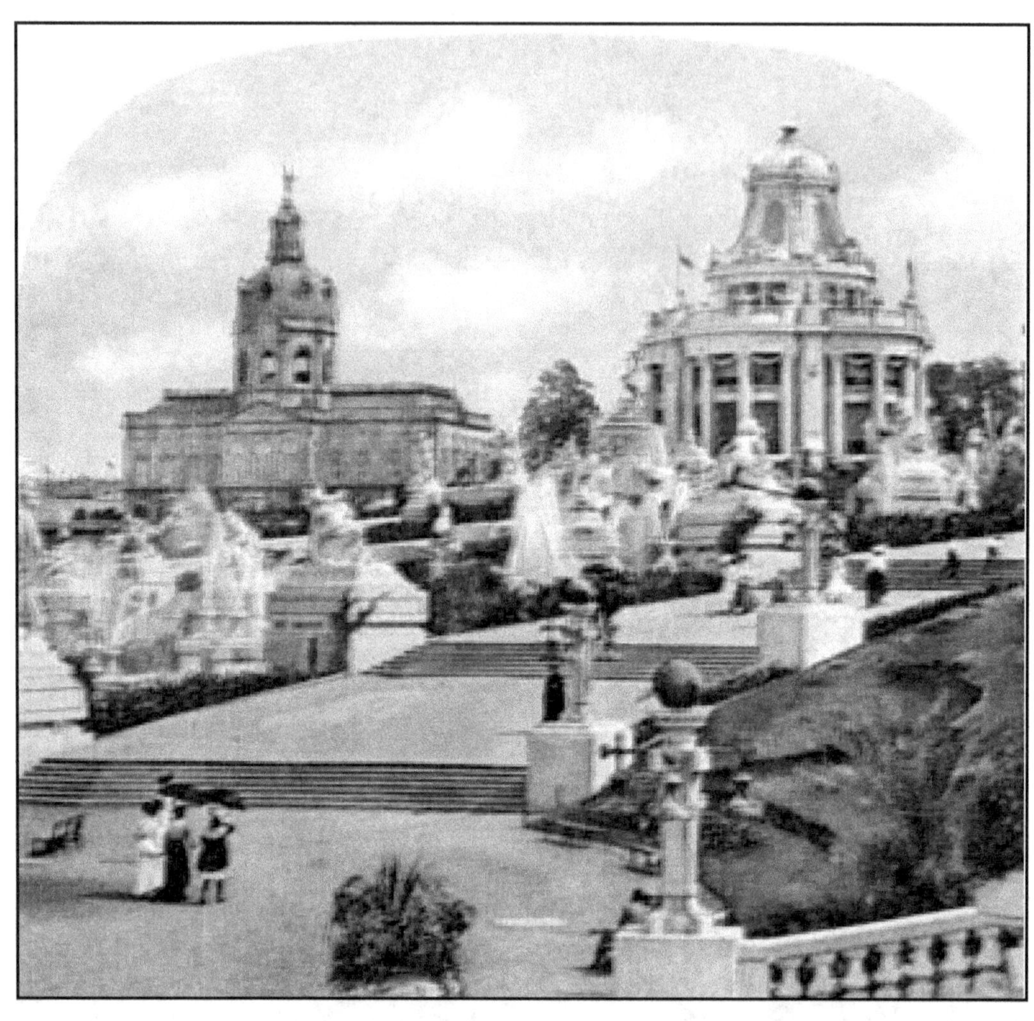

No. 27. Grand Stairway of Cascade Garden

The view from the foot of the grand stairway in Cascade Garden, just below Festival Hall, looks toward the east restaurant pavilion, at the end of the east colonnade of states, and to the German House just beyond. A faithful reproduction of the Charlottenburg Schloss, erected by Frederick of Prussia, the German building displays personal treasures of the German Emperor including rare Gobelin tapestries, gold and silver plate. *(St. Louis World's Fair)*

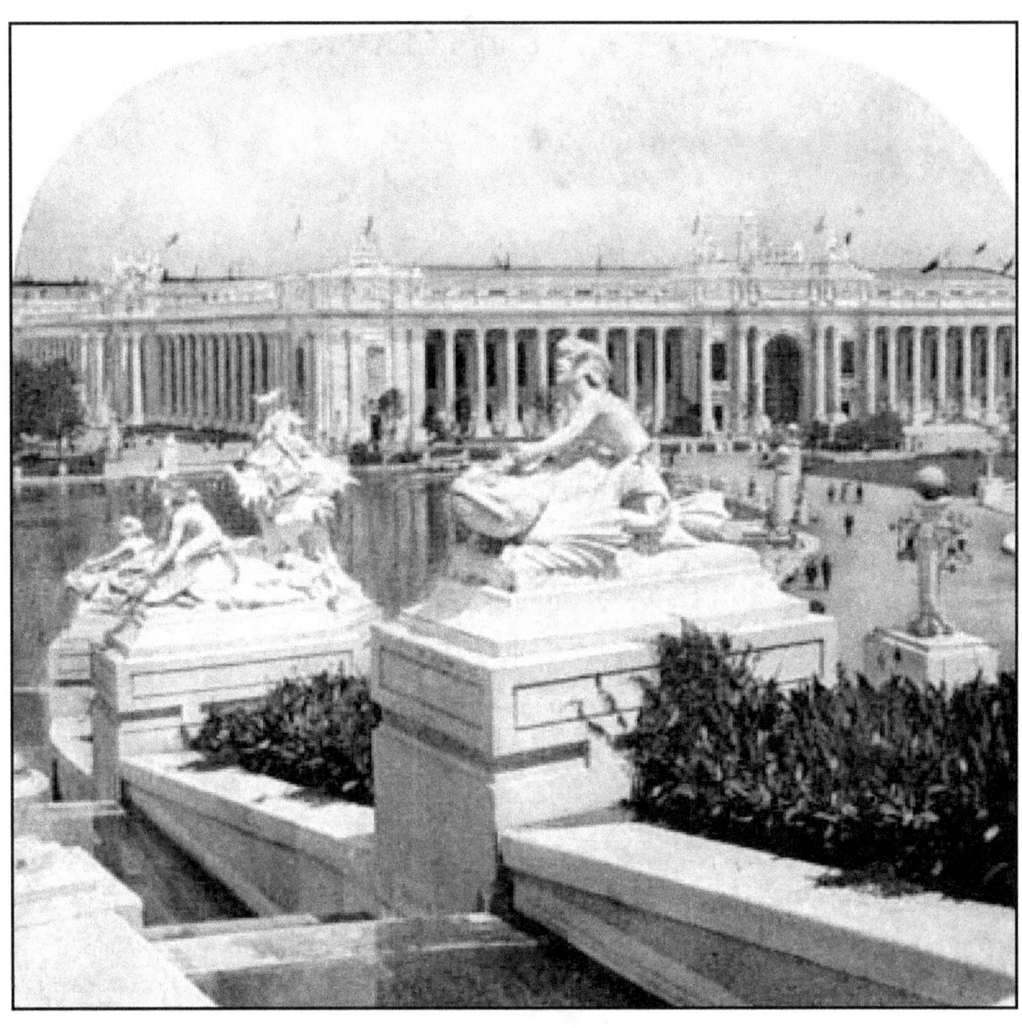

No. 28. General View Across Grand Basin

It has been remarked that at previous expositions there were but two or three good views, while the Louisiana Purchase exposition has hundreds. Of these the view from Festival Hall over the Grand Basin ranks easily among the first. Here one has the glorious stretch of water, with its surface gently rippled by passing gondolas and launches, seen from the steps leading down from Festival Hall. *(St. Louis World's Fair)*

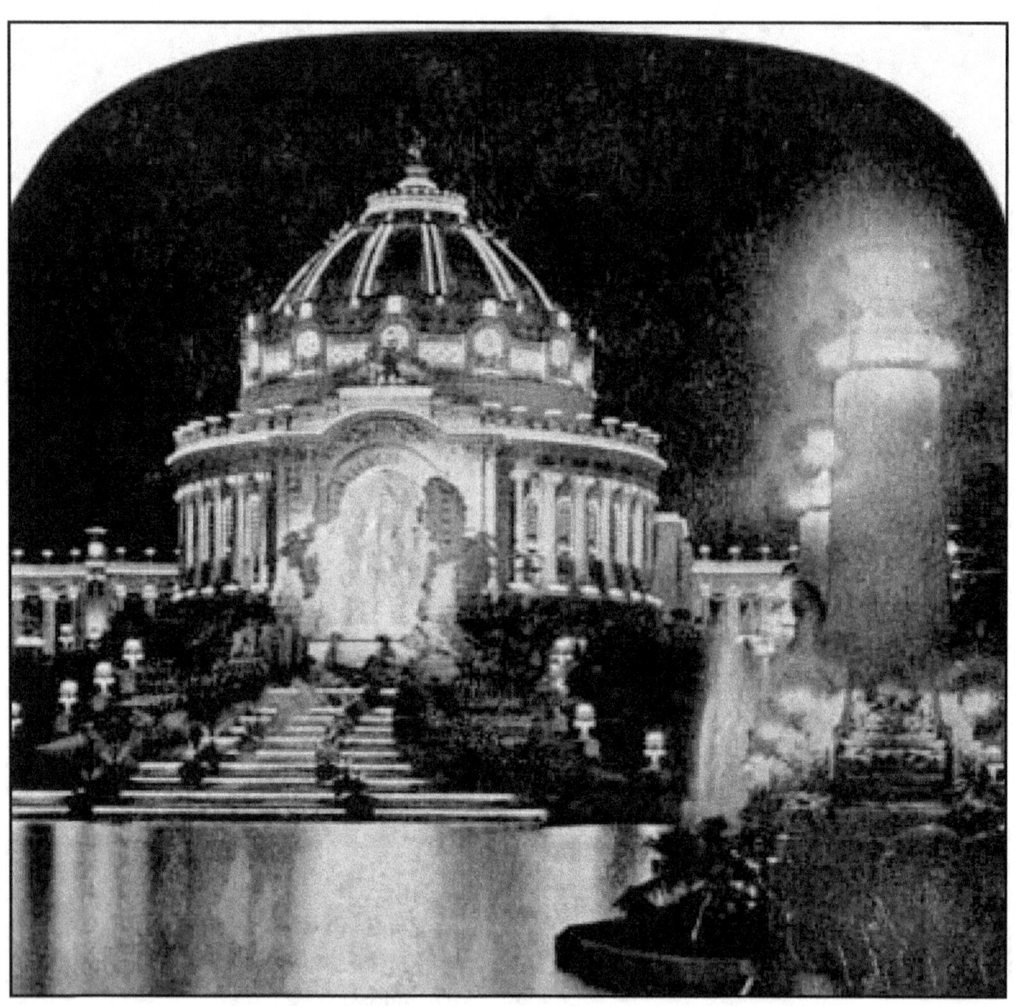

No. 29. Festival Hall at Night

Night works a transformation at the Fair. Every graceful line and curve is softened, every mass of color is subdued, everything one most wishes to see is under the witchery of the effulgence produced by uncounted lights. The scene is beautiful by day, but at night it is another picture and an entrancing one... The visitor who has seen the Exposition only by day has not seen half. Festival Hall, rising stately and majestic from the Colonnade of States. ... At times the whole cascade picture is illuminated in green, then again in red or in white, and all the while searchlights play ... Here is the Center of the Exposition. (*Universal Exposition*)

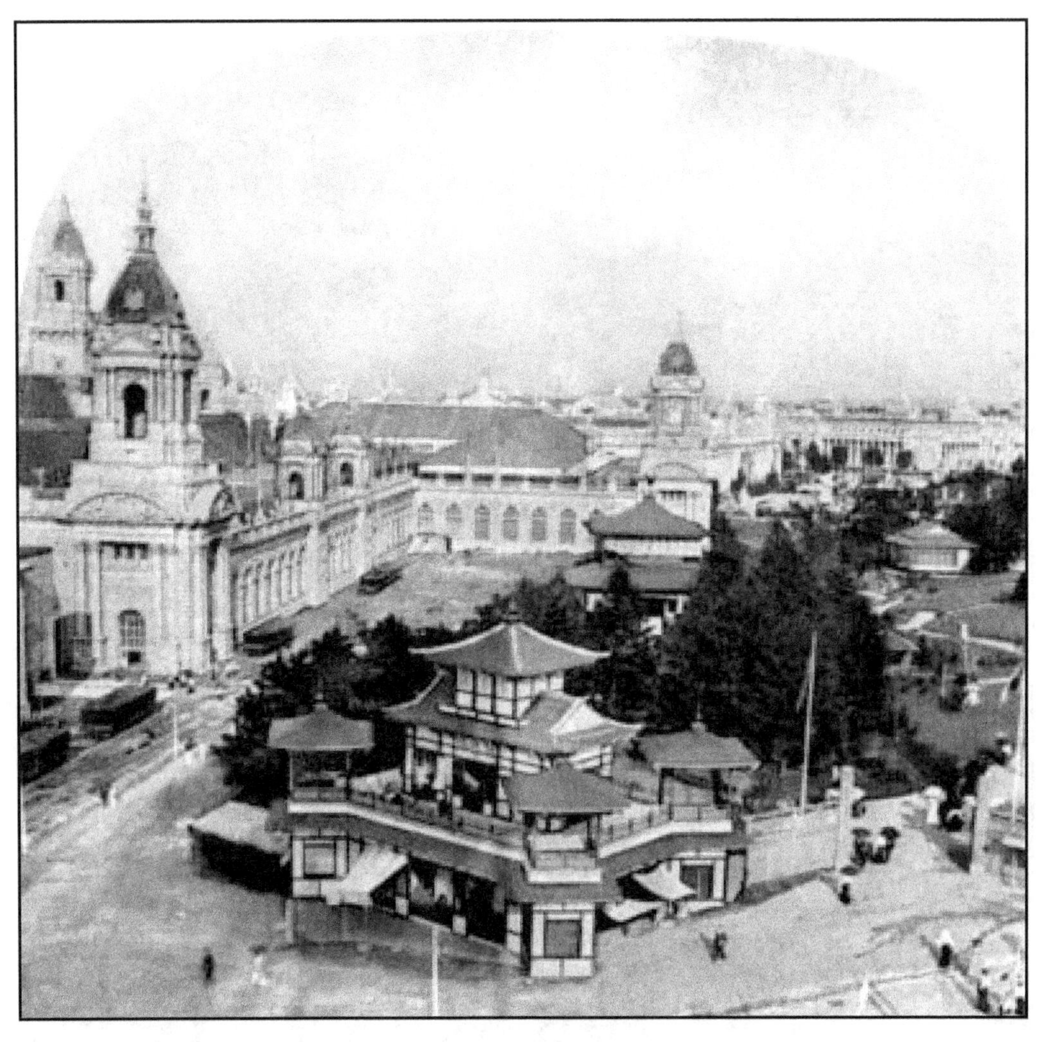

No. 30. Japanese Tea House, Palace of Machinery

The large hillside area which is occupied by Japan lies east of the Observation wheel and southwest of the Palace of Machinery. The beautiful pavilion shown... is used as a tea house, and is modeled after the Kikakuji Palace still standing at Kioto after 480 years of service. In the upper rooms are models of Japanese idols and images, and on the first floor one stops to take tea, whether he cares for it or not, just for the pleasure of being served by the dainty and charming maidens whose English is as limited as it is delightful. (*Universal Exposition*)

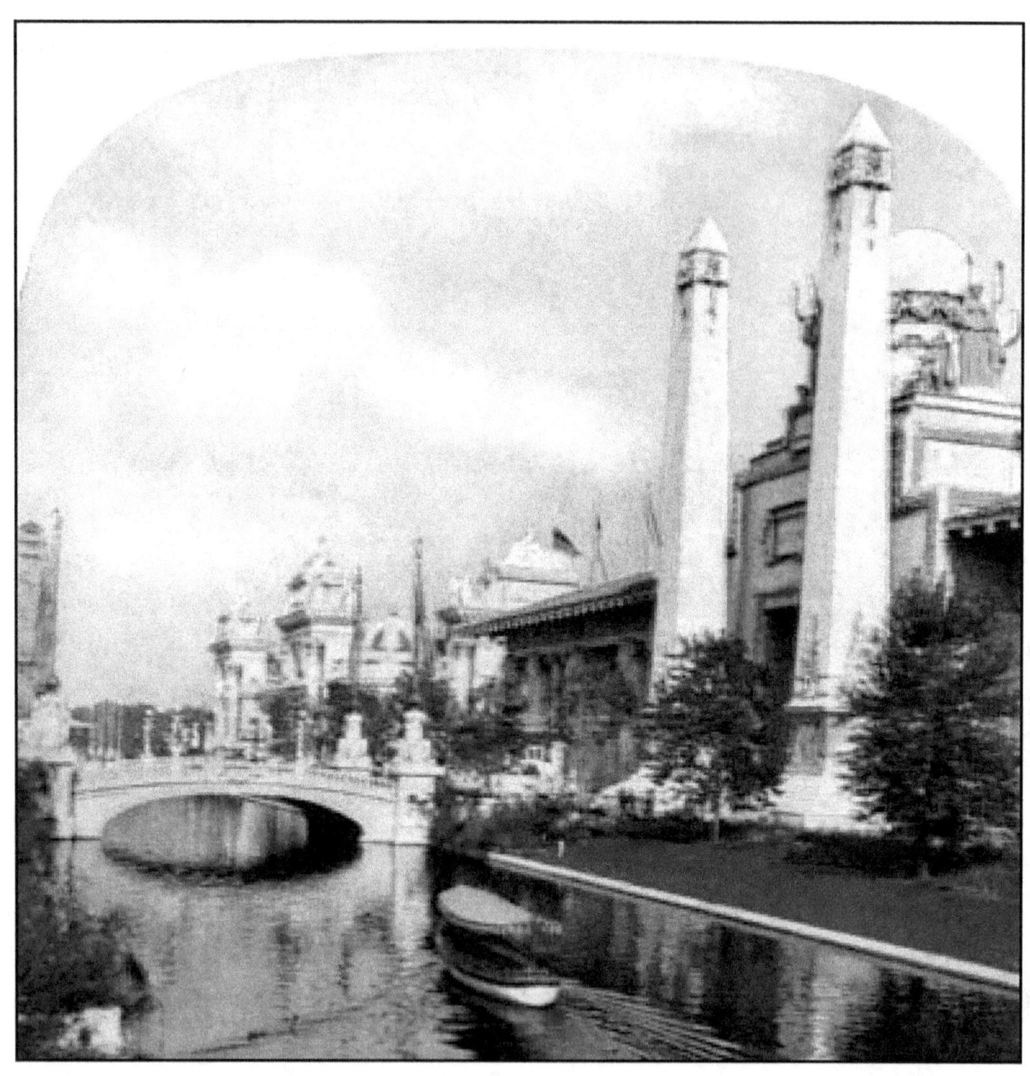

No. 31. Palace of Mines and Metallurgy

The architect of the Palace of Mines and Metallurgy offers something entirely new in Exposition construction. We can all discover the tall Egyptian obelisks that flank the square Egyptian entrances but the bulbous domes far aloft are nature's favorite form. The open corridors and overhanging roof suggest coolness. The building is 525 by 750 feet and covers nine acres. It is the largest building ever erected for a mining exhibit and cost $500,000. (*Universal Exposition*)

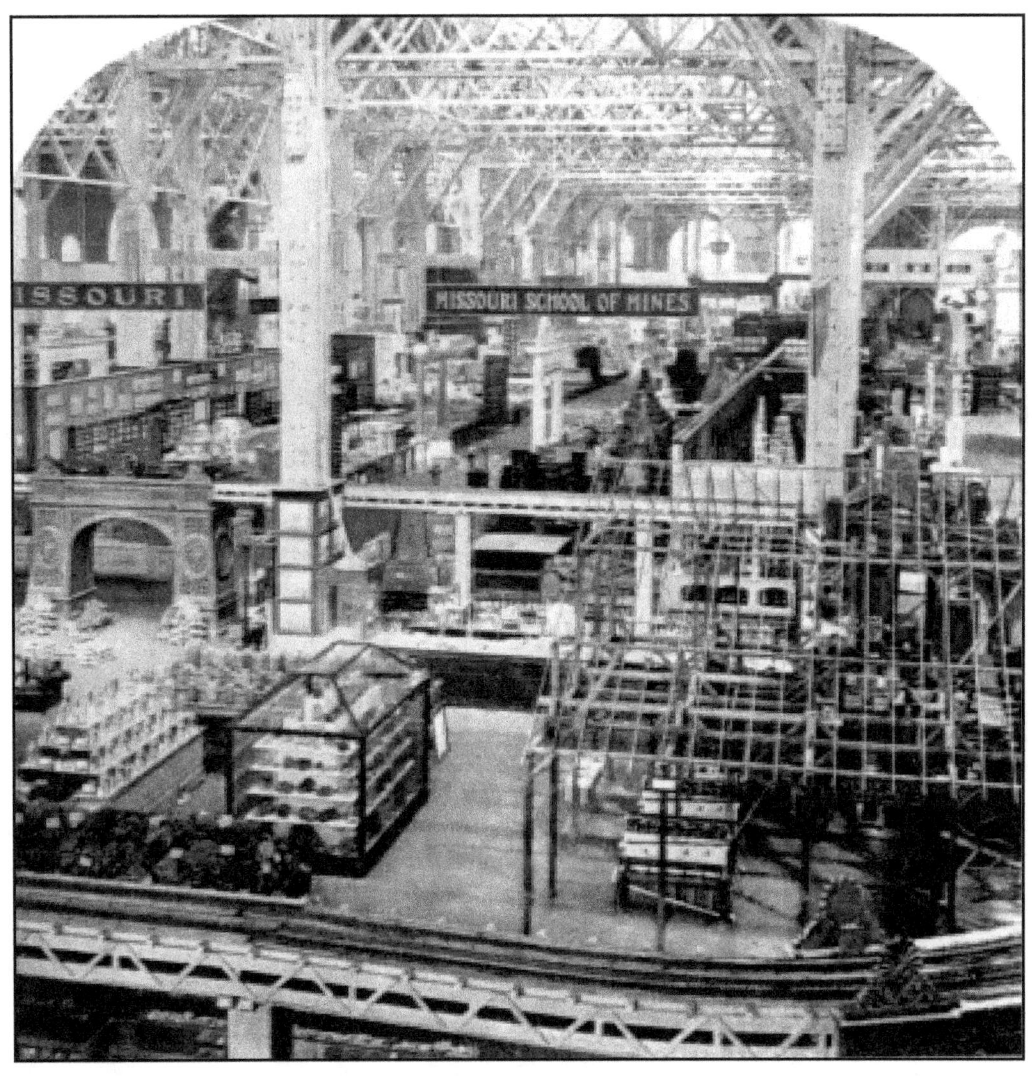

No. 32. Palace of Mines and Metallurgy

The Mines and Metallurgical exhibit embraces everything from clays to precious metals and gems. Mine engineering in its latest development is clearly portrayed. Ore crushing and concentrating processes are shown. Primitive methods of smelting copper ores by Mexican Indians are shown in an exhibit in the Mining Gulch. A modern art pottery is also a feature of the gulch, wherein the processes of manufacture may be noted. (*Universal Exposition*)

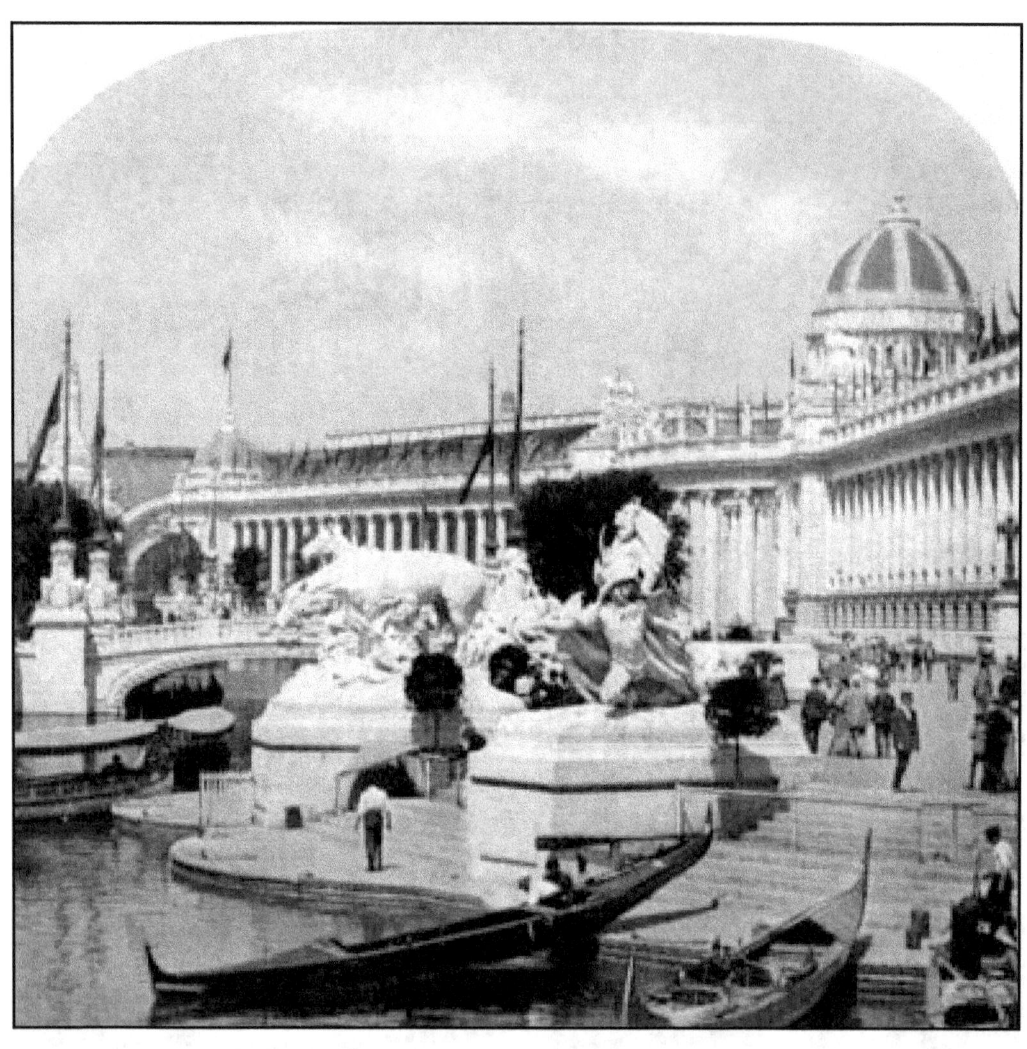

No. 33. Palace of Varied Industries

The long colonnades, domes, and towers are the distinguishing features in the architecture of the Palace of Varied Industries. It has the same dimensions as the Palace of Manufactures, being 525 feet wide by 1,200 feet in length and covering an area of fourteen acres. The exhibits within this beautiful palace are gathered from many states and countries. Germany and Japan are rivals in the extent of space covered, but their rivalry ends there, for the exhibits are radically different. (*Universal Exposition*)

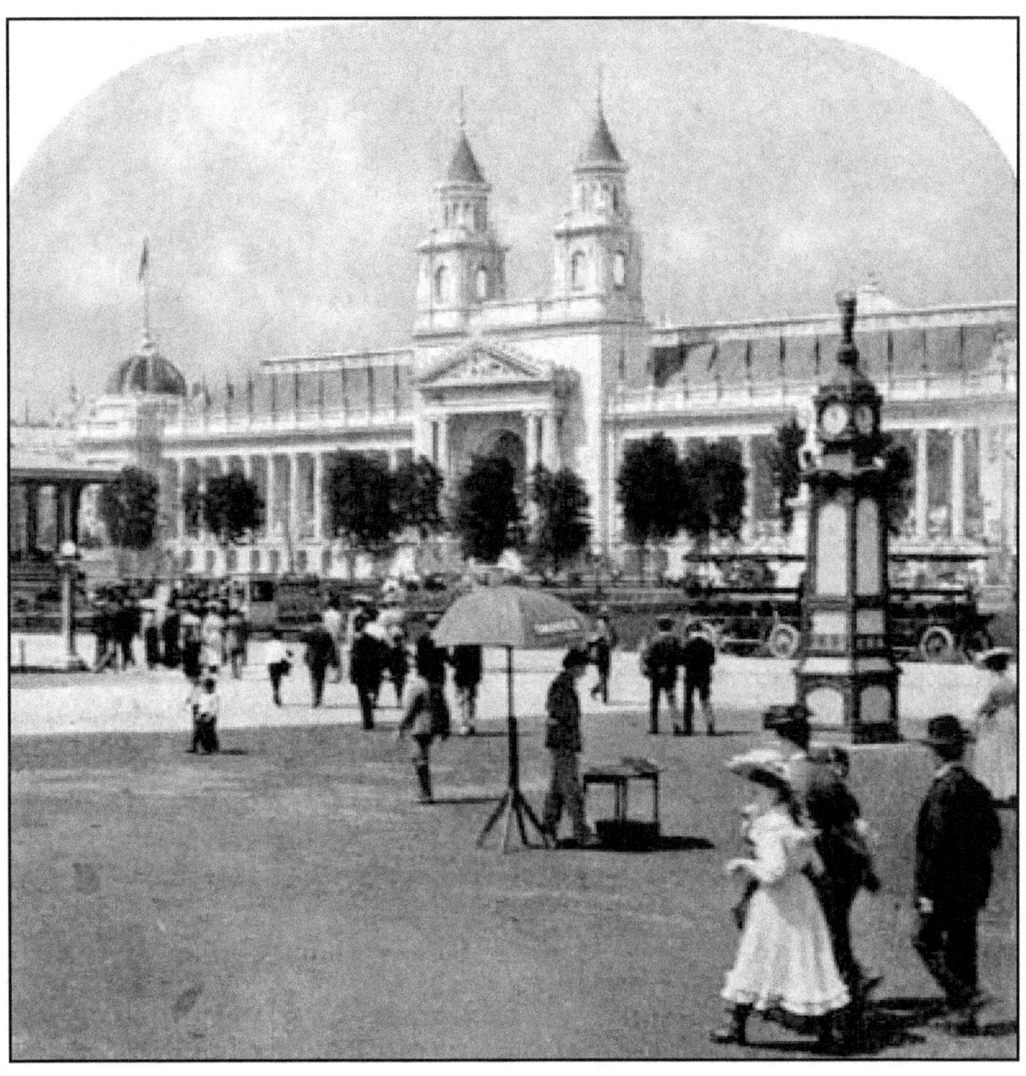

No. 34. Palace of Varied Industries

Germany occupies a large area in the northeastern corner, the installation for which is very elaborate. In this building the exhibits are those of art industries such as art pottery, cut glass and art glass, office and household furniture, brushes, fine leather articles, jewelry, silversmiths' and goldsmiths' wares, clocks and watches, products in marble, bronze, cast iron, wrought iron, paper hangings and upholsterers' decorations. The Japan exhibit occupies a very large space in the southwestern corner with a beautiful temple as its entrance. (*Universal Exposition*)

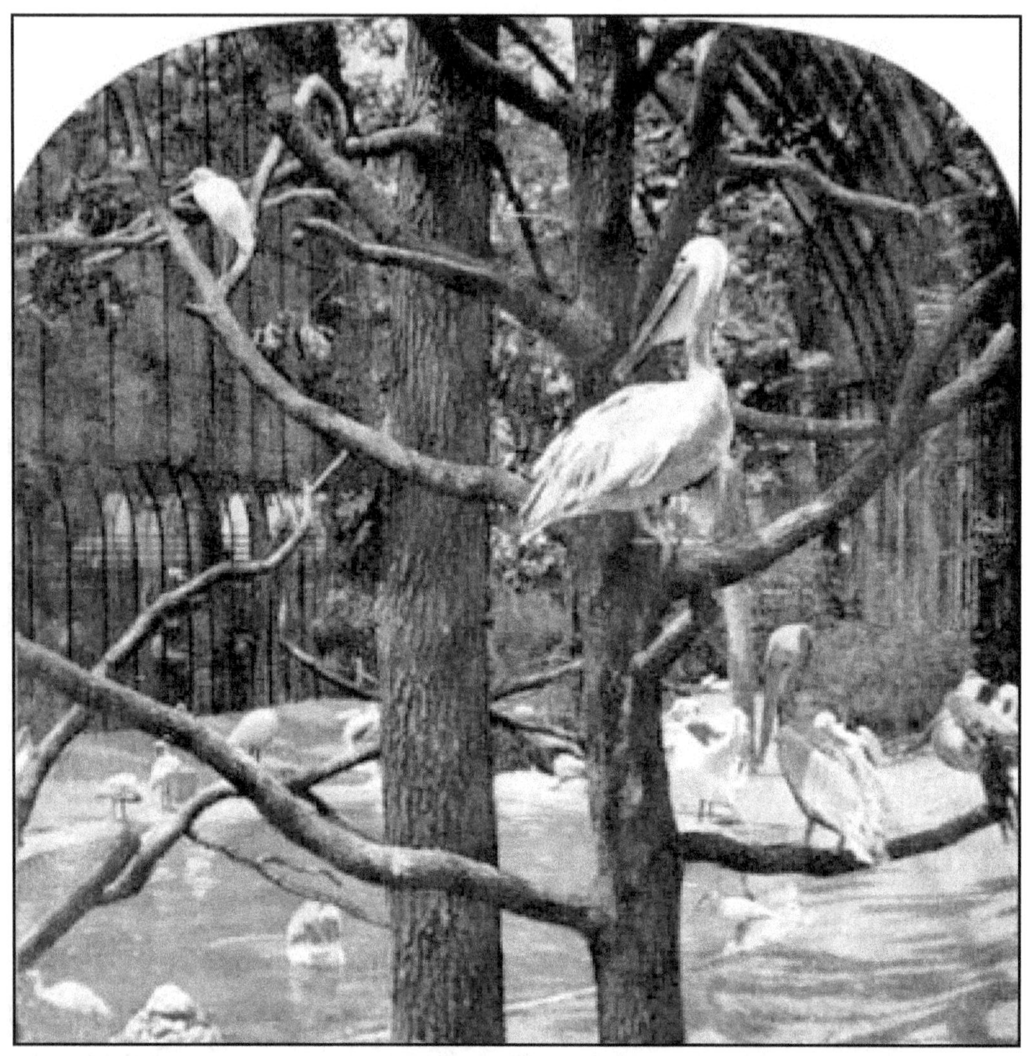

No. 35. The Happy Family in Mammoth Bird Cage

It was indeed a happy family in the great cage of the United States Government. Birds from sea and land, river and forest, large and small, plain and gorgeous, were there, and all seemingly content to dwell together and to be looked at the thousands who crowded around them. There was the pelican, crane, oyster-catcher, sandpiper, grouse, partridge, prairie-hen, bob-white, the golden, belted and piping plover, the Godwit, yellow-legs, and woodcock dozens of ducks and geese, herons and bitterns, owls and boobies, gulls and kittywakes, grebes and puffins, hawks and pigeons, woodpeckers and humming-birds, orioles, jays, finches, and blackbirds. *(original 1904 caption)*

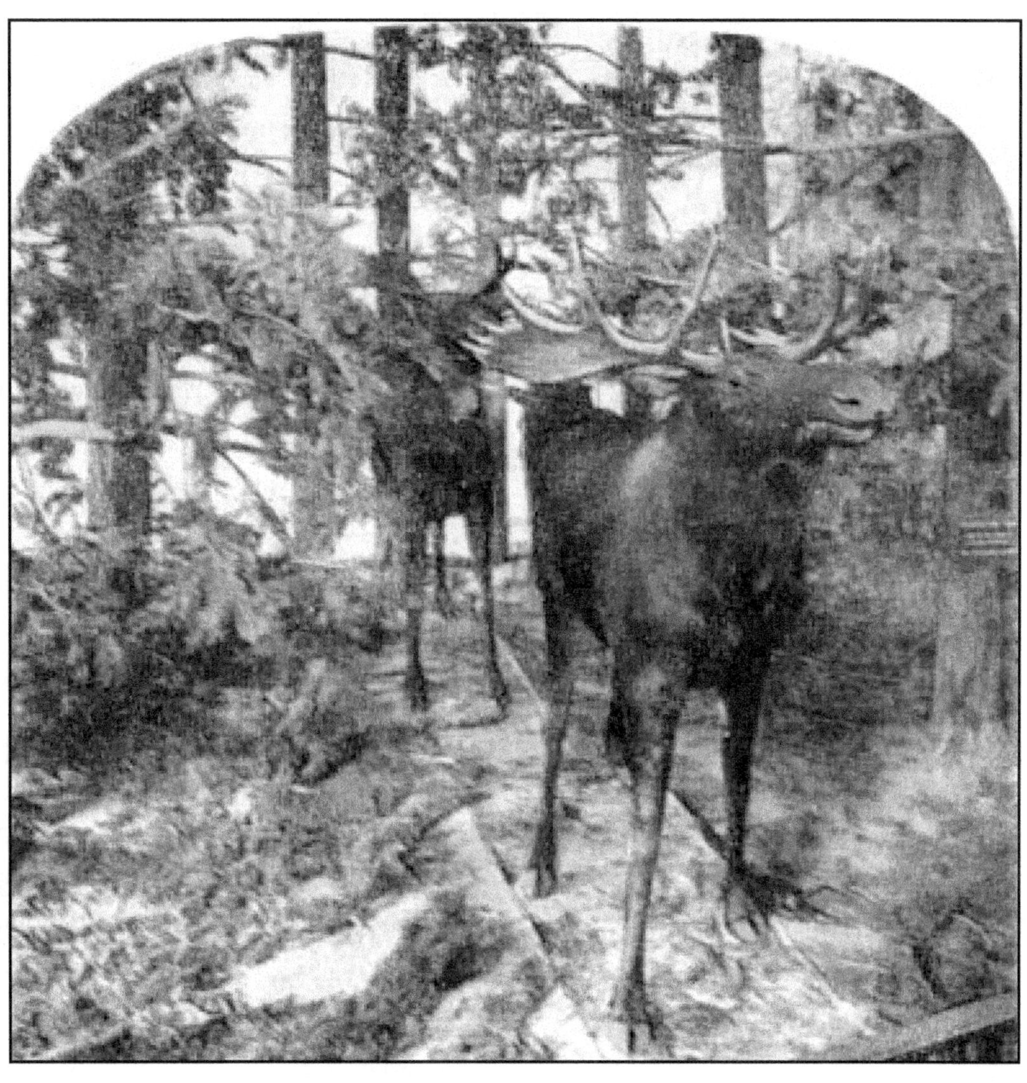

No. 36. Moose in Minnesota Game Exhibit

In the Forestry, Fish and Game Building, Minnesota had a very elaborate display of her sources of wealth. There were tanks with fresh water fish, and a realistic piece of forestry and game in the shape of a real forest of trees, with wild animals mounted in natural poses and with a painted background blending with the real objects. *(original 1904 caption)*

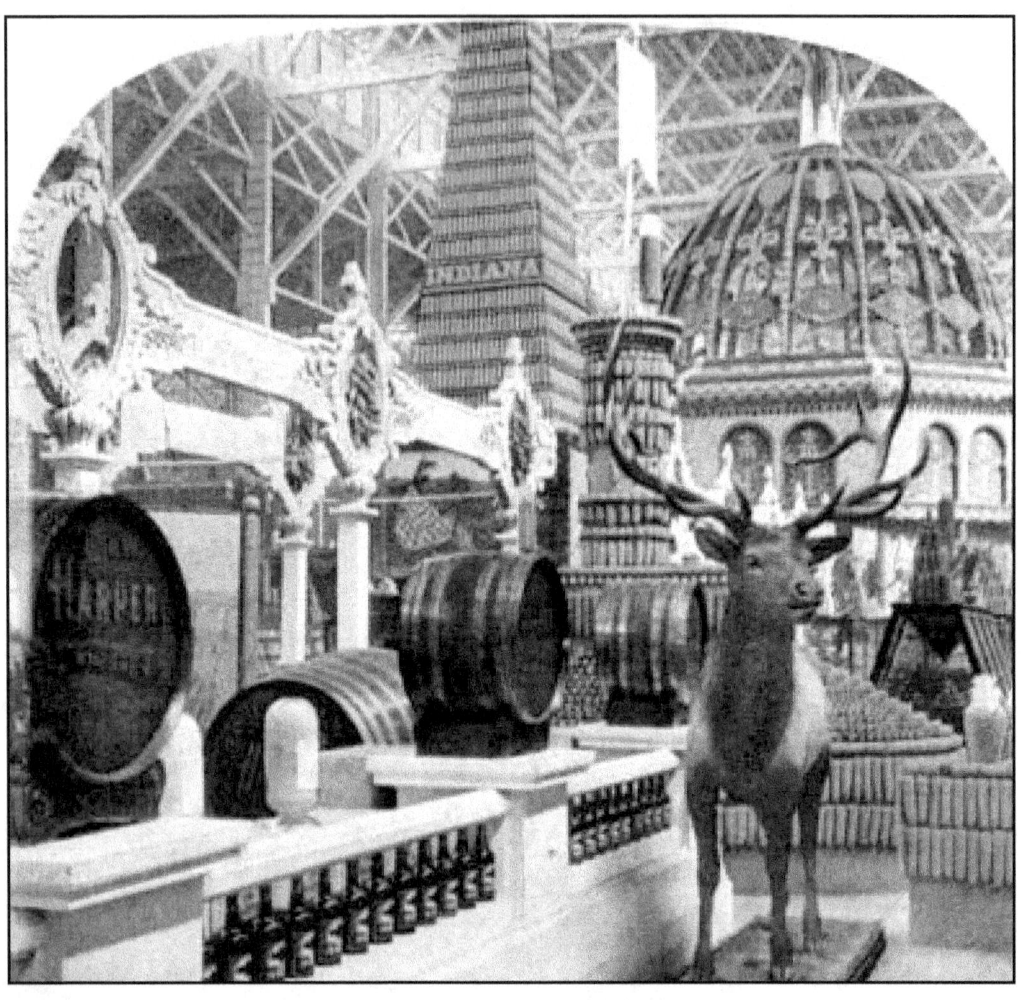

No. 37. Indiana and Missouri Grain Exhibit

Indiana's chief industry is agriculture.The alluvial valleys of the streams and the drained prairies offer the most fertile soil, a light, sandy loam, and the farmers produce every year agricultural staples in the value of $200,000,000, chief among which is corn, of which they raise about 180,000,000 bushels. Missouri is a great country for raising corn, oats and a superior grade of wheat. All kinds of fodder grasses also grow abundantly, and fruits from apples to figs and nectarines, are successfully cultivated. In the southern part a large quantity of wine is made, and Missouri grapes are famous. The exhibits of these two states went far to demonstrate the claim of the United States to the name of the richest country in the world. *(original 1904 caption)*

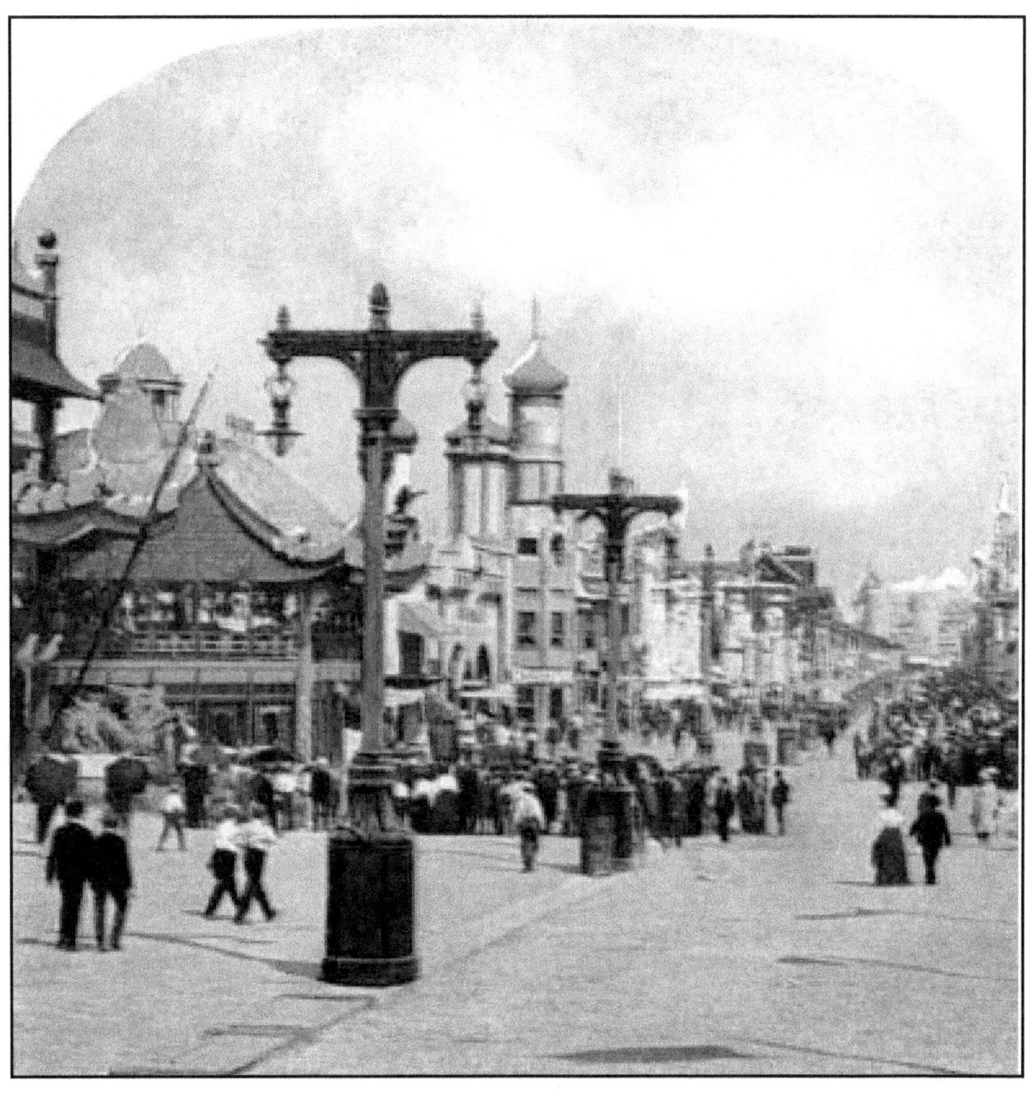

No. 38. General View of "The Pike"

The Pike is a street a mile long, solidly lined with amusements more varied, more elaborate and more costly than any previous exposition has ever contained. Some fifty entertainments have been installed, at a total cost of several millions. When night comes, and the exhibit palaces are closed, the throng is on the Pike. Everyone on the grounds takes a stroll down the Pike, to see the life and motion and color and light, to hear the bands and listen to the ingenious gentlemen whose wits are sharpened in the competition for patronage. *(St. Louis World's Fair)*

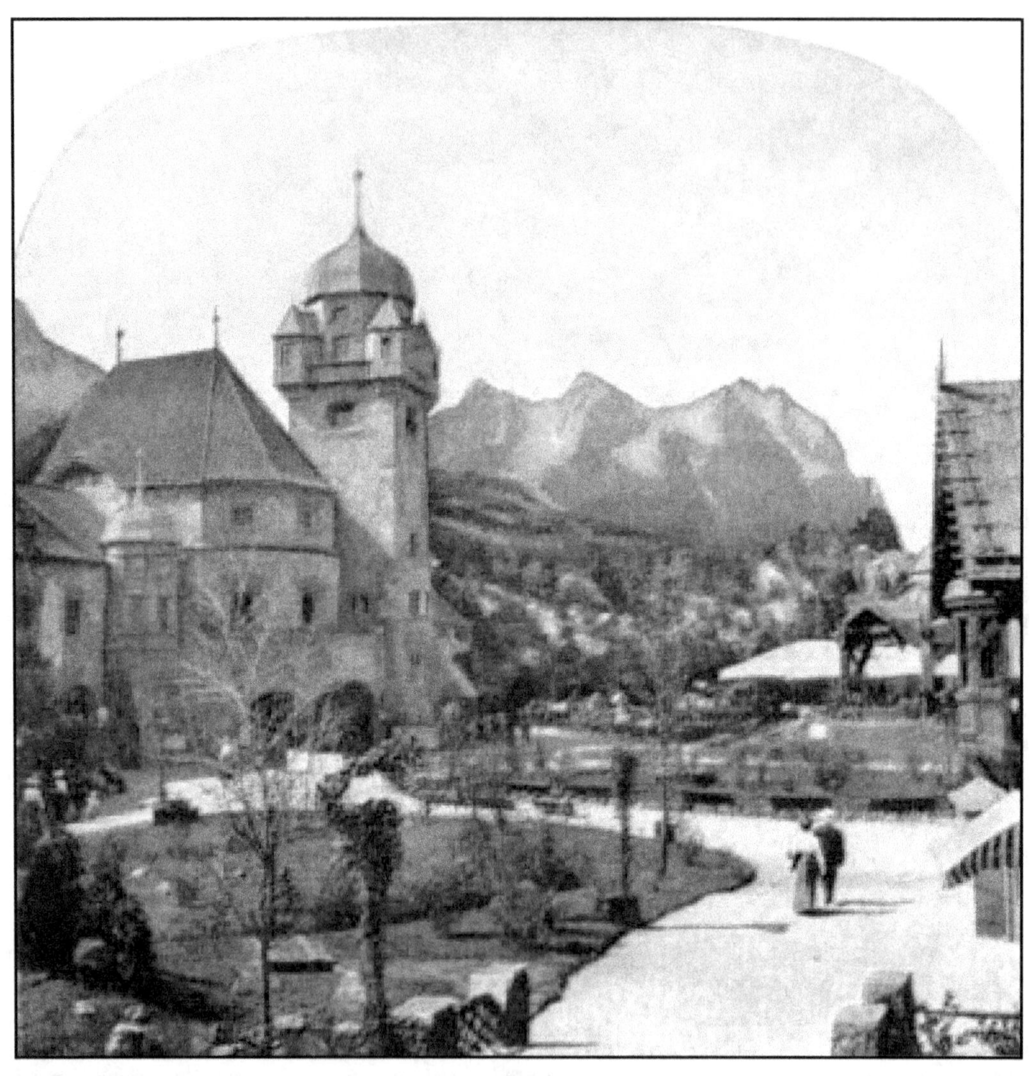

No. 39. The Castle in the Tyrolean Alps

The concession "Tyrolean Alps" was the most popular among all the amusement resorts on the Pike. Thousands wended their way there every night, when the great palaces had closed, to spend a few hours in these most restful surroundings. Our picture represents a mountain castle and council hall with verandas and terraces, overshadowed by jagged, snow-capped peaks in the background. *(original 1904 caption)*

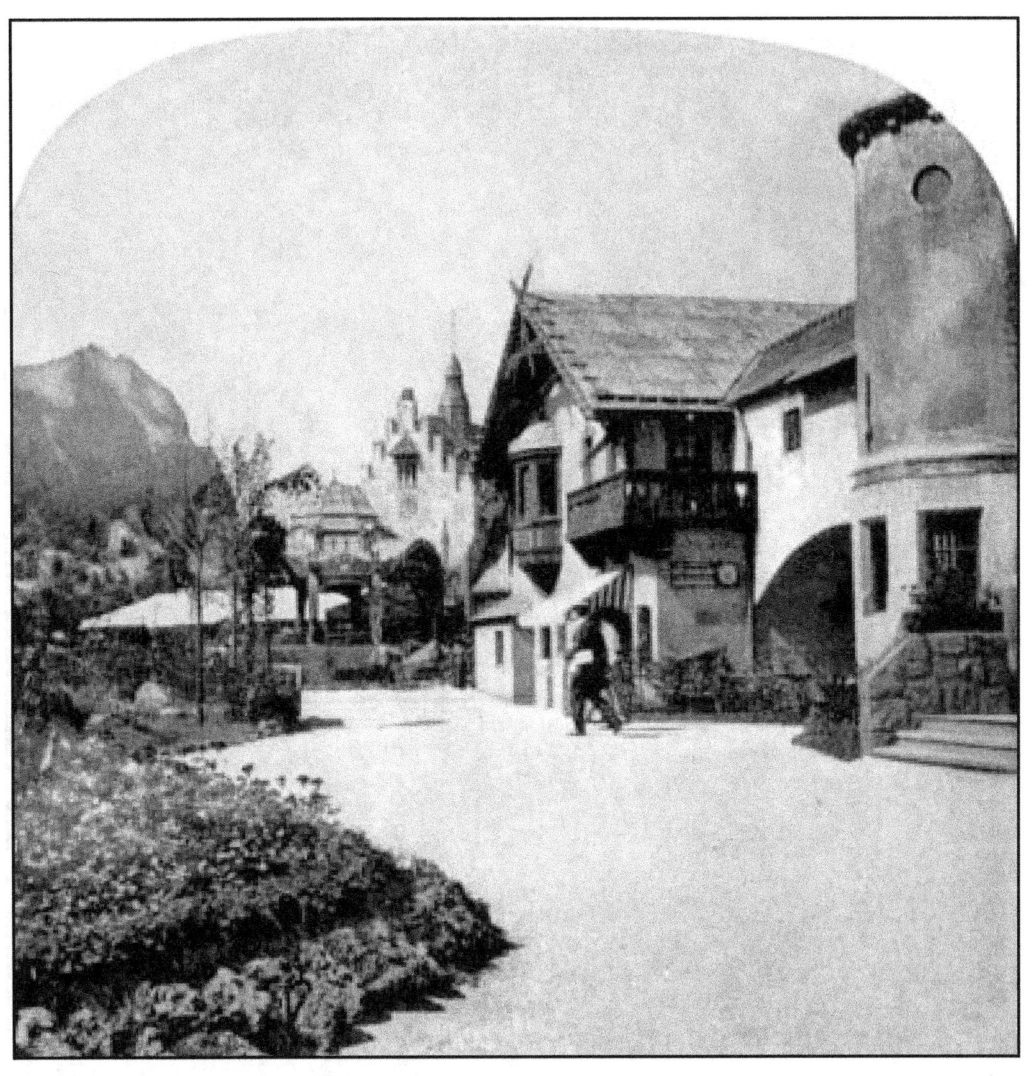

No. 40. View in the Tyrolean Alps Village

The grounds covered 250,000 square feet, contained 100 buildings, and the whole was such a splendid imitation of real Alpine scenery in the Tyrol that everybody was charmed with it. To carry out the illusion, two troupes of genuine Tyroleans alternately entertained the visiting crowds with their "yodlers" and native mountain songs and dances, greatly admired by the Germans and Austrians who flocked thither to hear them, and by many Americans. *(original 1904 caption)*

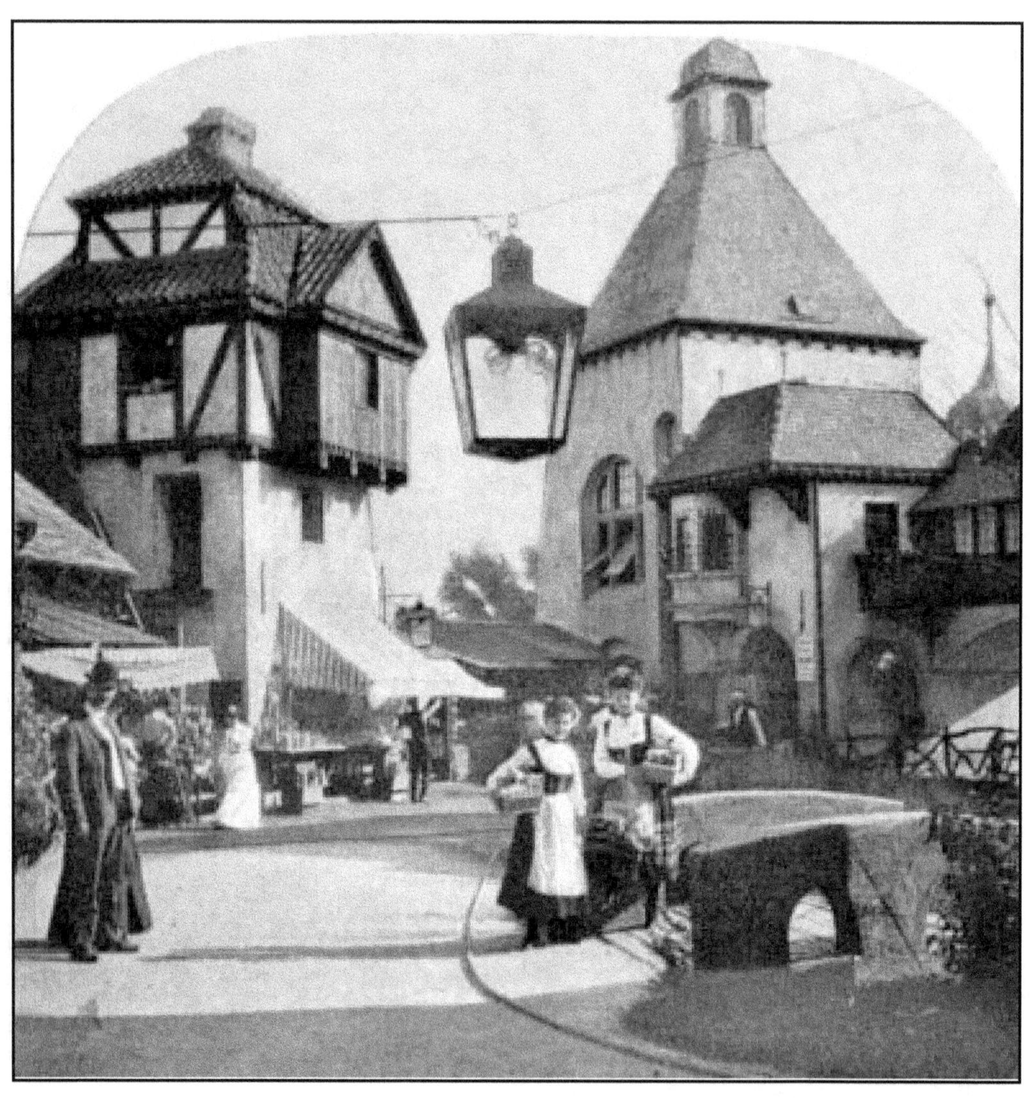

NO. 41. A PICTURESQUE CORNER IN THE TYROLEAN ALPS

The most delightful local feature of the concession "Tyrolean Alps" on the Pike were the choruses of Tyrolean singers. There were two of these, both consisting of genuine mountaineers from Tyrol, rivaling each other in every respect. The voices were exceptionally fine and strong, and the singing was wholly the natural, untutored art of the peasants of Tyrol. These troupes recruit themselves every winter in their native mountains and soon after Christmas go forth on a tour of the principal large cities of Germany. *(original 1904 caption)*

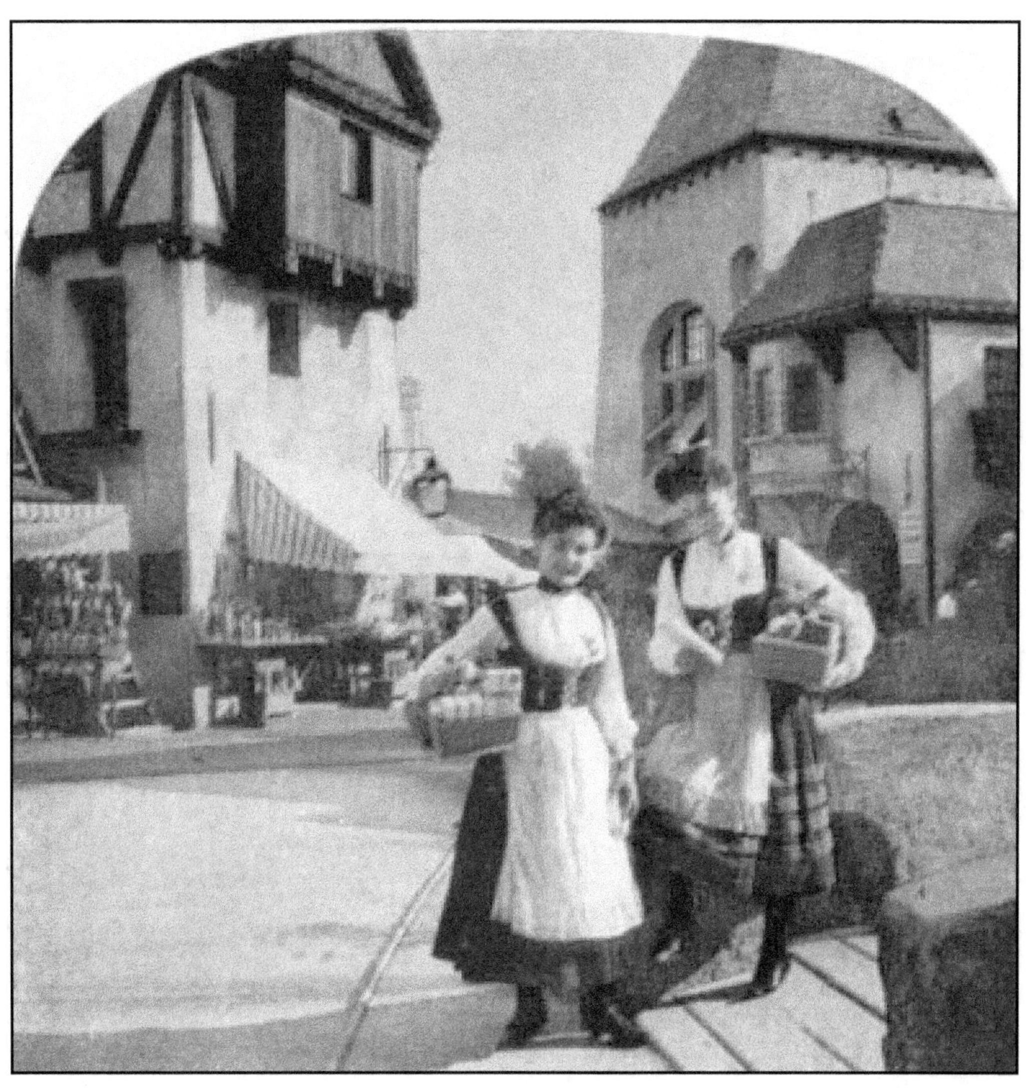

No. 42. Bon Bon Girls in the Alpine Village

To a stranger, especially an American, it is amazing to find a finely developed ear and a capital voice in a rough looking country lad who can hardly read, but who is able to join with a second or third voice in a song which he has not heard before. It is not so easy, however, to hear these people sing in Tyrol. They are shy, and to enjoy a musical treat of this kind one must strike into unfrequented paths and if possible visit a lonesome Alp-hut up in the clouds. *(original 1904 caption)*

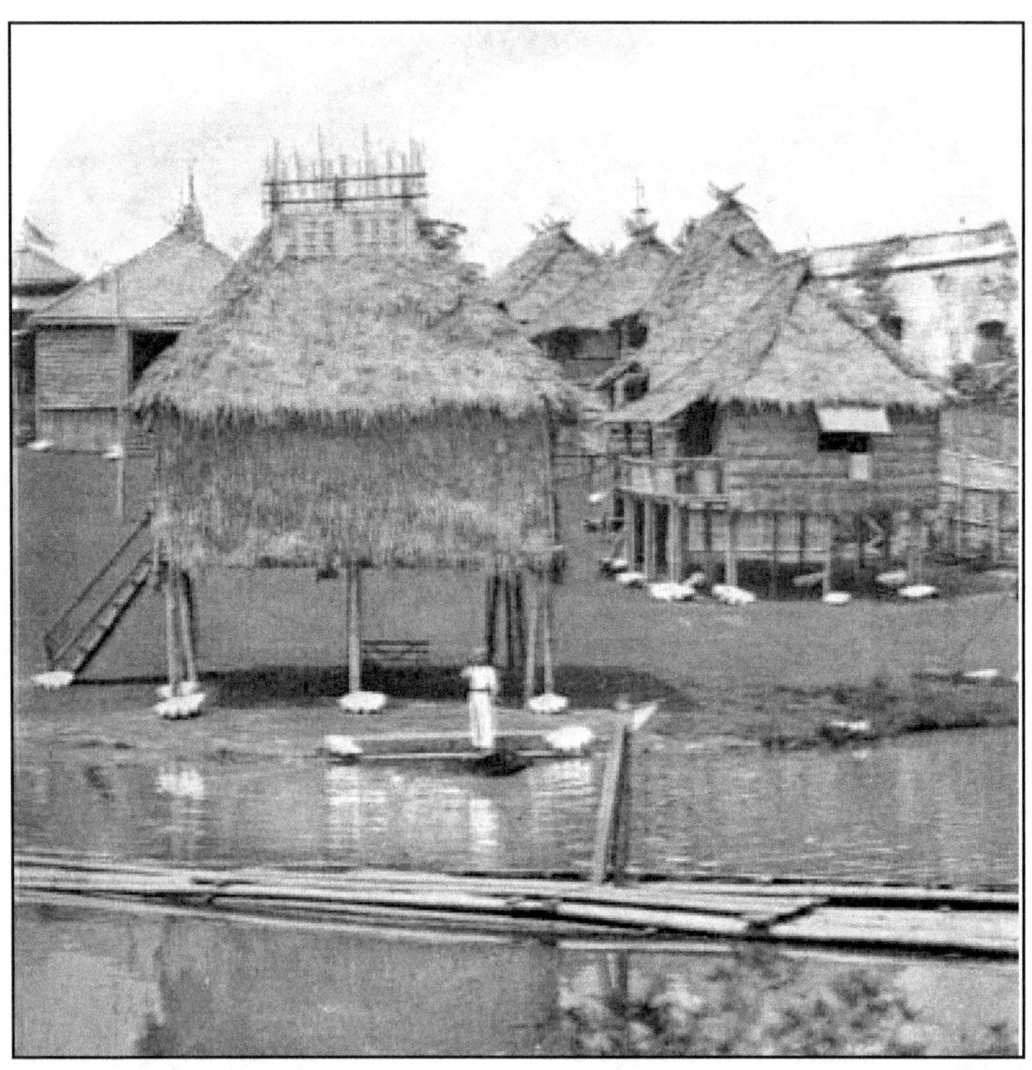

No. 43. Visayan Houses in Philippine Village

The Visayan Islands compose the largest and central group of the Philippine Archipelago, south of Luzon and north of Mindanao, with a total land area of 23,500 square miles. The houses of the Visayans, as shown in the picture, are raised above the ground on poles of bamboo, for sanitary and other reasons. They remind the beholder of the similar dwellings found in the moors of Switzerland, remnants of the time when our Caucasian ancestors also lived in primitive houses on stilts. *(original 1904 caption)*

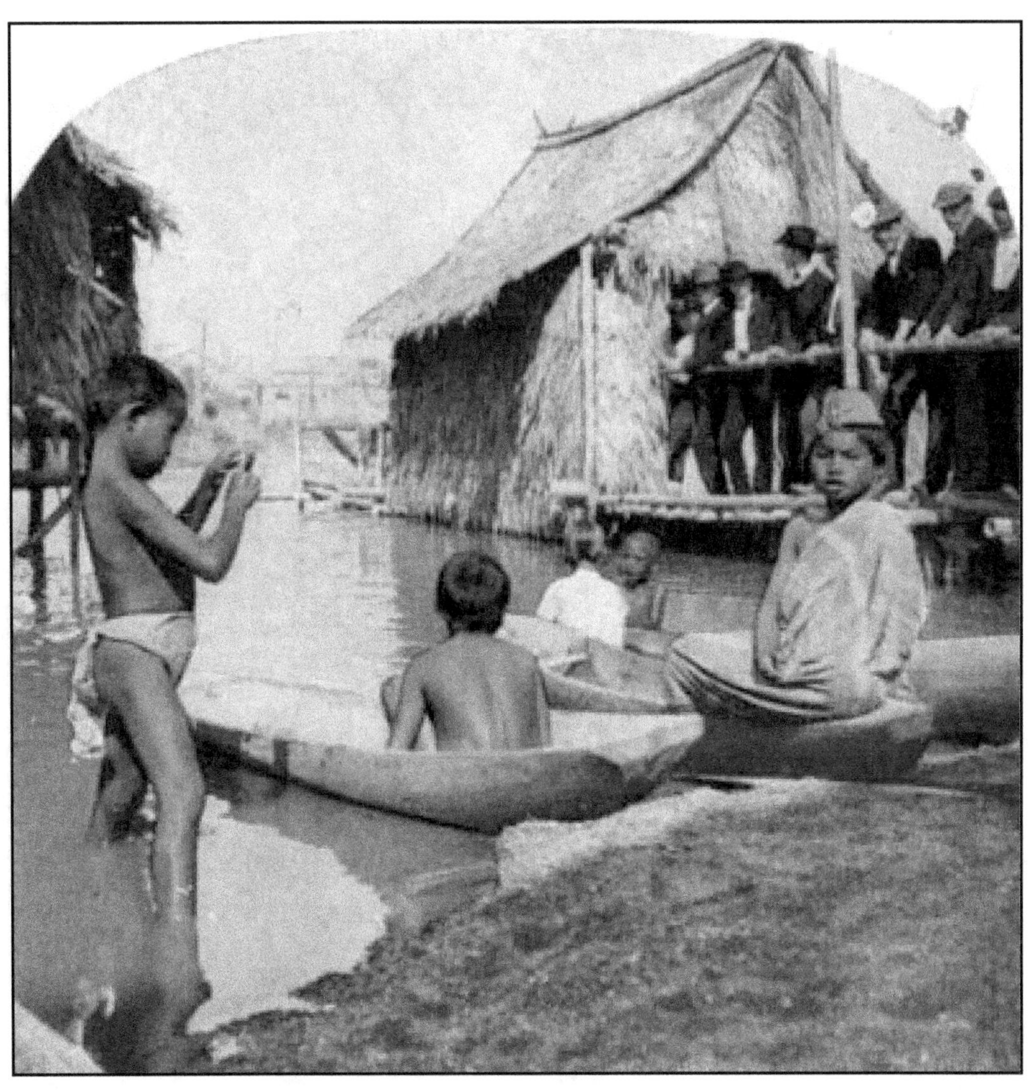

No. 44. Visayan natives, Philippine Village

There are about 490 islands in the group, of which Bohol, Cebu, Leyte, Masbate, Negros, Tanay, Romblon and Samar are the largest. All the islands are well wooded, producing excellent varieties of hardwoods and many resin and gum trees. The trepang, pearl shell and pearl fisheries are quite important. *(original 1904 caption)*

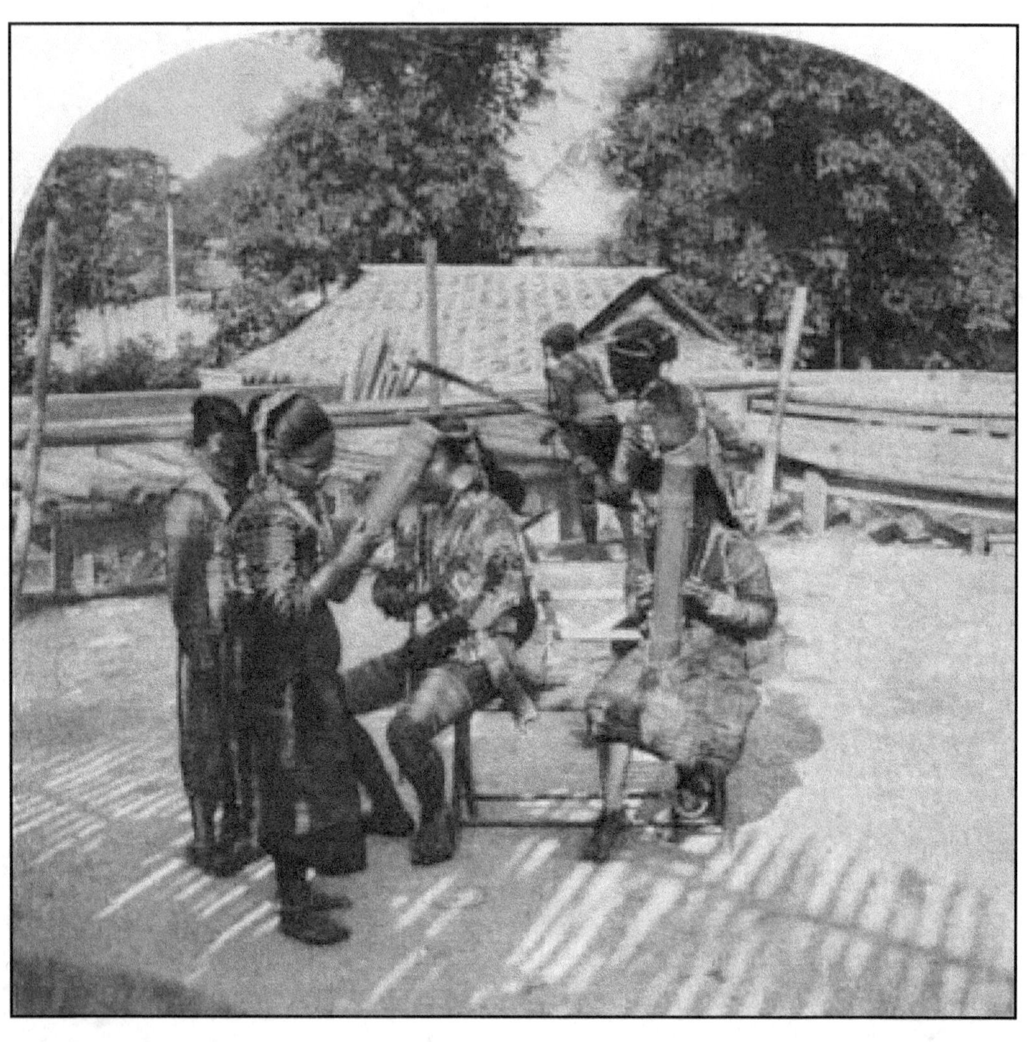

No. 45. Bagabos Maidens, Philippine Village

In Cebu was found the first coal discovered in the Philippines. Gold, silver, copper and iron also are mined to some extent. The islands produce cane sugar mostly and the weaving of the sugar sacks is a large industry. *(original 1904 caption)*

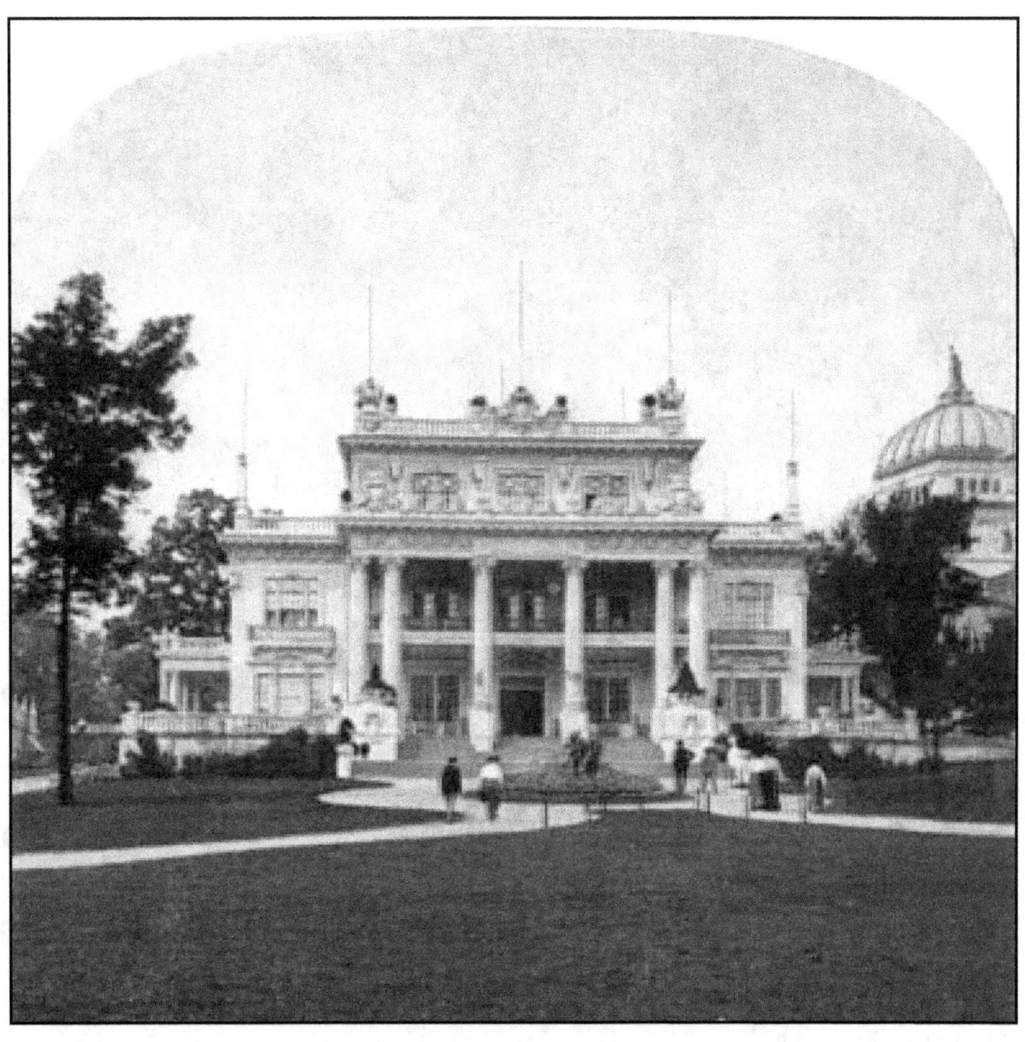

No. 46. Kentucky State Building

Near the five-pointed structure of Texas stood the Kentucky State Building, a rich elaboration of the Colonial style. The central feature was the great reception hall extending through three stories with two galleries. In the center of the main floor was the statue of George Rogers Clark of Kentuckian fame. The walls of all the rooms were ornamented with Kentucky paintings, and on the two upper floors were displayed the famous embroideries and fancy needle work from the convents of the state. In one room, amid other interesting furniture, stood the desk at which Stephen Collins Foster wrote the words of My Old Kentucky Home." *(original 1904 caption)*

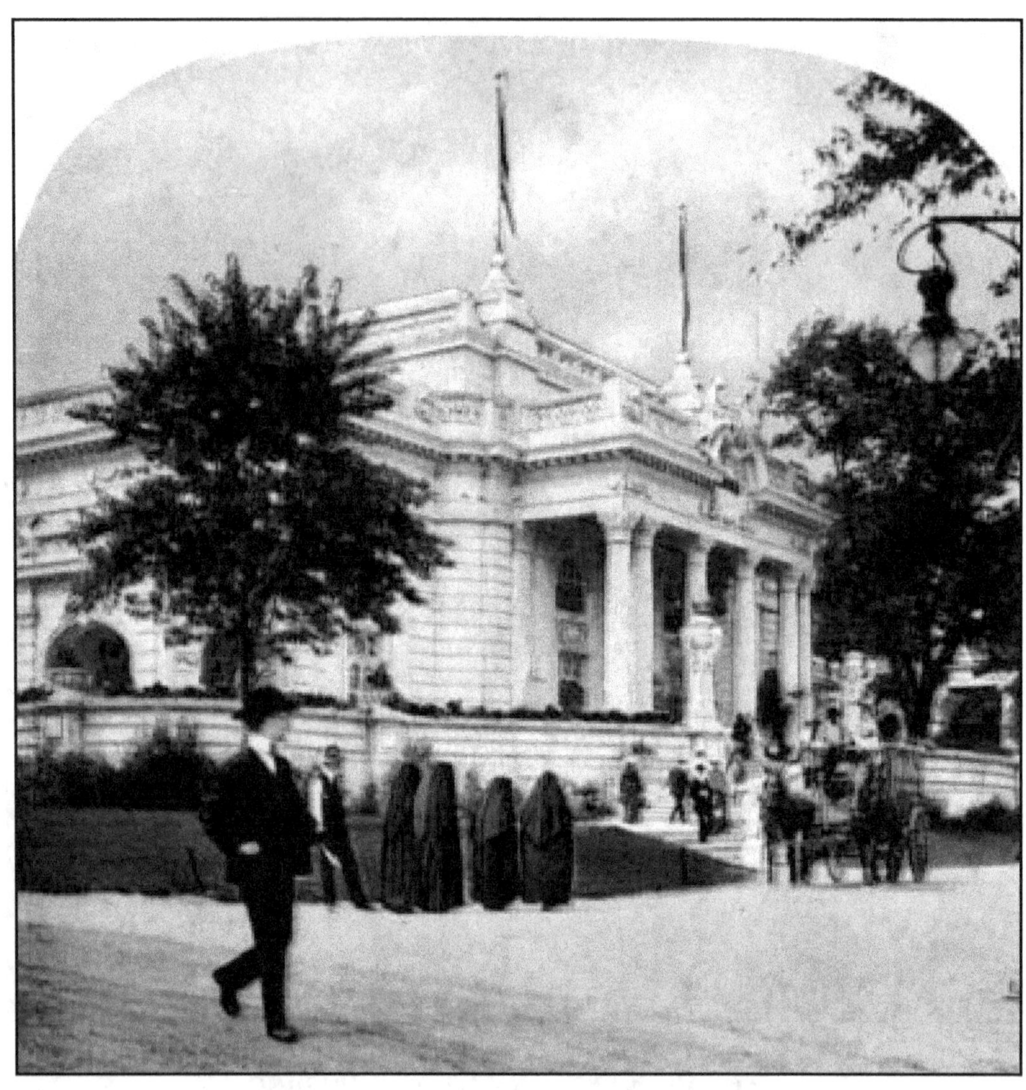

No. 47. Indiana State Building

Broad verandas decorated with a profusion of flowers and potted trees and shrubs added a decidedly homelike charm to the Indiana State Building, the richly sculptured portal of which was supported by six beautiful Corinthian columns. The main stairway in the interior was monumental. This building contained a complete set of the books of all the authors of Indiana, among which many a visitor recognized his favorite reading. The exhibition of Indiana artists, too, was very large and a great credit to the state. On the first floor of the State Pavilion was a lunch room for basket lunchers, largely patronized by the citizens of Indiana and other states. *(original 1904 caption)*

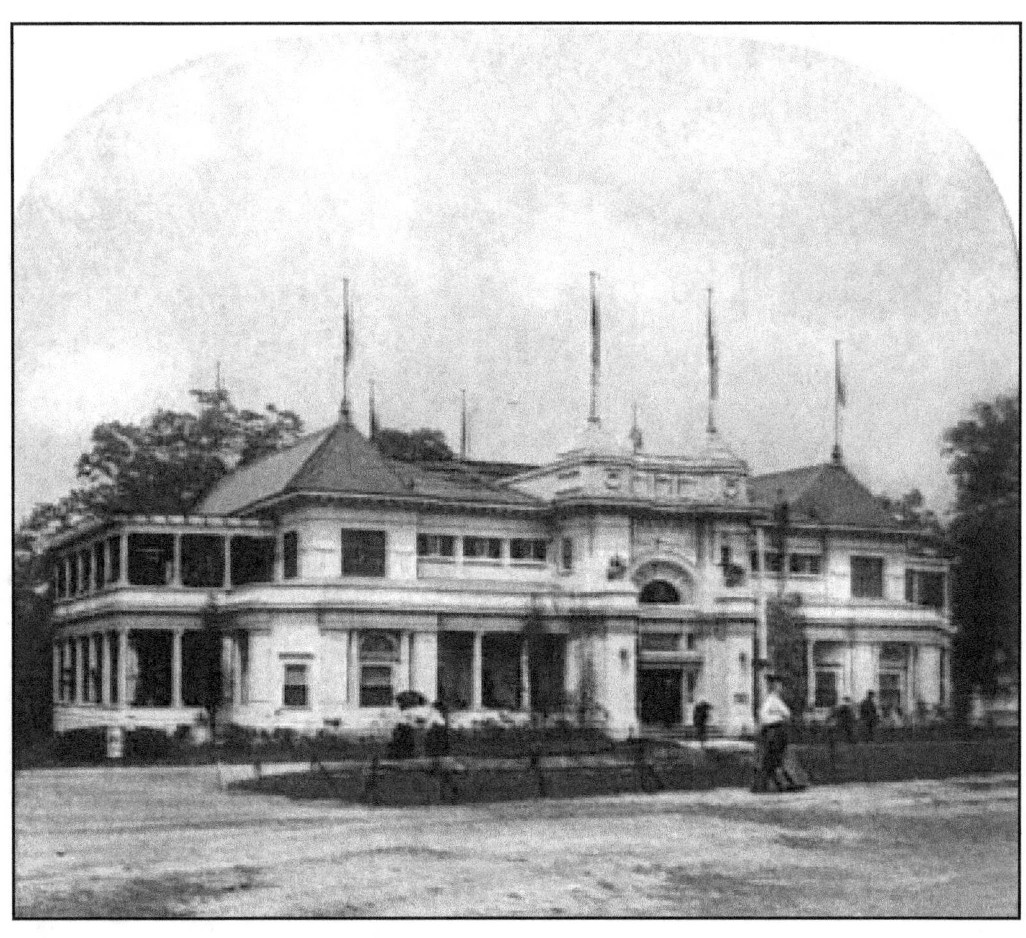

No. 48. The Kansas State Building

Of all the State buildings facing on Commonwealth Avenue, none is more home-like or more popular than that of Kansas. Opening from its great central reception hall are rest rooms for the ladies and smoking and reading rooms for the gentlemen, post-office and check room, emergency hospital, and day nursery where Kansas mothers may leave their little ones. The reception hall is surrounded, at the line of the second floor, by a gallery, the walls of which are covered with paintings by Kansas artists. The building and furnishings cost $40,000. *(St. Louis World's Fair)*

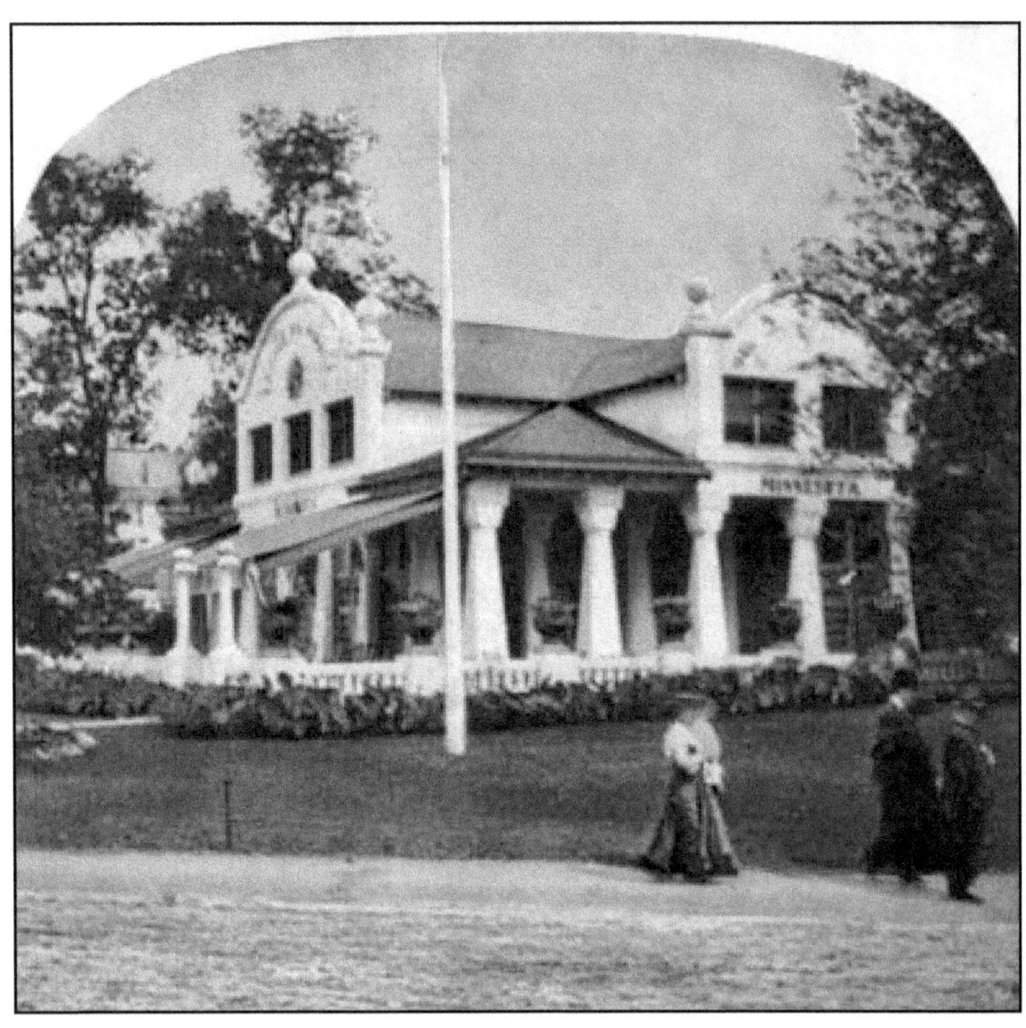

No. 49. The Minnesota State Building

The Minnesota Building represents an expenditure of over $16,000 and is a two-story structure. It is of the Greek Byzantine style. The furniture was largely furnished by the mechanical schools of the State. (*Universal Exposition*) Minnesota produces one-seventh of all the wheat raised in the United States, one-fifth of all the barley, and ranks fourth in the value of all cereals raised. Thousands of acres of swamp land worth $2.00 an acre have been reclaimed by the ditch work system of the State Drainage Commission and are worth $10.00 an acre today, and many thousands of acres more are waiting to be so reclaimed. *(original 1904 caption)*

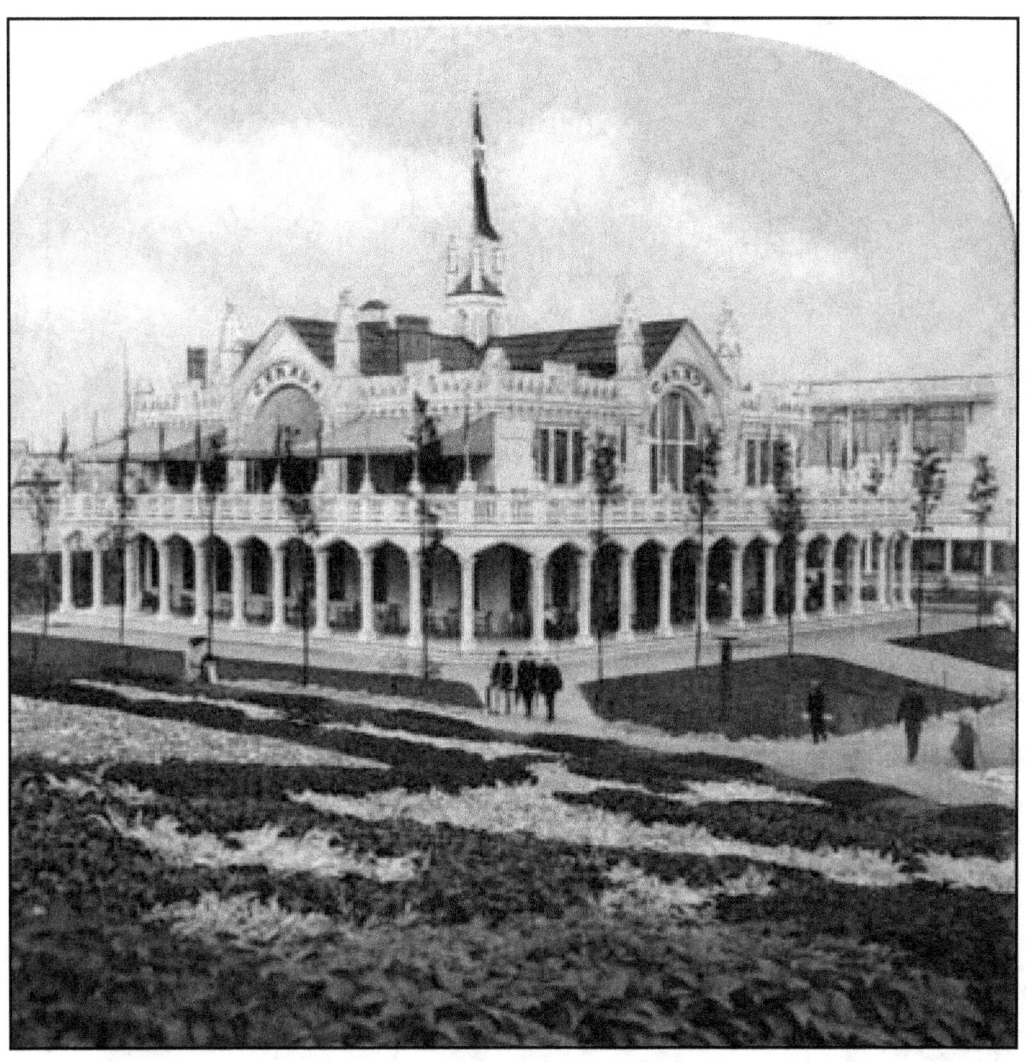

No. 50. The Canadian Building

The style of the Canadian Building was the Gothic of the times of Henry VII. The spacious verandas of the building were much in favor with those who wished for a cool place where to rest, as they were very centrally located between the Agricultural Palace, the Floral Clock and the Forestry, Fish and Game Building. The Dominion was well represented in all the large palaces, owing to the untiring efforts of the Commissioner of Expositions for Canada, Sir William Hutchinson. *(original 1904 caption)*

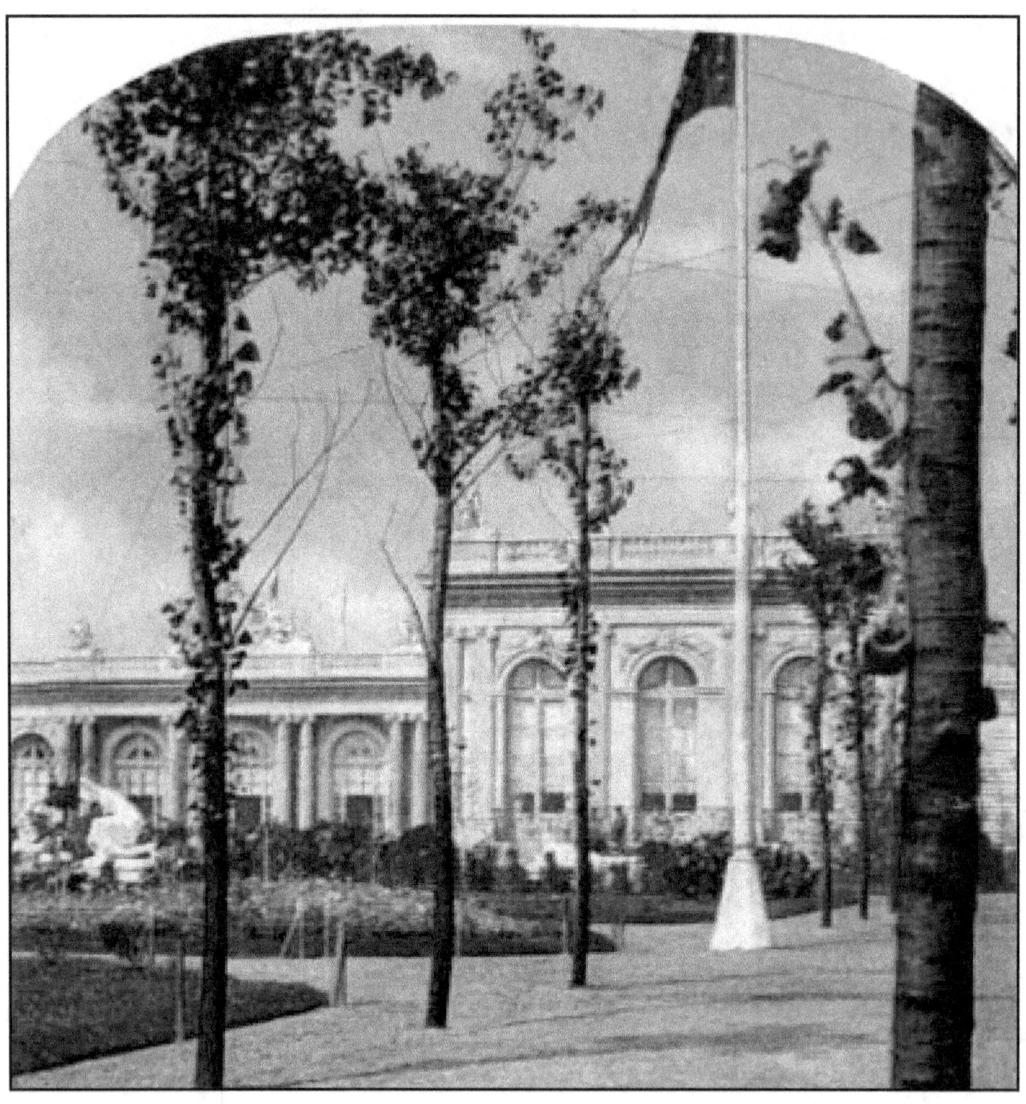

No. 51. The French Government's Building

The French Government selected as a model for its pavilion the Grand Trianon at Versailles, built by Louis XIV, and the building was surrounded by a plat of fifteen acres, laid out as a French garden with fruit trees trimmed in geometrical designs and a charming group of rock and water. The pavilion contained a beautiful display of priceless old tapestry and other historic articles of French art. There was also a large collection of invaluable Sevres porcelain, considered the finest in the world. *(original 1904 caption)*

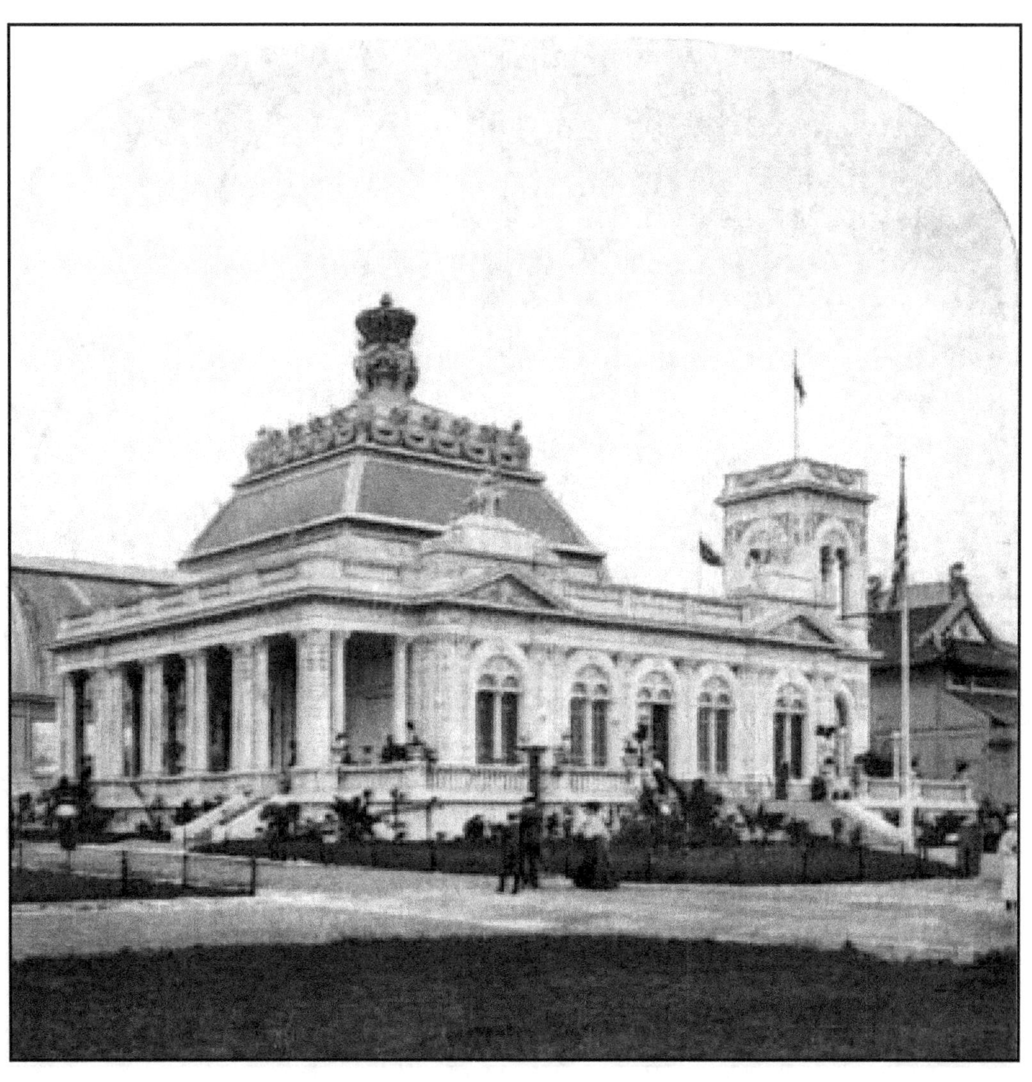

No. 52. Cuba's Pavilion

A well appointed dwelling-house of Havana of the present day is reproduced as the Cuban building opposite the Brazil building and adjoining the Chinese pavilion. The building was designed by the state architect of Cuba, Salvador Guartella. The ahded veranda on the south and open terrace on the east are attractive resting places for Exposition sightseers. (*Universal Exposition*)

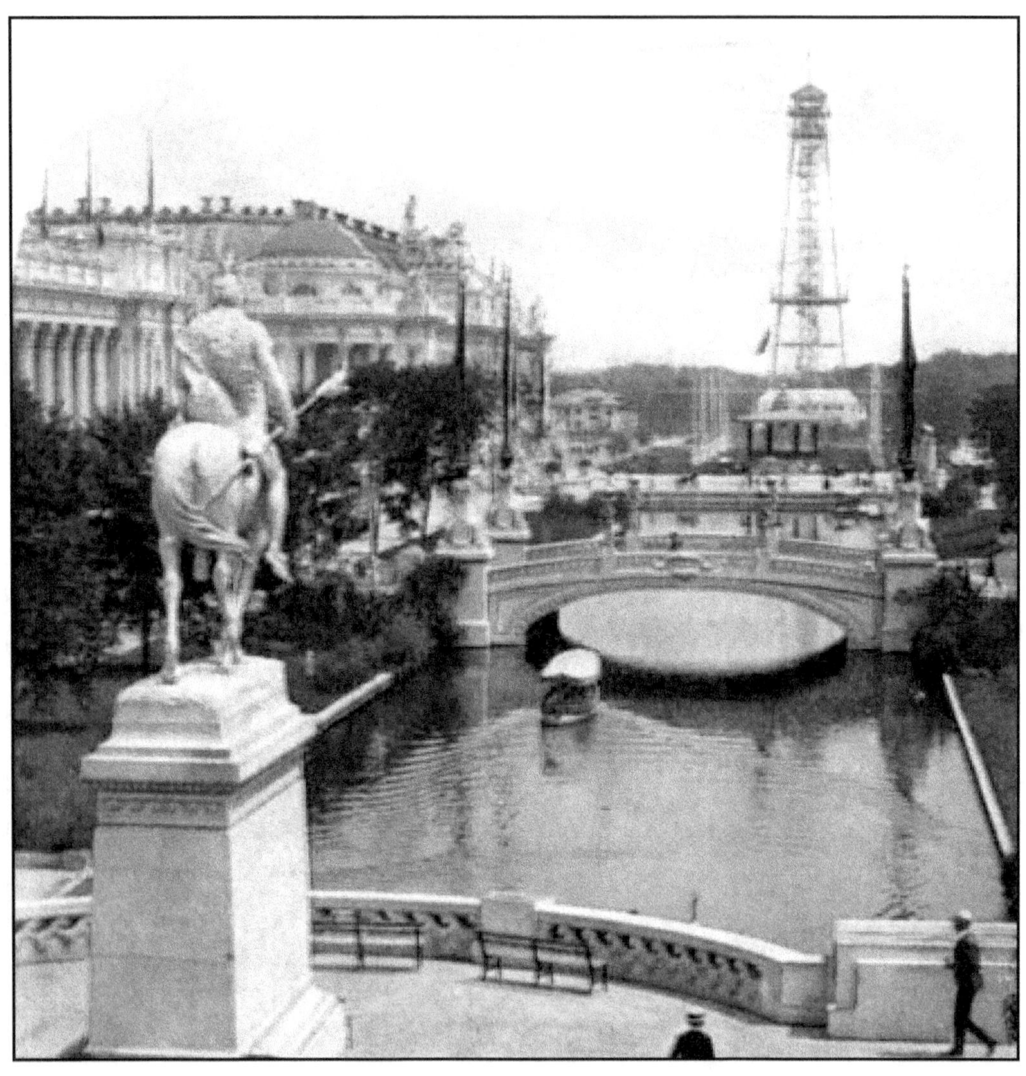

No. 53. East Lagoon, Palaces Education, Manufacture

This view looks from the east restaurant pavilion, at the east end of the colonnade of states, down across the east lagoon to the Buffalo Tower (or wireless tower) in the distance. An elevator in the Buffalo Tower took visitors nearly 300 feet up to overlook the fair grounds. The Palace of Education is to the near left, with the Palace of manufacture just beyond it. The Plaza of Orleans lies just beyond the bridge. *(St. Louis World's Fair)*

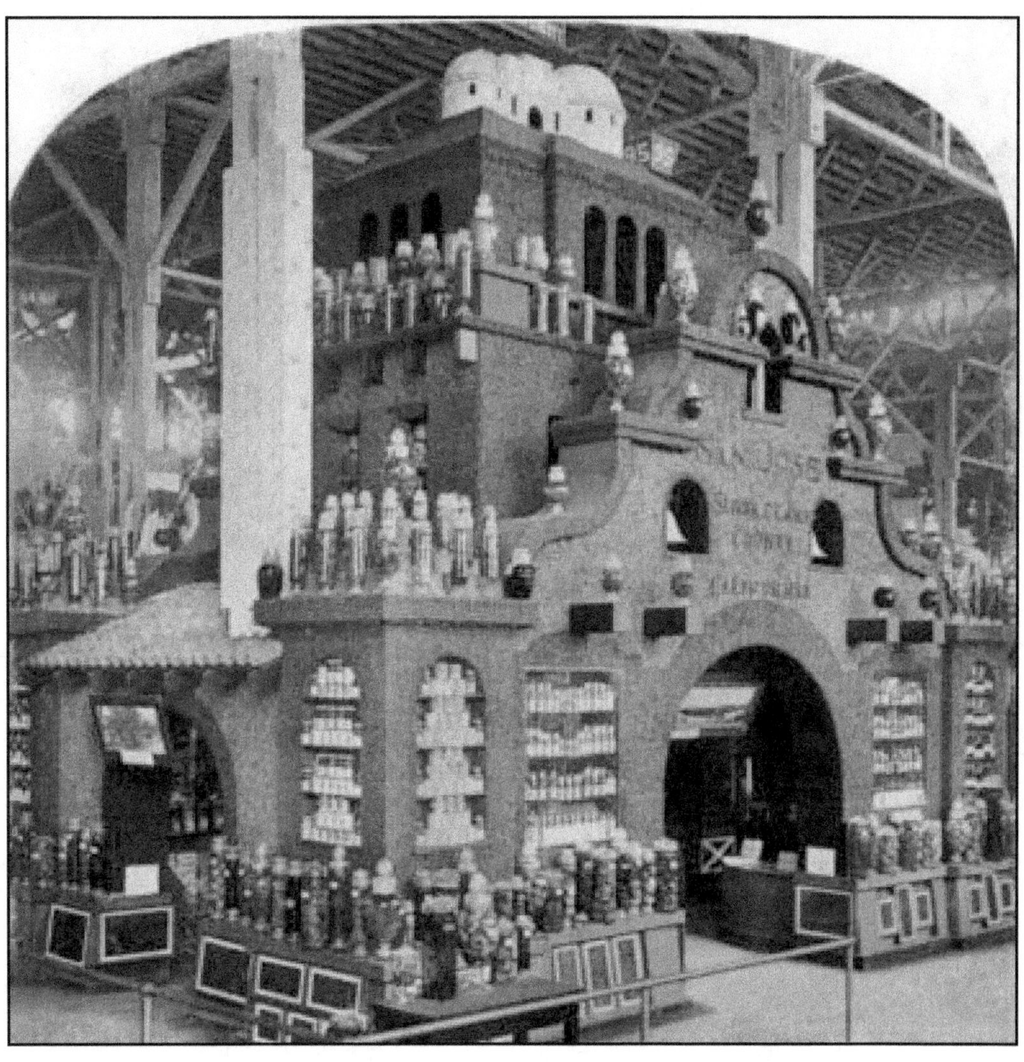

No. 54. California's Exhibit of Fruit

In the Palace of Agriculture a large area was devoted to the exhibition of California. Fruits were prominent and in endless profusion. The array of table delicacies was tempting to the most exacting gourmet. The wine growers of the state had made great efforts. Curiosities were a horse done in hops, a bear in prunes and the great seal of the state reproduced in beans. There were also large bales of alfalfa, the great forage plant, which is harvested five times a year. Some counties demonstrated by maps and charts the conditions of climate, temperature and rainfall prevailing with them, to prove the superiority of their region as a farming country. *(original 1904 caption)*

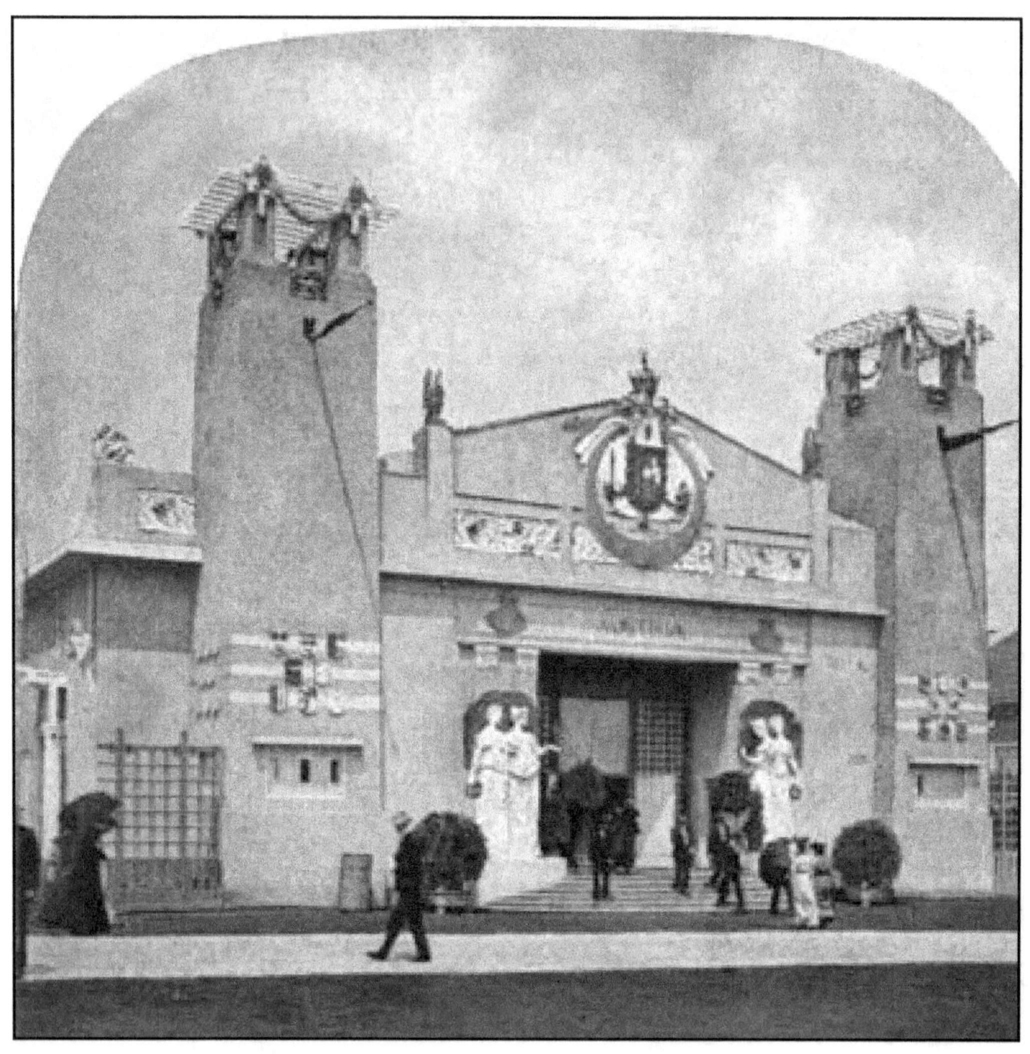

No. 55. The Austrian Building

Something new in architecture—totally different from every accustomed style, but certainly pleasing to the eye, was the Austrian Pavilion, consisting of a central hall with two broad wings. Frescoes and statuary of modern art, so-called, were used very effectively as decorations of the plain exterior walls. The wide front door opened into a reception hall, the principal ornament of which was a large bust of Emperor Francis Joseph. The Society of Artists of Vienna exhibited in the eastern most room. In the center of this room stood the bronze equestrian statue of Rudolph of Habsburg, the founder of the present dynasty. *(original 1904 caption)*

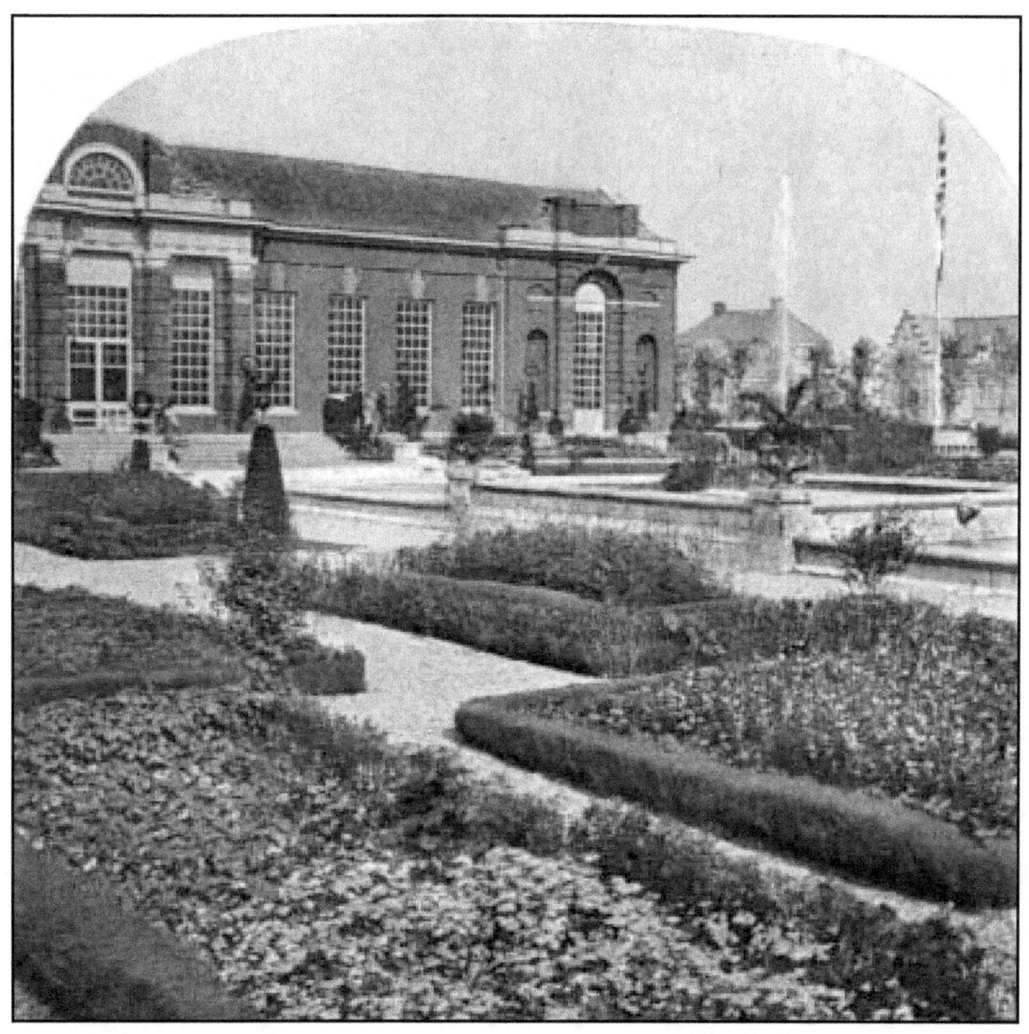

No. 56. England's Building and Gardens

The orangery was a reproduction of the banquet hall at Kensington Palace, England, built 200 years ago and designed by Sir Christopher Wren. One wing was divided into four rooms which showed the surroundings of British royalty. There was an Elizabethan breakfast room, furnished in oak, a Georgian dining room with furniture of genuine Chippendale mahogany, and a clock that was over 300 years old. The third room was an exact reproduction of Queen Anne's reception room, in which the latest portrait of King Edward VII hung above a beautifully carved chest of great age. The fourth room, furnished in satin wood, represented a modern English tea room. *(original 1904 caption)*

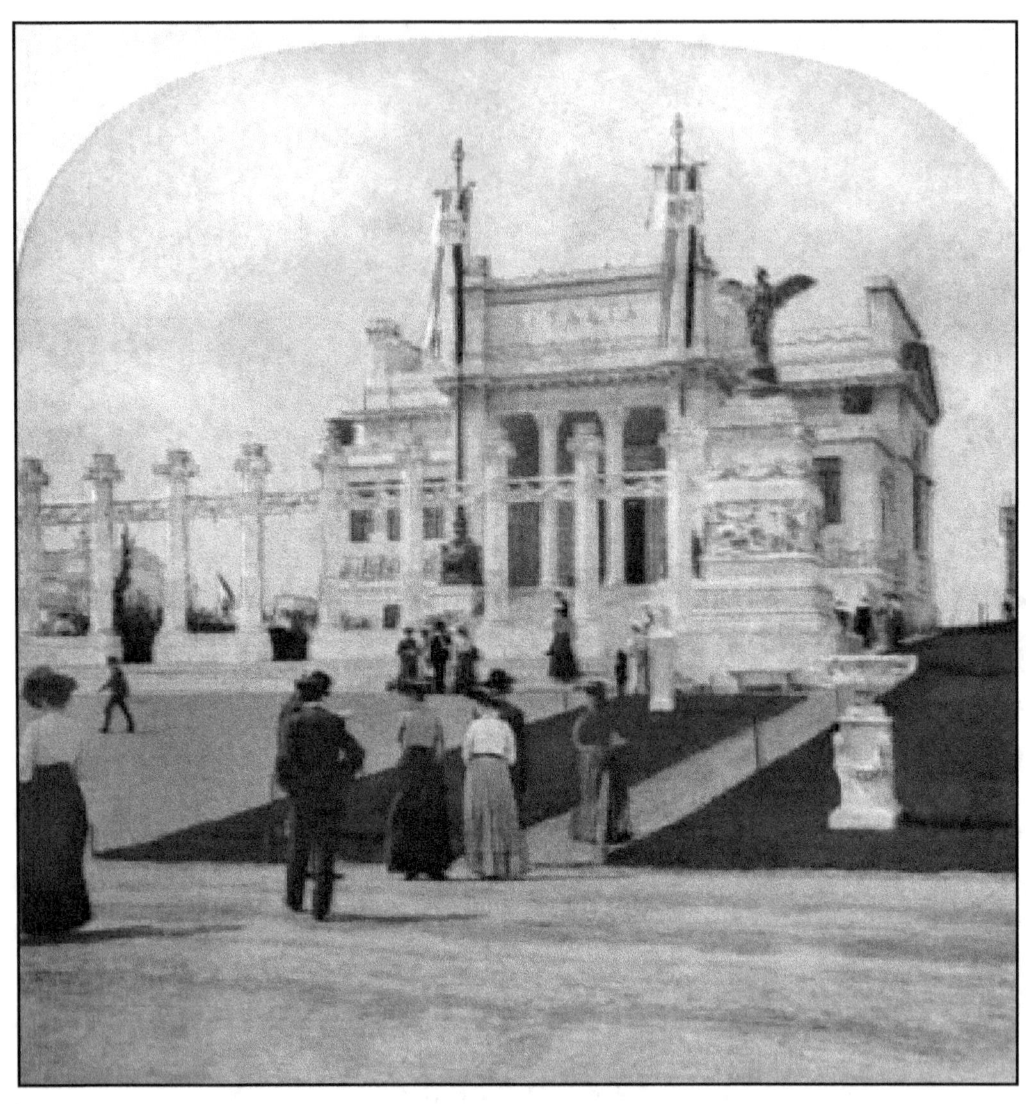

No. 57. The Italian Building

The Italian Pavilion is a gem of Old Roman architecture, the visitor entering through a peristyle of Ionic Columns and Italian Garden. (*Universal Exposition*)

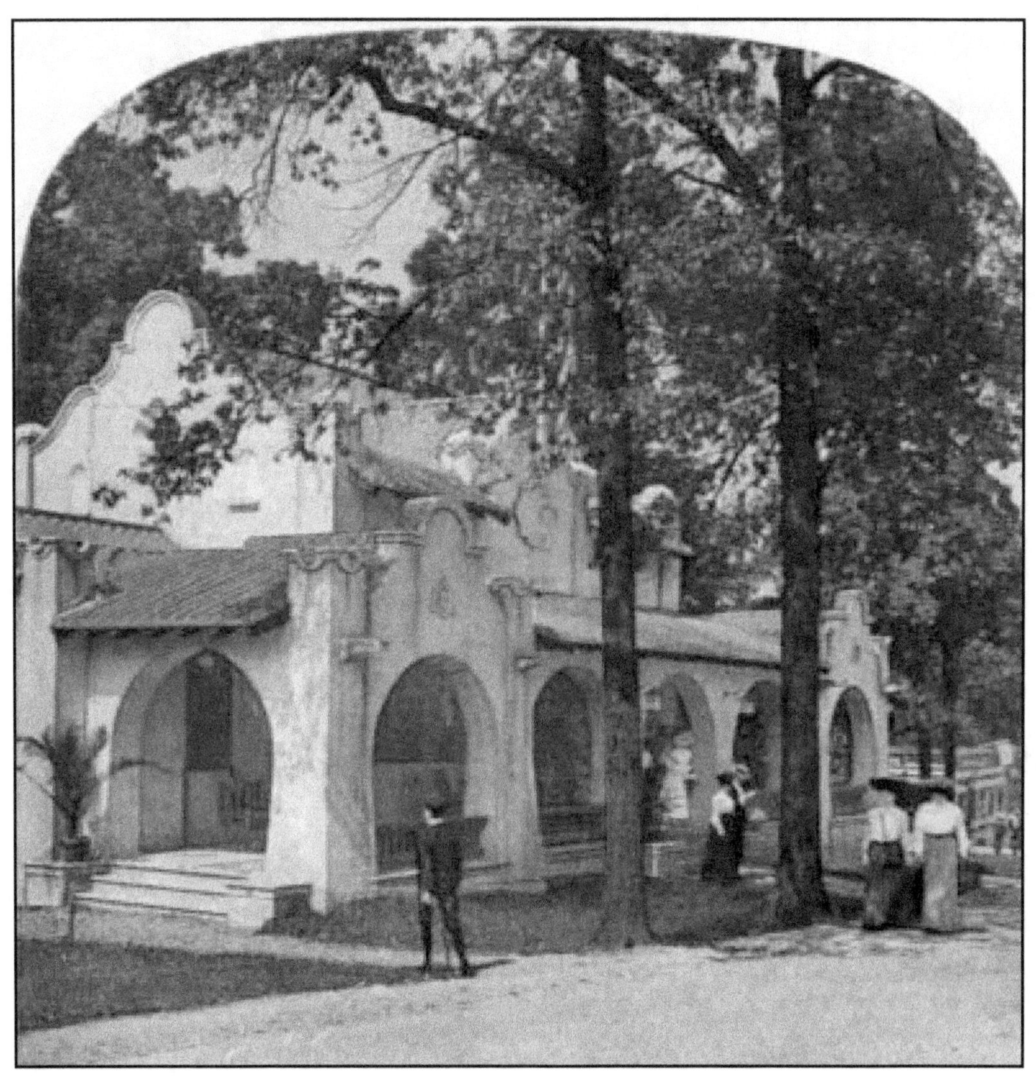

No. 58. New Mexico's State Building

New Mexico Building is in the style of the Spanish renaissance, and stands at the junction of two streets opposite the Montana Building. (*Universal Exposition*)

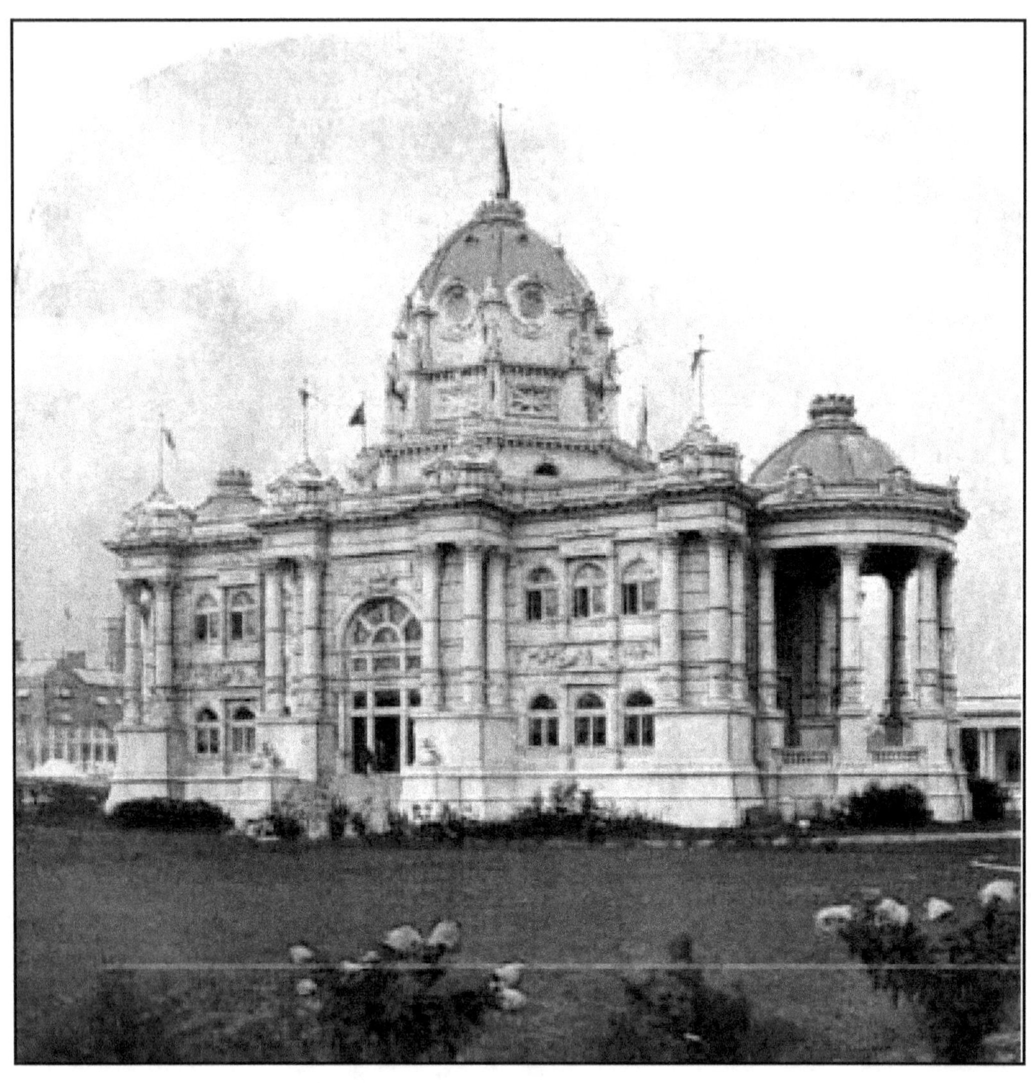

No. 59. The Brazilian Building

One of the buildings that attracted most attention was that of Brazil. Its great dome rose to the height of 138 feet. Brazil, the greatest among the South American republics, took great pains to call attention to her industries, especially coffee growing. Many visitors availed themselves of the chance to ascend to the top of the great dome, from where a wonderful view of the Exposition grounds was obtainable. At night the building was ablaze with thousands of electric lights. *(original 1904 caption)*

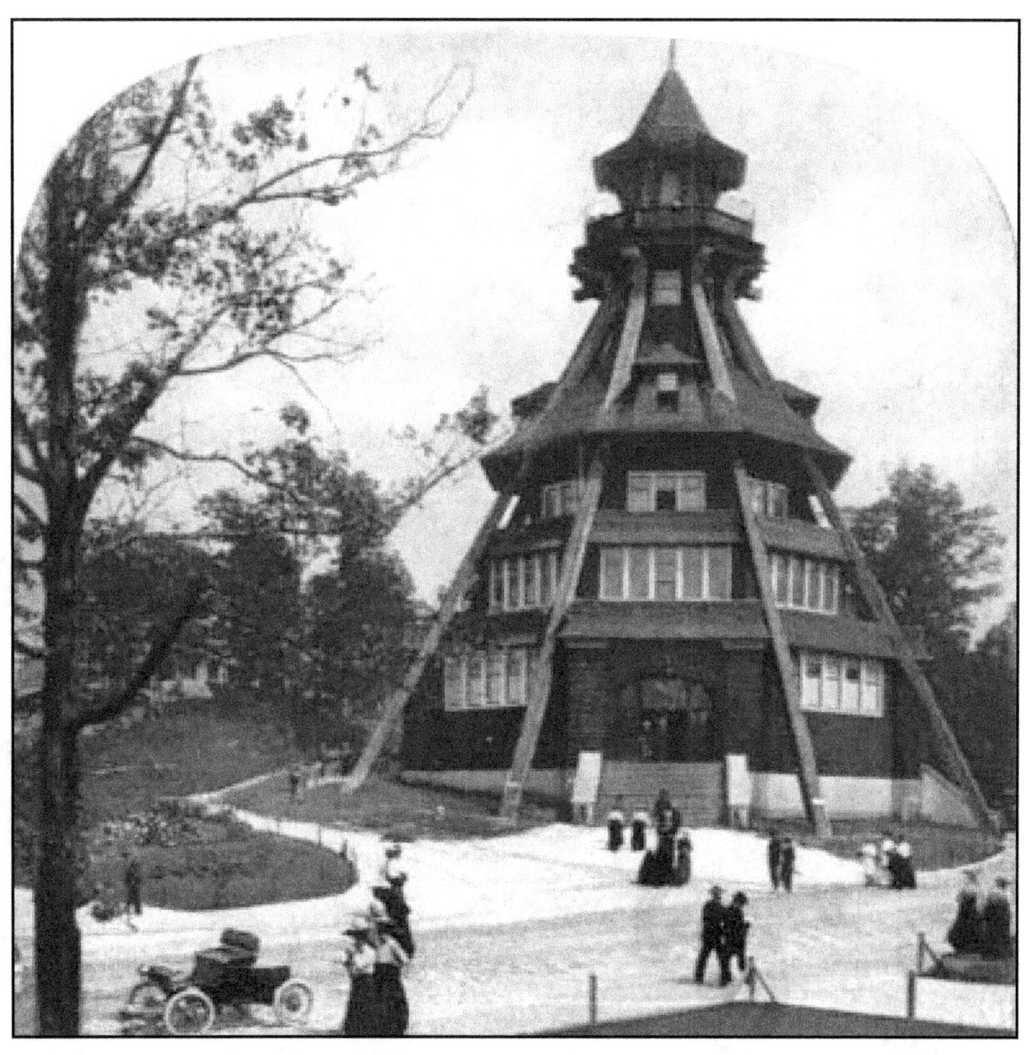

No. 60. The Washington State Building

The Washington State Building was certainly the most unique of all the state buildings. It was constructed entirely of wood and furnished an impressive demonstration of the state's unlimited resources in timber. Eight massive beams, two feet square in thickness and 100 feet long, each cut from a single tree, formed the supporting skeleton of the towering structure. The dome was 114 feet above the ground. The five octagonal floors contained exhibits of the products of Washington state, and many paintings of the unrivaled, magnificent scenery of the state. *(original 1904 caption)*

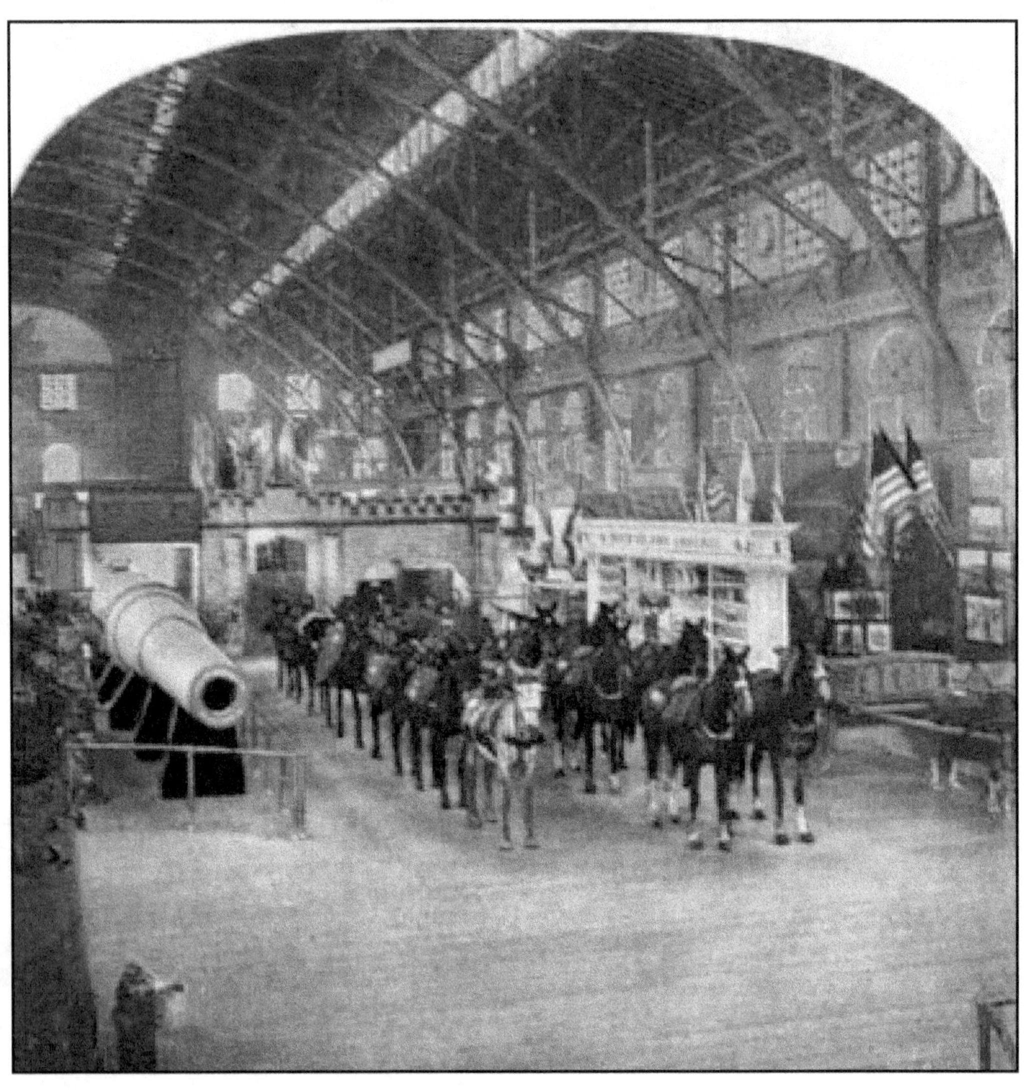

No. 61. War Department Exhibit

A section of the War Department exhibit shows a mountain artillery battery packed with the horses and mules needed to haul it over rough terrain, along with a full-scale model of a twelve-inch coastal defense rifle (at left). *(St. Louis World's Fair)*

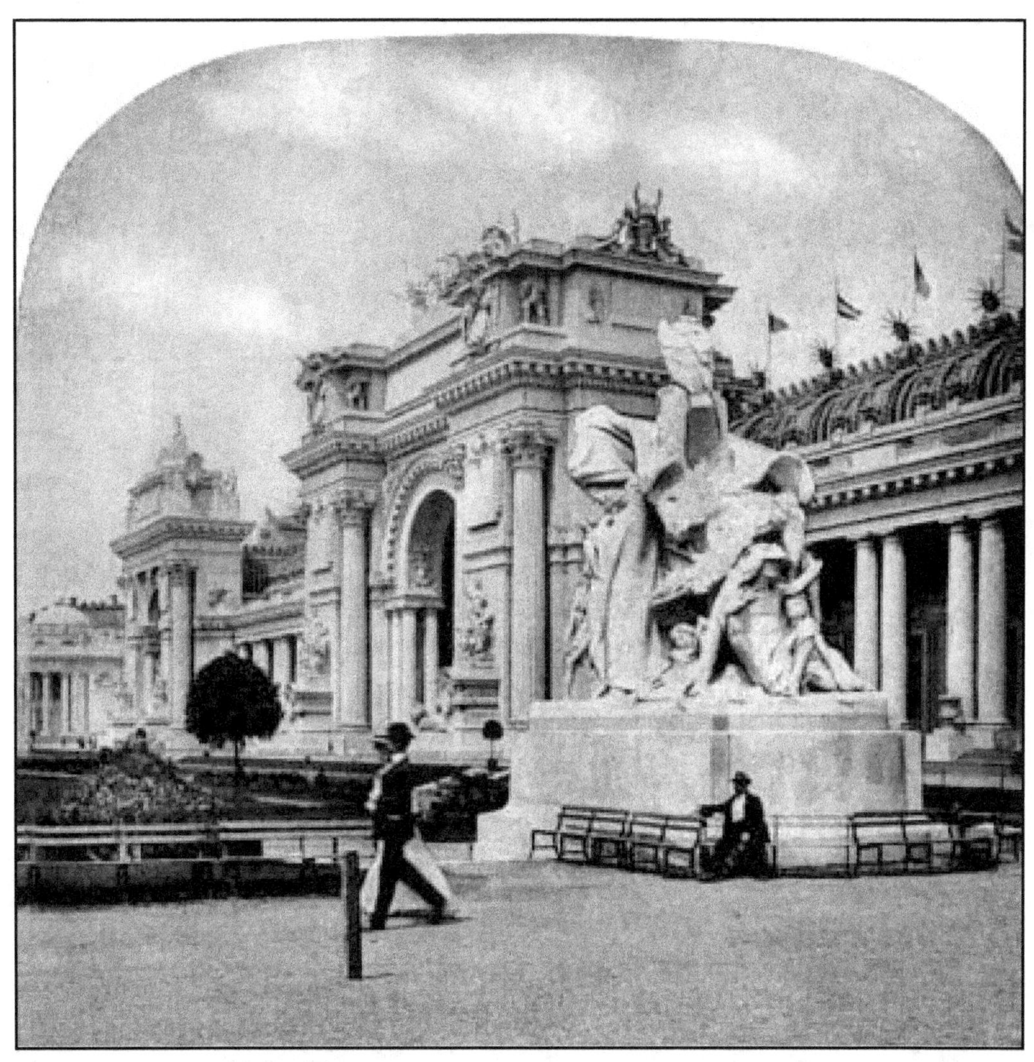

No. 62. Palace of Liberal Arts

One of the great architectural triumphs of the Exposition was the the Palace of Liberal Arts. The height of the doorway was ninety feet. The fluted Ionic columns ornamenting it measured nearly 100 feet from base to top of capital. The Palace covered nine acres. On April 30, 1903, on the 100th anniversary of the Louisiana Purchase, President Roosevelt dedicated the Exposition in this building. Inside this splendid structure were displayed exhibits of the country's achievements in the graphic arts, in musical instruments and similar classes of human activity. *(original 1904 caption)*

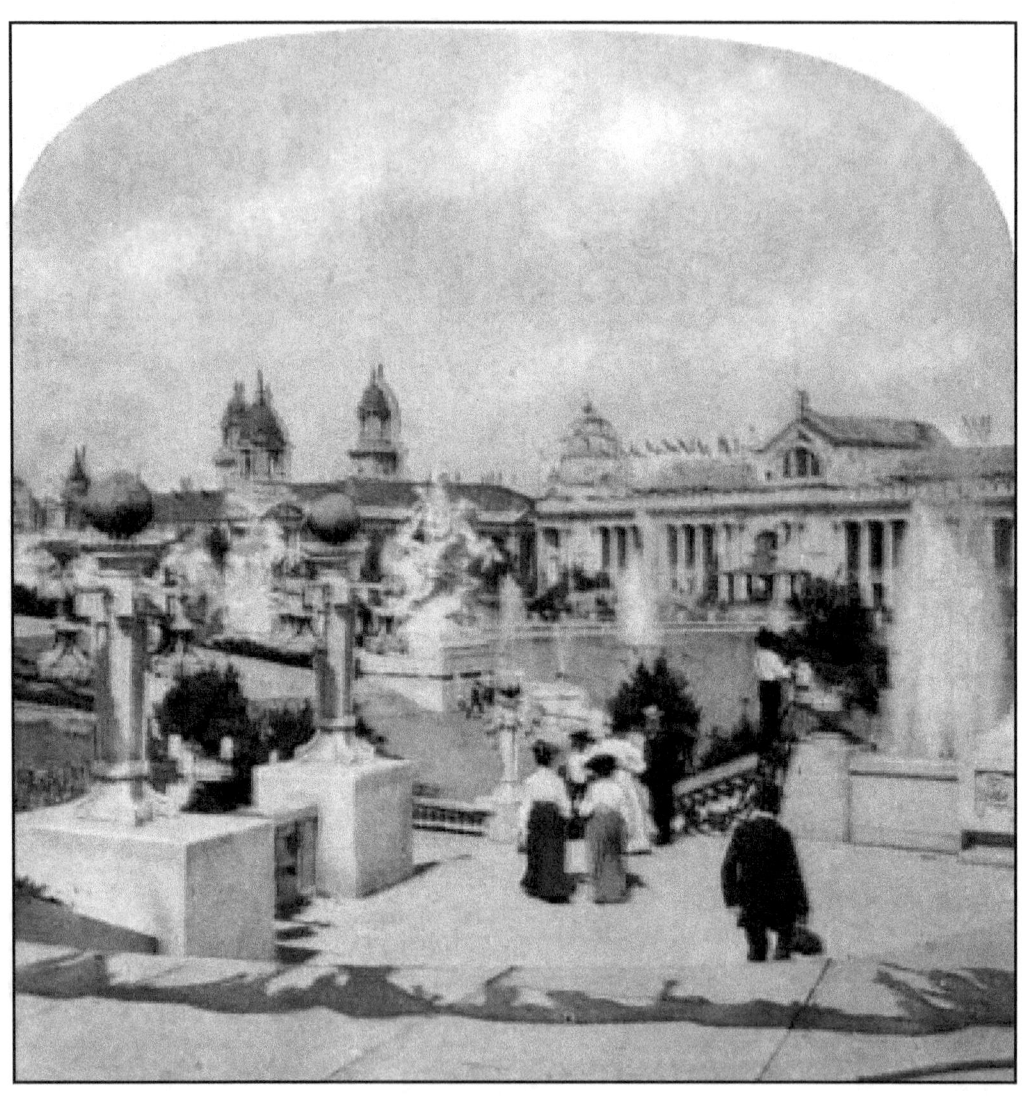

No. 63. Grand Stairway and Cascade Gardens

The Grand Basin into which the cascades emptied, was a part of the lagoon system which encircled the Palace of Education and the Palace of Electricity. Being the heart of the Exposition, a round trip on the lagoon afforded the easiest and most profitable way of viewing the magic splendor of this fairyland. *(original 1904 caption)*

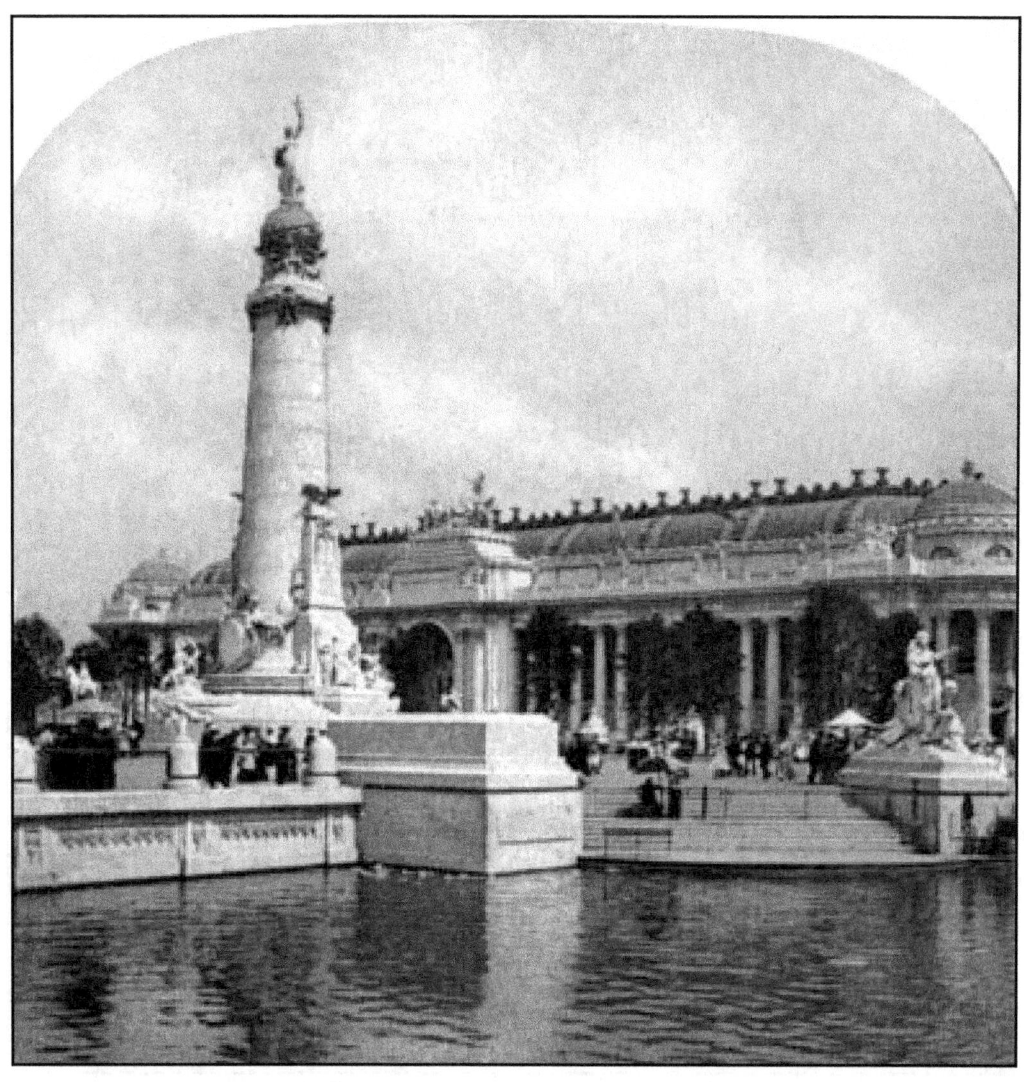

No. 64. St. Louis Monument, Palace of Manufacture

There is but one monument in the Exposition grounds, the magnificent Louisiana Purchase monument that stands at the head of the Plaza of St. Louis, directly opposite the central cascade. It is a majestic shaft, 100 feet high, and is crowned by Carl Bitter's colossal statue of Peace. At the base, on the side facing the Grand Basin, is a group of statues showing the commissioners in the act of signing the Louisiana treaty. At the two sides are symbolic figures of the Missouri and Mississippi rivers. On the side facing the Plaza is the speaker's stand from which many noted visitors have already addressed the exposition throngs. (*Universal Exposition*)

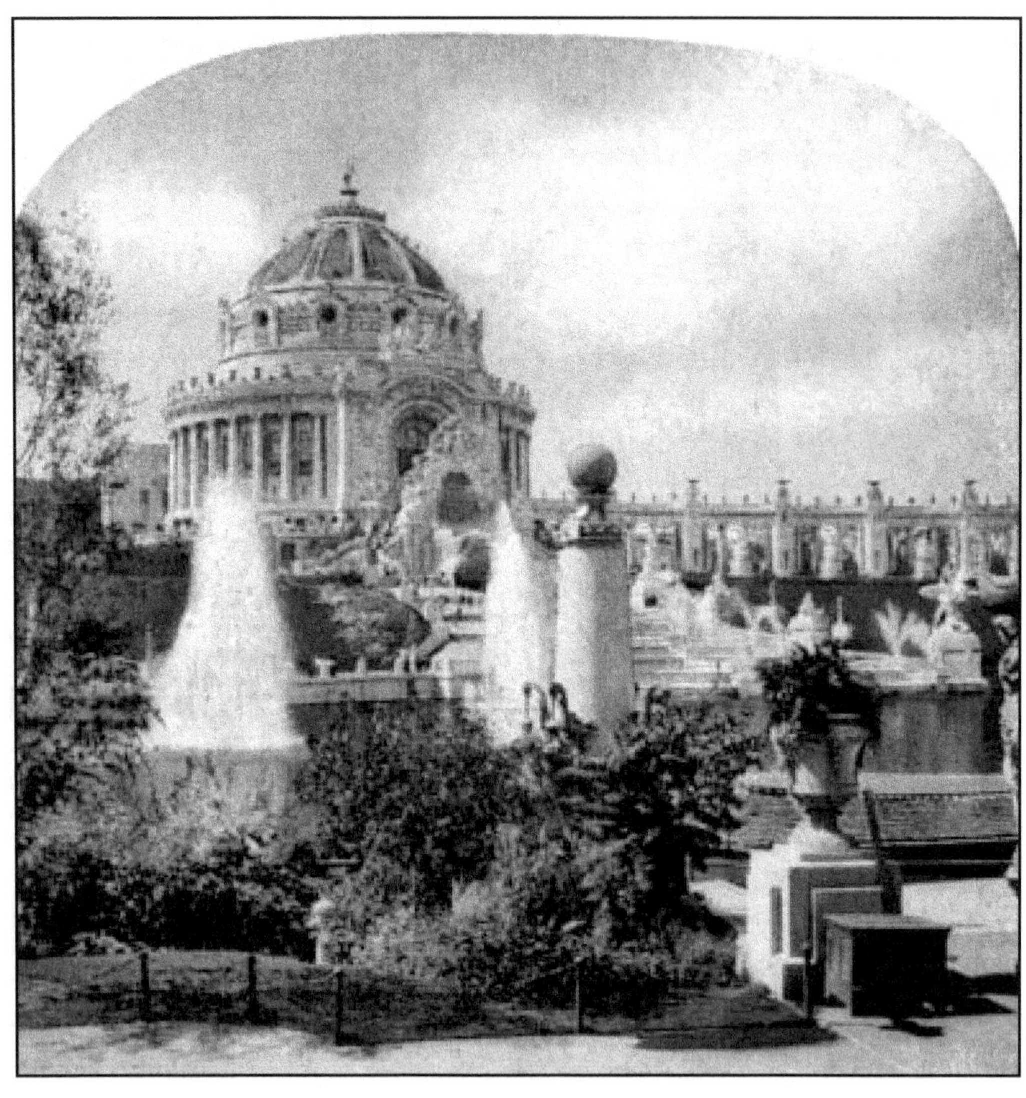

No. 65. Festival Hall and Cascades

The circular Festival Hall was 200 feet in diameter and 200 feet high. The auditorium within contained seats for 3,500 people and a stage large enough for a chorus of hundreds of voices. The largest pipe organ in the world was part of the equipment. It had 10,059 pipes and 140 stops. The interior was planned by E. L. Masqueray of New York, who also designed the colonnades and the cascades with their rich sculptures. *(original 1904 caption)*

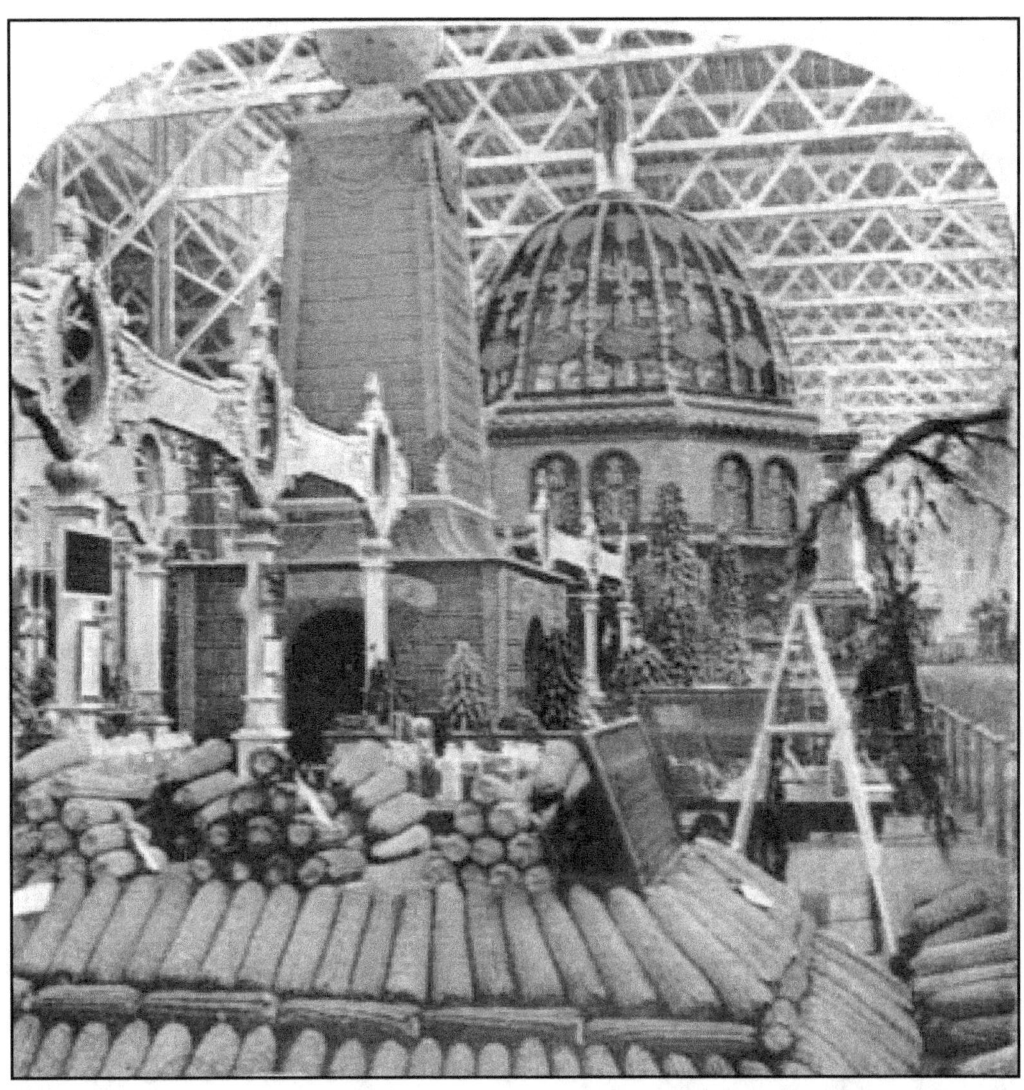

No. 66. Nebraska Corn and Grain Exhibit

Geologically, Nebraska is probably the most distinctly agricultural state in the Union. The strata of rock are covered by a deep surface material known as bluff deposit or loess, by glacial drift and sand hills. This loess, often 100 feet deep, is a light sandy loam of glacial origin and of almost inexhaustible fertility. A peculiar feature of Nebraska are the sand hills, covering about 15,000 square miles in the northern part of the state, which are formed of drifting sand. The wind carries the sand from the side over the crest, lodging it on the opposite side, and when the wind shifts, the process continues in a new direction. *(original 1904 caption)*

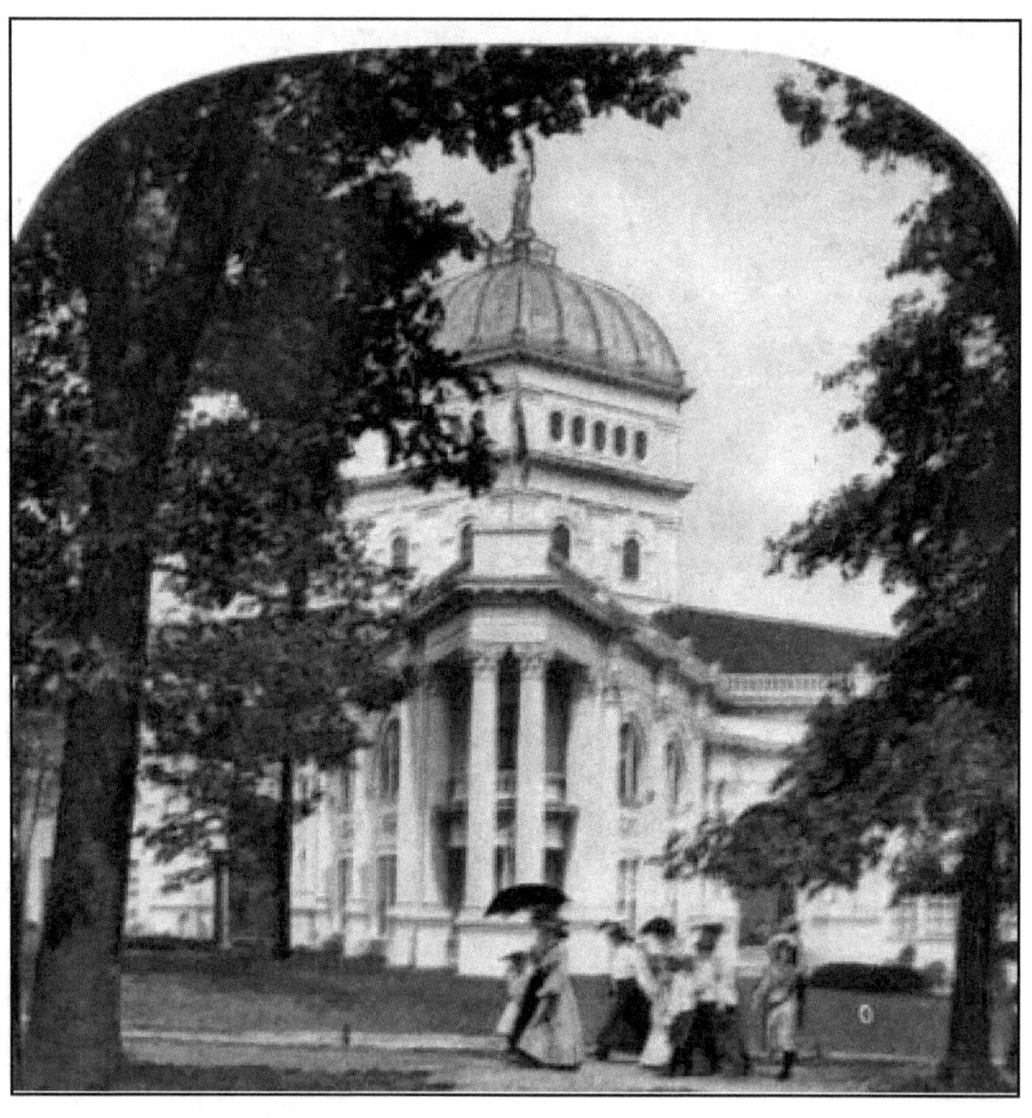

No. 67. The Texas Building

The Texas Building is a massive structure in the form of a five-pointed star, with a center dome rising 132 feet from the ground. Native woods and marble of Texas are used in the interior finishing of the building. (*Universal Exposition*)

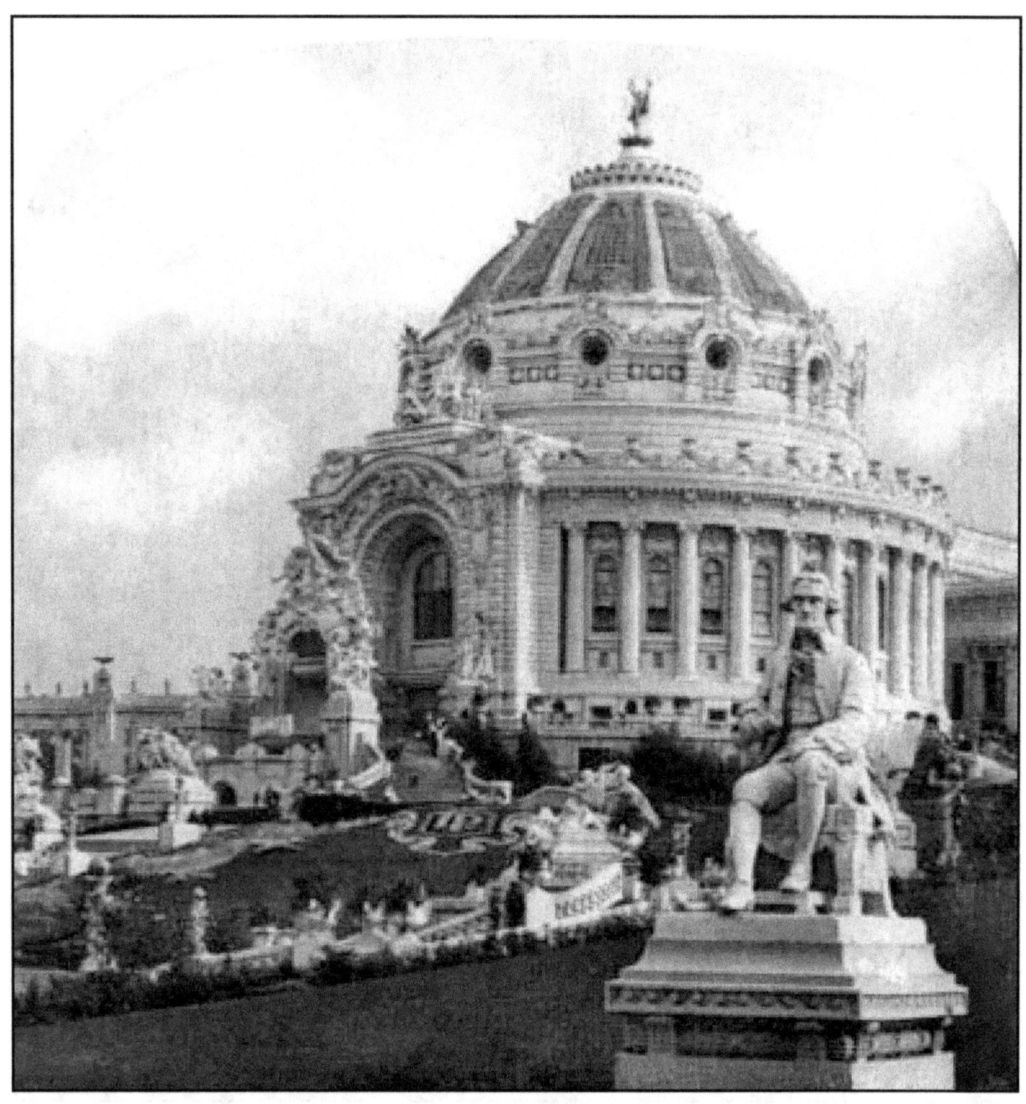

No. 68. Festival Hall and Statue of Thomas Jefferson

If the drafting of the Declaration of Independence had not sufficed to make the name of Jefferson immortal, his initiative in the Louisiana Purchase and the conclusion of that great achievement would have served to place his name forever in the annals of America. The sculptor represented Jefferson as gazing far ahead into the nation's future. Jefferson, while sending his envoys to Paris, sent at the same time an expedition to the far northwest to learn the extent and nature of the territory which the Louisiana Purchase finally embraced. *(original 1904 caption)*

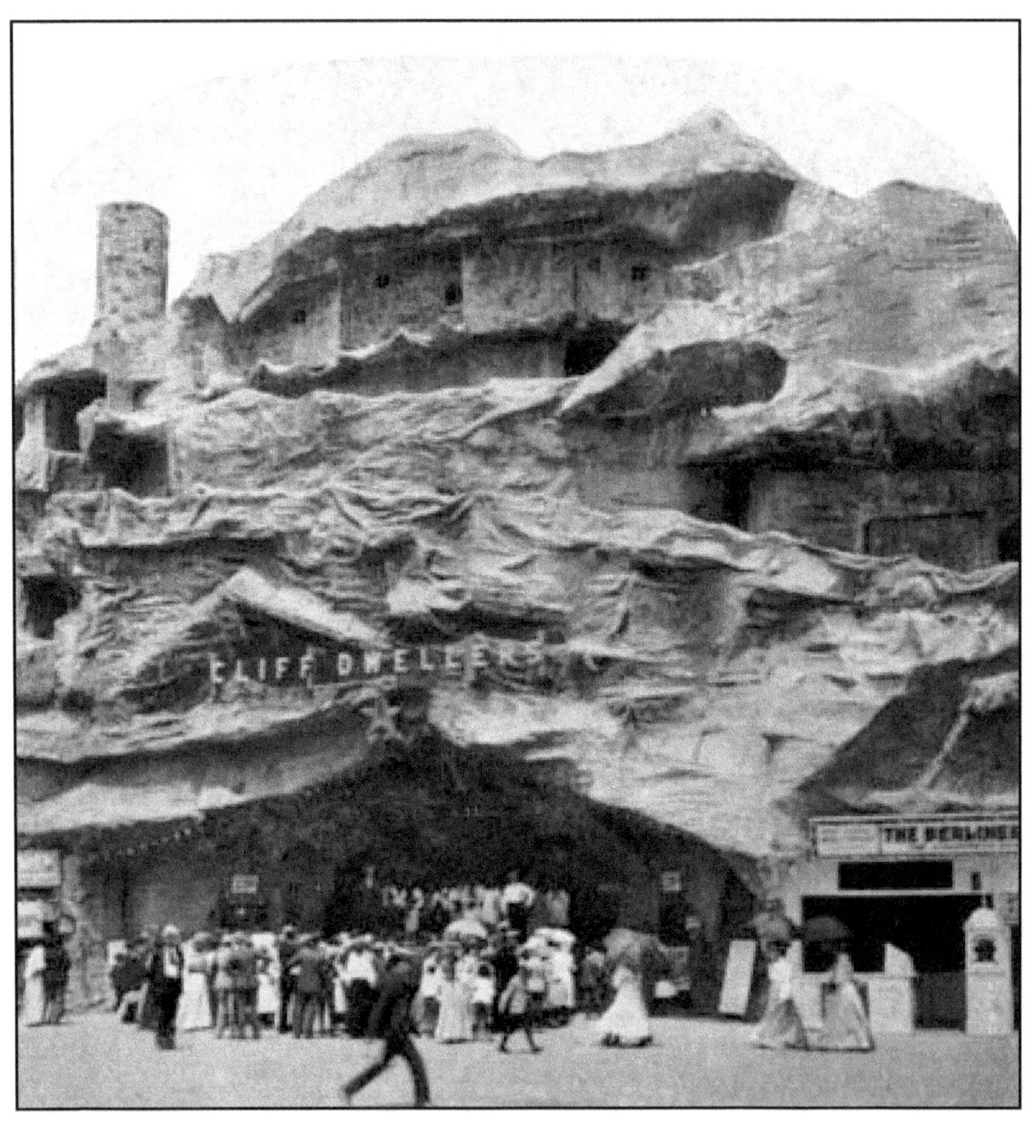

No. 69. Entrance to "Cliff Dwellers" on the Pike

The representation of these strange habitations in New Mexico and Arizona, built hundreds of feet above the level of the valleys, carved out of the soft rock hundreds of years ago by people of whom we know very little, was visited by great crowds. The utensils and relics that have been found in these dwellings were shown and proved that these people had a certain degree of culture. The Pueblo Indians are believed to be the descendants of the race of cliff dwellers, but nothing definite is known about the matter. *(original 1904 caption)*

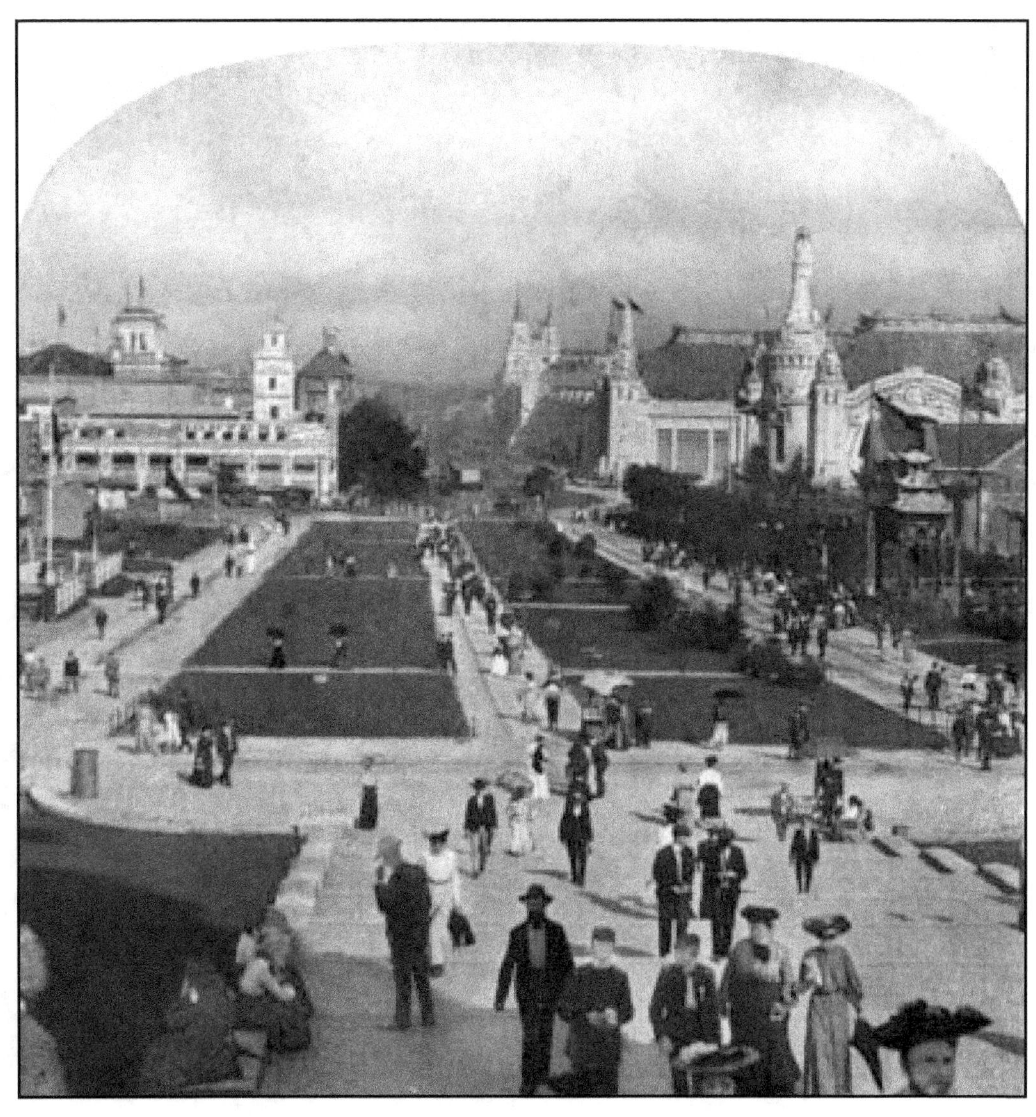

No. 70. The Grand Plaza from Administration Building

The view from the Administration Building's steps overlooks the Grand Plaza. The Great Britain building is on the right, with the Palace of Transportation just beyond. On the left is the Pike entertainment area in the distance. *(St. Louis World's Fair)*

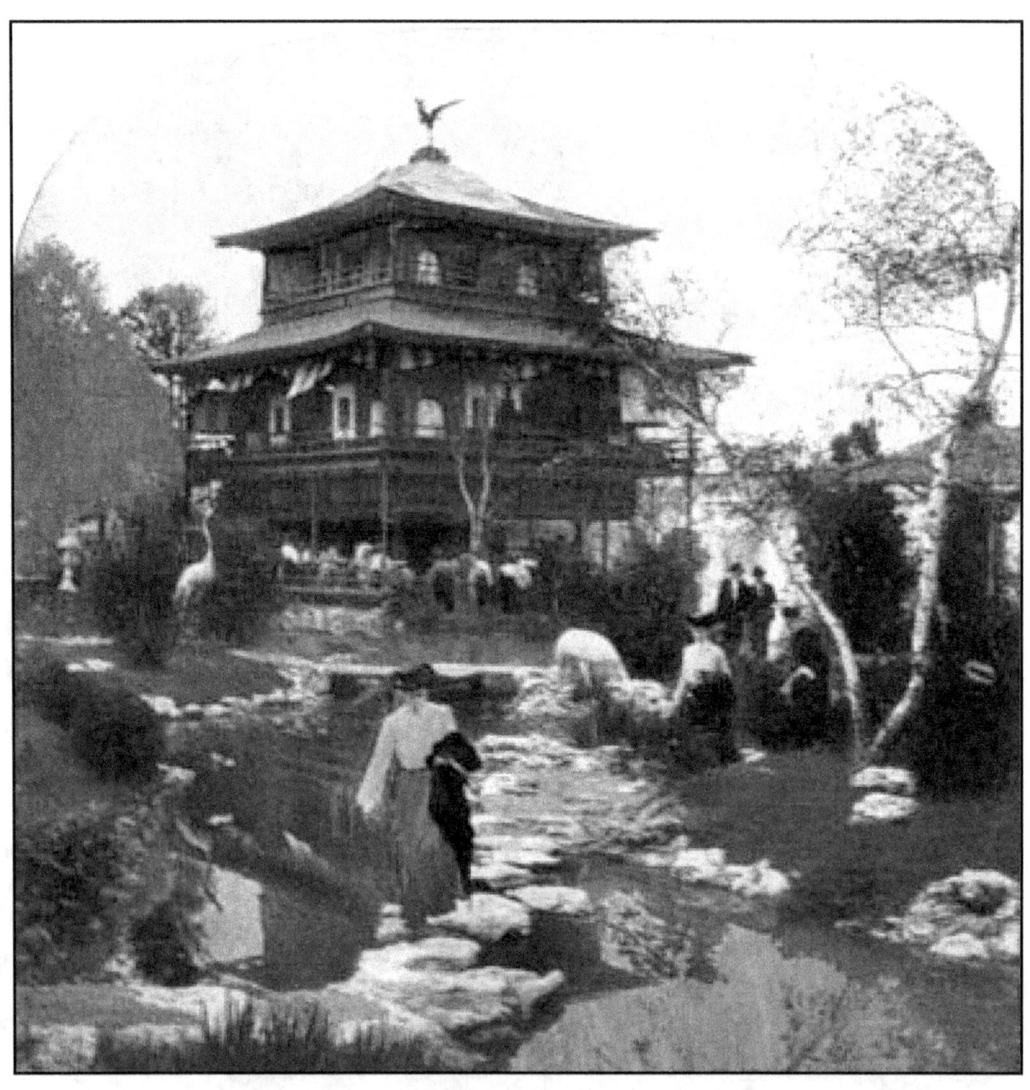

No. 71. Japanese Tea House and Gardens

The pavilion seen in our picture was used as a tea house, and was modeled after the Kikakuji Palace in Kioto. The upper floor was filled with Japanese images, and on the first floor dainty Japanese maidens served tea. The gardens with their tiny rivulets with stepping stones, their pretty pagodas and rock work, their Japanese flowers, vases, fountains and cranes made a picture of enchanting beauty. *(original 1904 caption)*

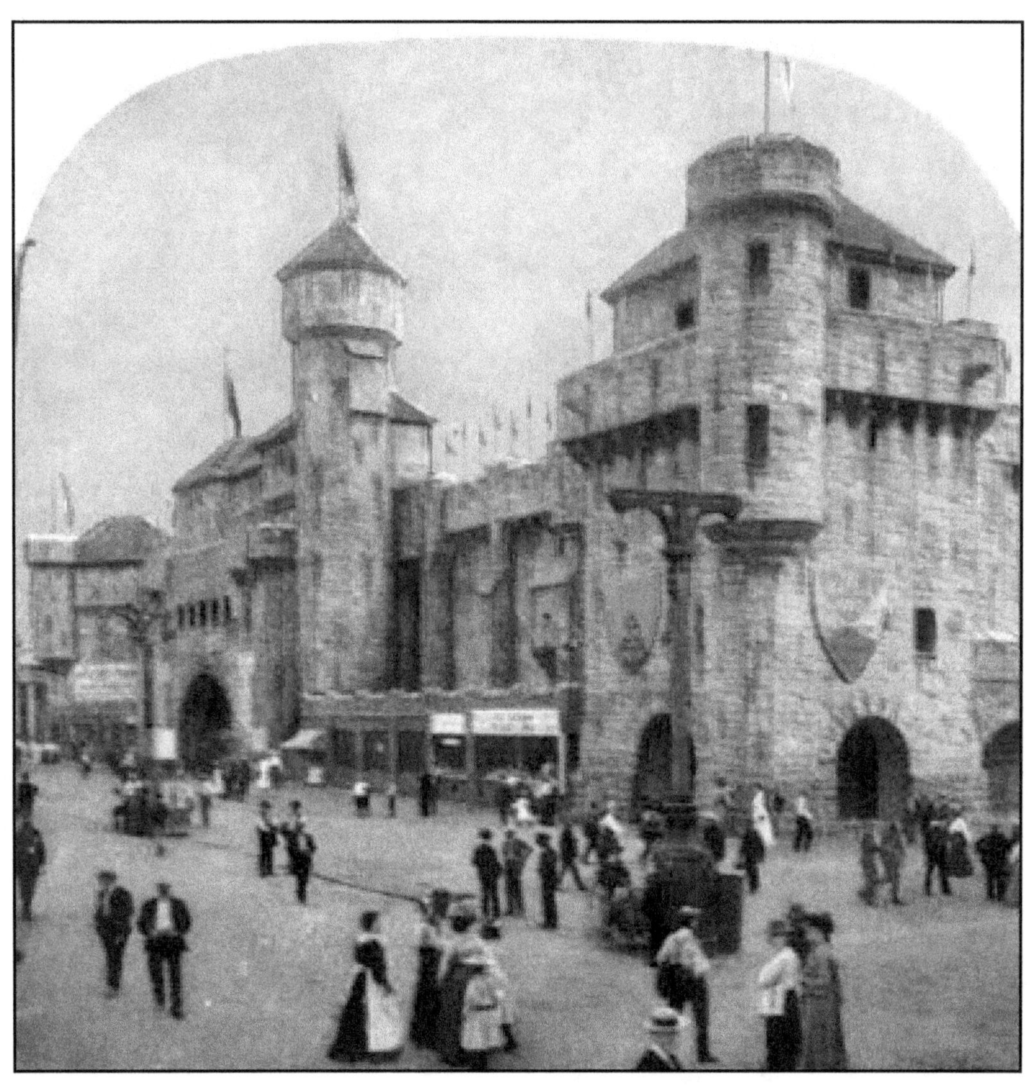

No. 72. "Battle Abbey" on the Pike

The Battle Abbey has a thrilling interest for soldiers and the children of soldiers. Two of the greatest Cycloramas of the world are here, the Battles of Gettysburg and Manassas, besides five dioramas of other historic battles, and a great museum of war relics in which one may spend a day without losing interest. (*Universal Exposition*)

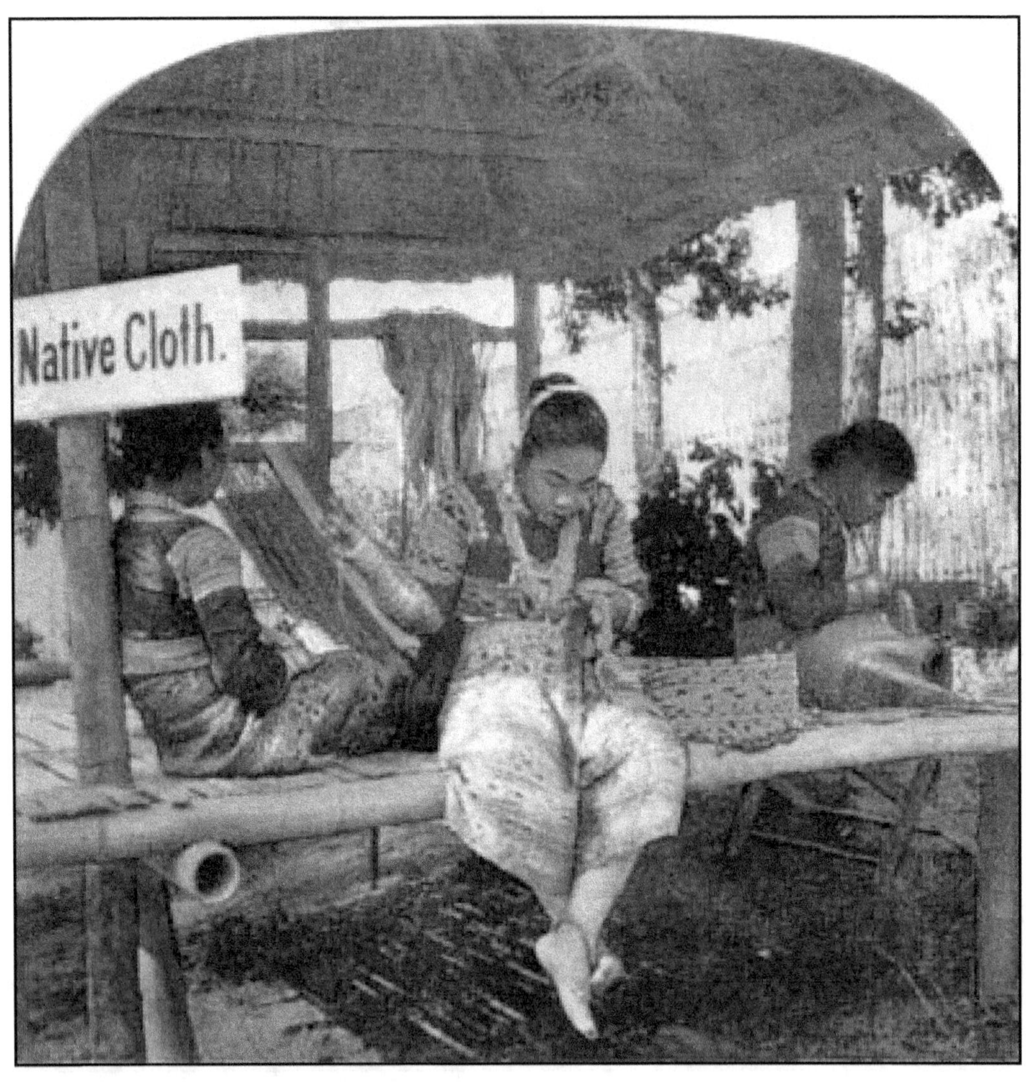

No. 73. Bagabos Women in the Philippine Village

The arrival of the colorful Bagabos from the Philippines was delayed until September, long after the opening of the fair. Because of cases of smallpox among them the visitors were held in quarantine. *(St. Louis World's Fair)*

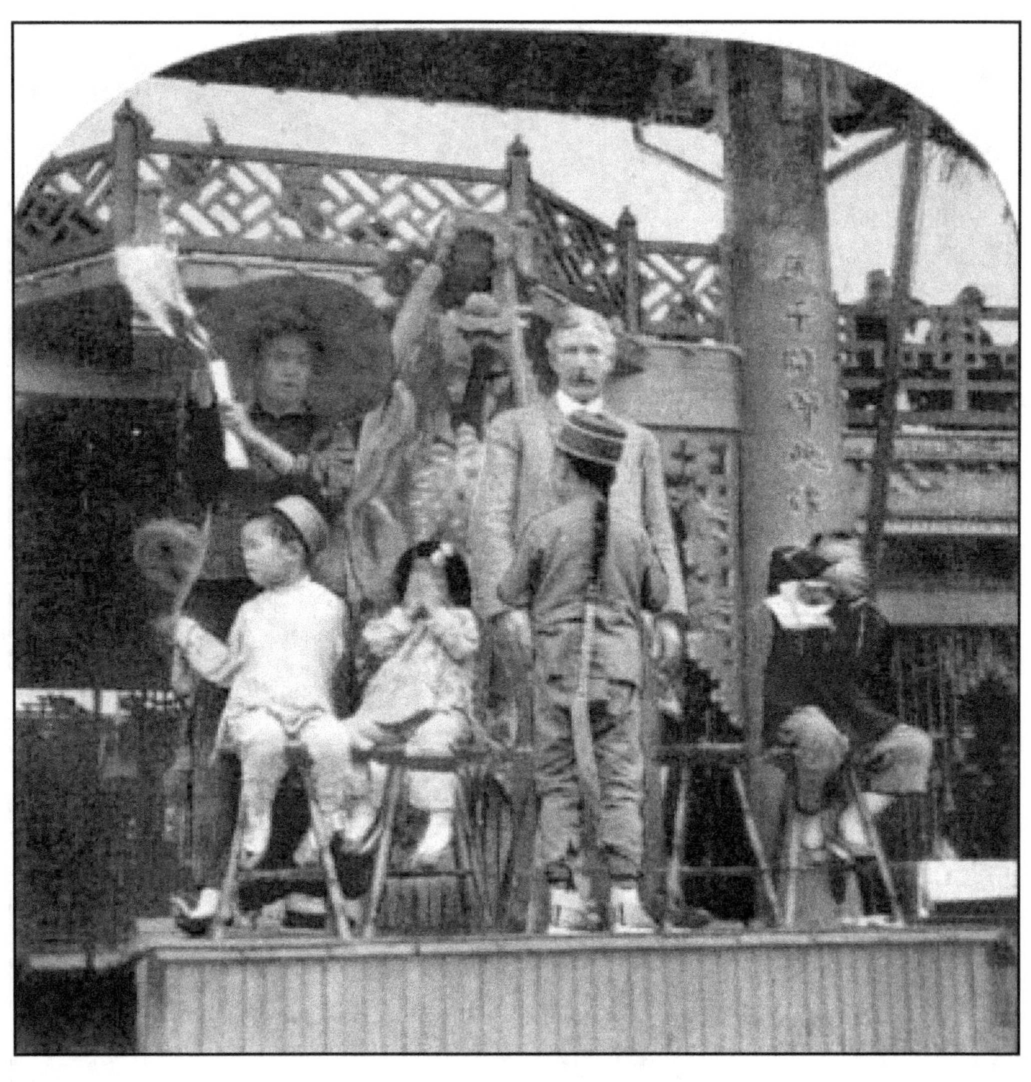

No. 74. Superstitious Chinese Children Covering Their Faces to Avoid Being Photographed

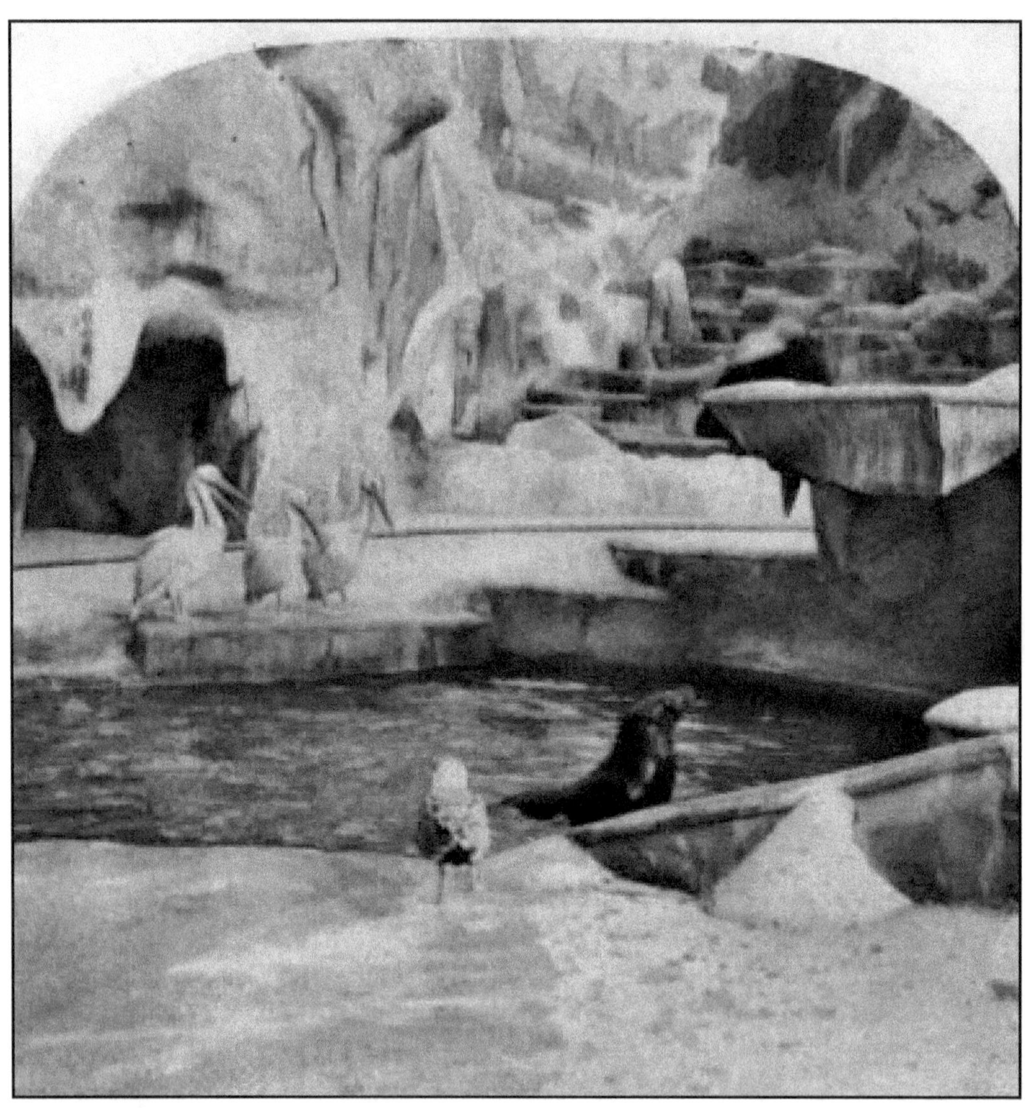

No. 75. Seal and Sea Fowl at Hagenbeck's Show

The love of wild animals may be a relic of the almost extinct savage taste in our natures; there is no doubt that a cage of tigers possesses a deep fascination for the average American. The Hagenbeck trained wild animal show offers cages of magnificently terrible wild creatures, and there is a continuous animal performance, but the most interesting scene within the enclosure is the so-called "Jungle" where tame and wild animals clamber over the rocks and cliffs almost within reach of the spectators. *(St. Louis World's Fair)*

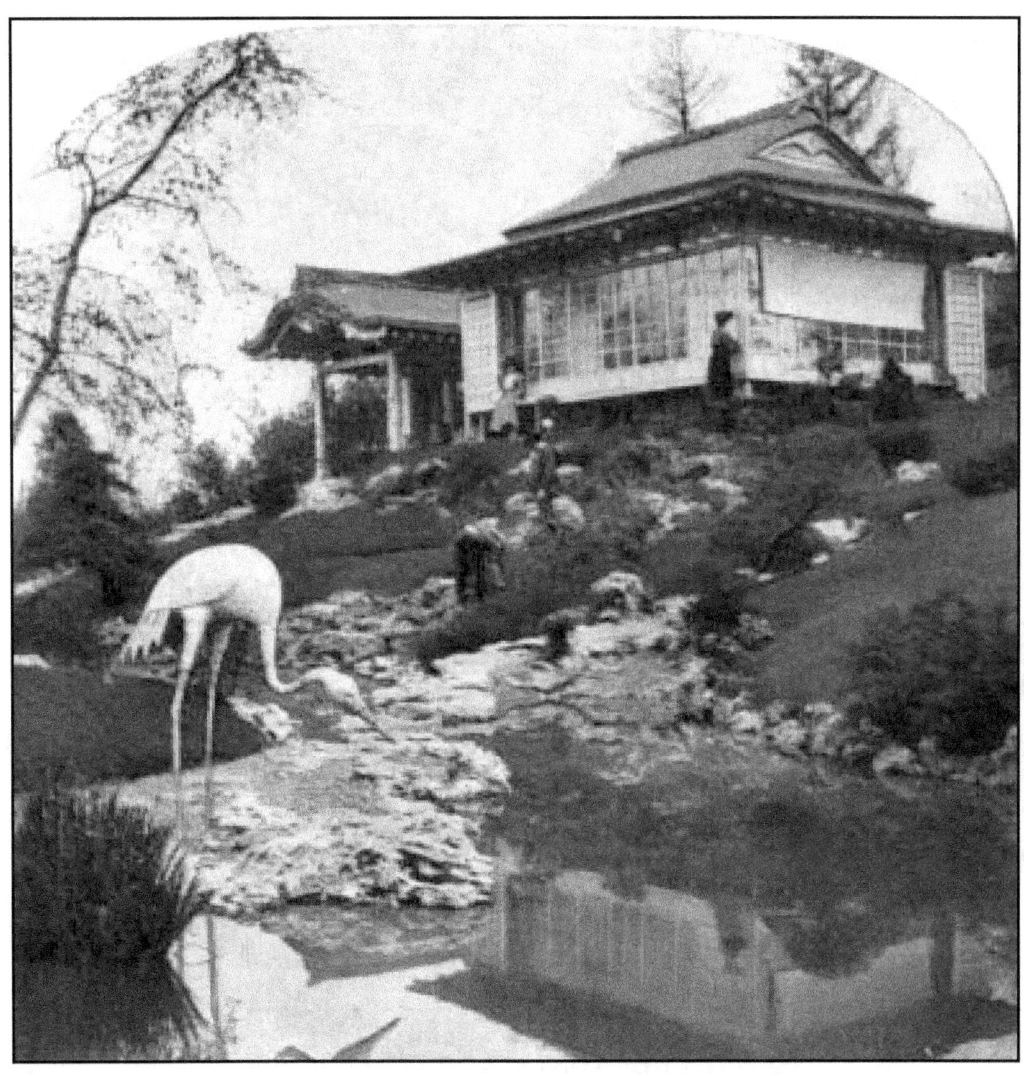

No. 76. Japanese Rest House and Gardens

The Japanese at home are not given to erecting large, isolated buildings, but collections of smaller and more varied structures. The national exhibit of Japan at the Fair is therefore in keeping with the spirit and taste of the people. Dainty gardens, with winding paths and green sward make the spot a pleasant one in which to enjoy the smiling hospitality of the Orientals. There are cascades and fountains, and plashing little streams spanned by quaint bridges or crossed by lines of stepping-stones. There are pretty pagodas, beds of flowering plants, and rock-work ornamented by giant cranes. (*Universal Exposition*)

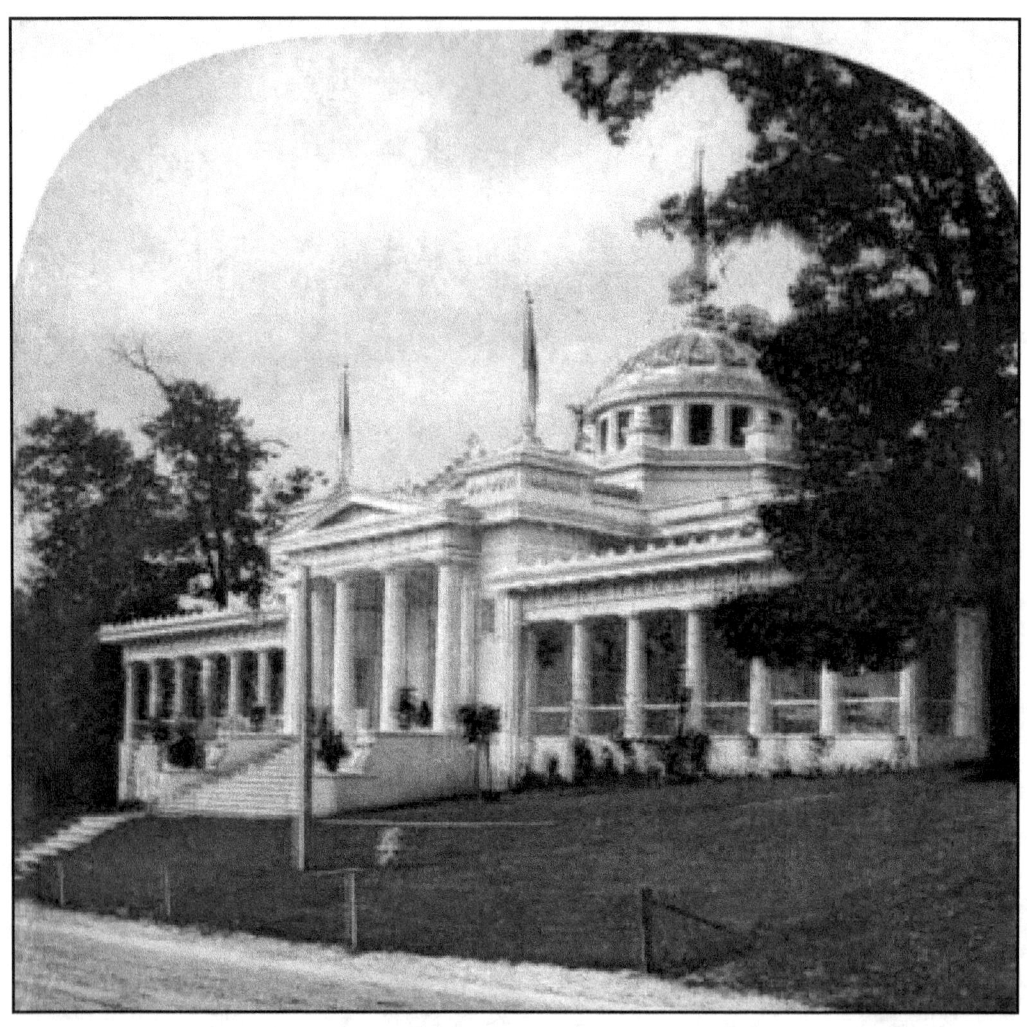

No. 77. The Montana State Building

On an elevation in the northwestern part of the Plateau of States, near the large bird cage, was the site of the Montana State Building. The spacious, handsome structure was of Grecian style with Doric columns, severe and stately in aspect. The cost of the structure amounted to $20,000, exclusive of the cost of furnishing it. Montana had exhibits of its products in five of the great palaces, those of Agriculture, Education, Forestry, Fish and Game, Horticulture and Mines and Metallurgy. In the one last named there was a collection of gold nuggets valued at $40,000, and an interesting display of copper ingots, representing the most valuable of the mineral resources of the state. *(original 1904 caption)*

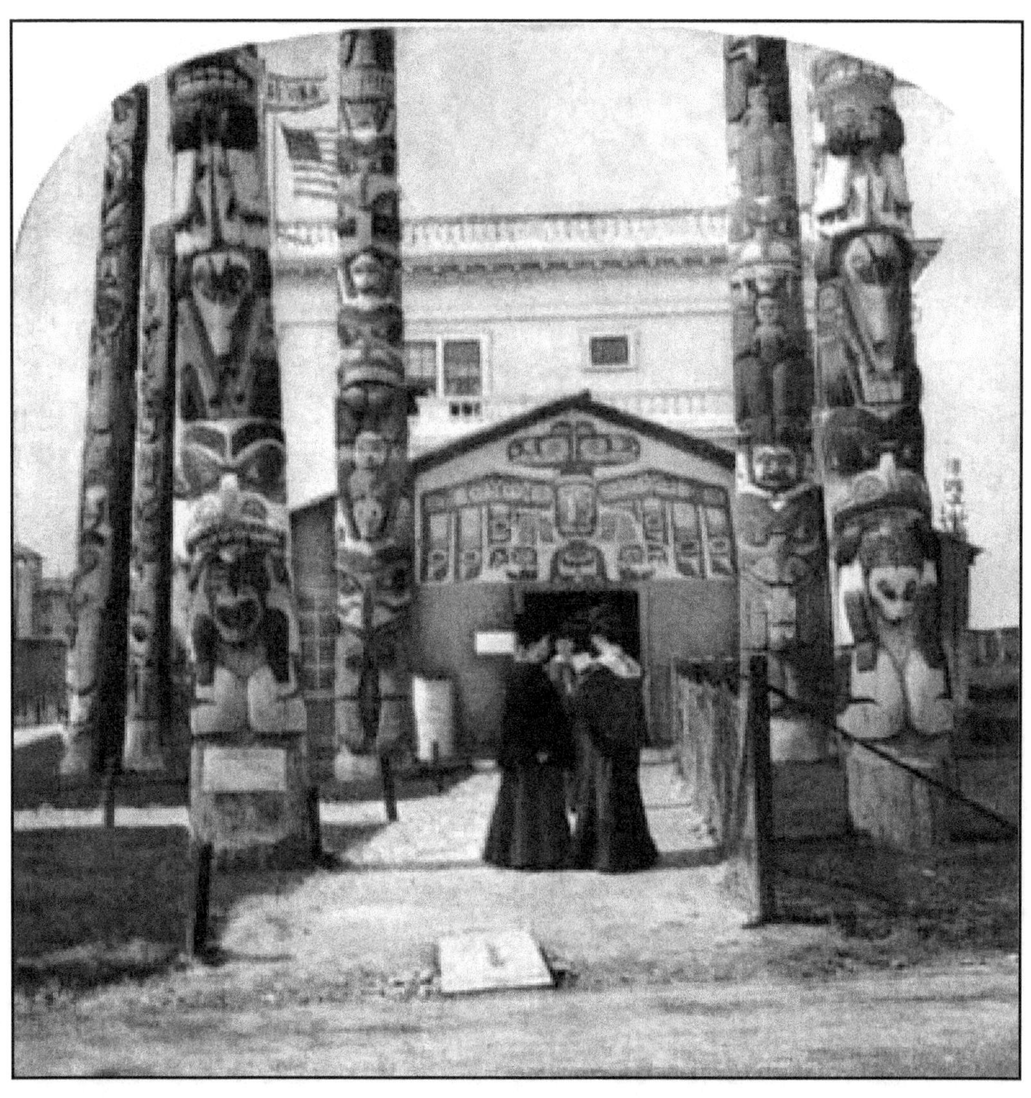

No. 78. The Alaska Building and Totem Poles

Alaska's comprehensive exhibit at the Fair occupies a space on the Olympian Way, in the western part of the grounds. The main building is 50 by 100 feet, with stately Ionic columns. Conspicuous in the group of buildings stand the tall totem poles, grotesquely carved, and with a ceremonial significance not commonly understood. They correspond in some sense to a coat-of-arms. *(St. Louis World's Fair)*

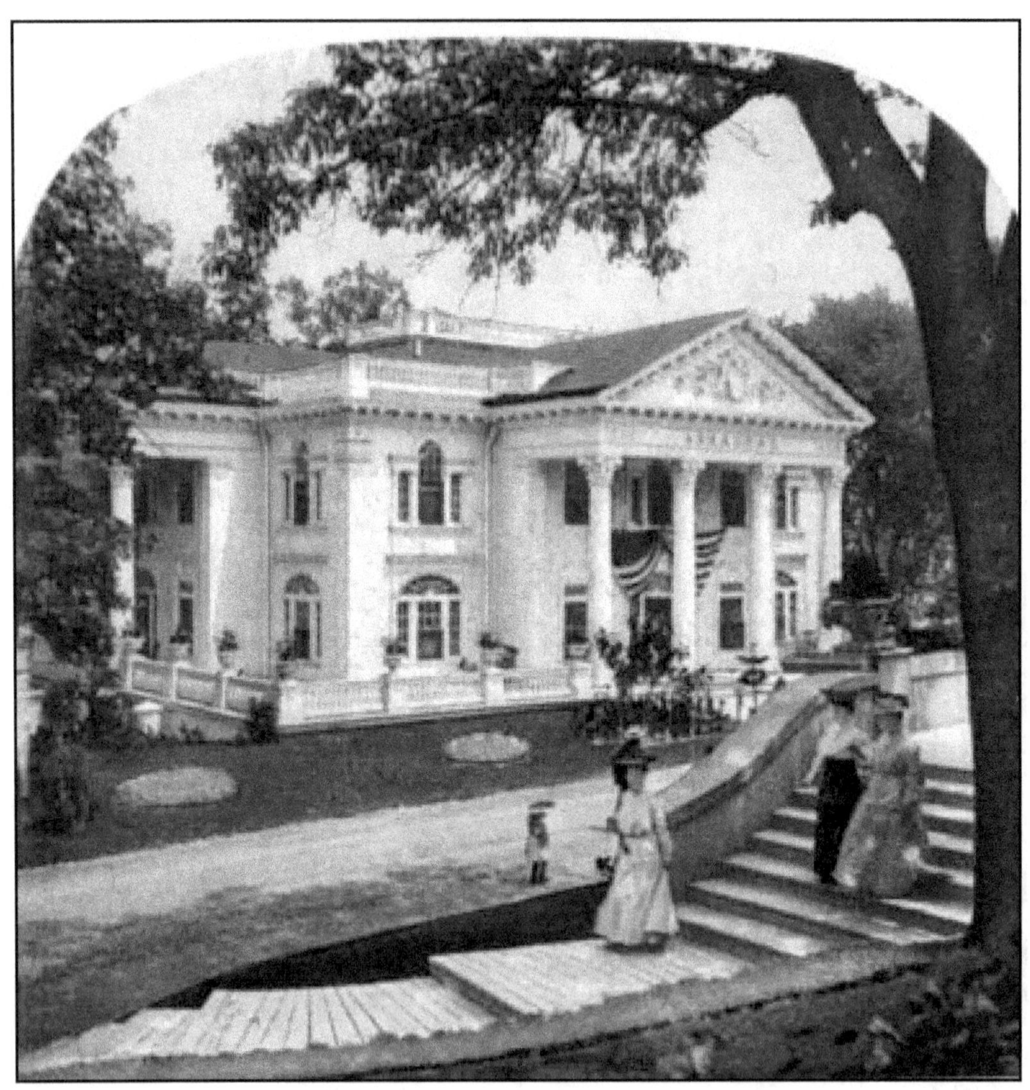

No. 79. The Arkansas State Building

The Arkansas State Building was set in a large, well kept garden, and its broad piazzas were a favorite resting place. The floors inside were made of native hardwood, with a wealth of inlaid work. The walls of the large reception hall were tinted green with a broad frieze of sky and clouds, which set off a profusion of apple boughs in blossom, the state's floral emblem. Among the handsome furnishings of the interior a mantelpiece of Eureka Springs onyx was the center of attraction. *(original 1904 caption)*

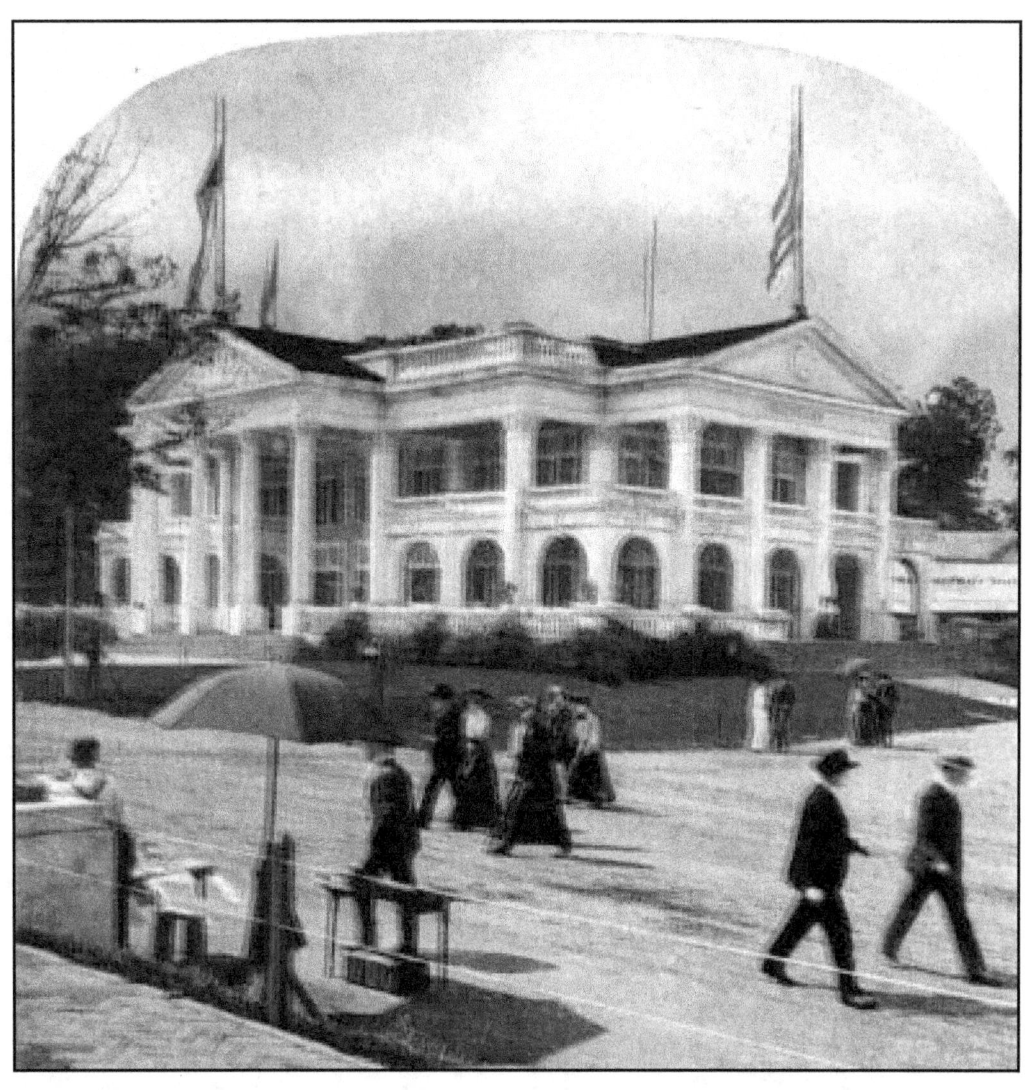

No. 80. The Michigan State Building

The Michigan building is in the Grecian style of architecture. It is built of cement and other materials which were contributed for this building. It is a large substantial and attractive structure. (*Universal Exposition*)

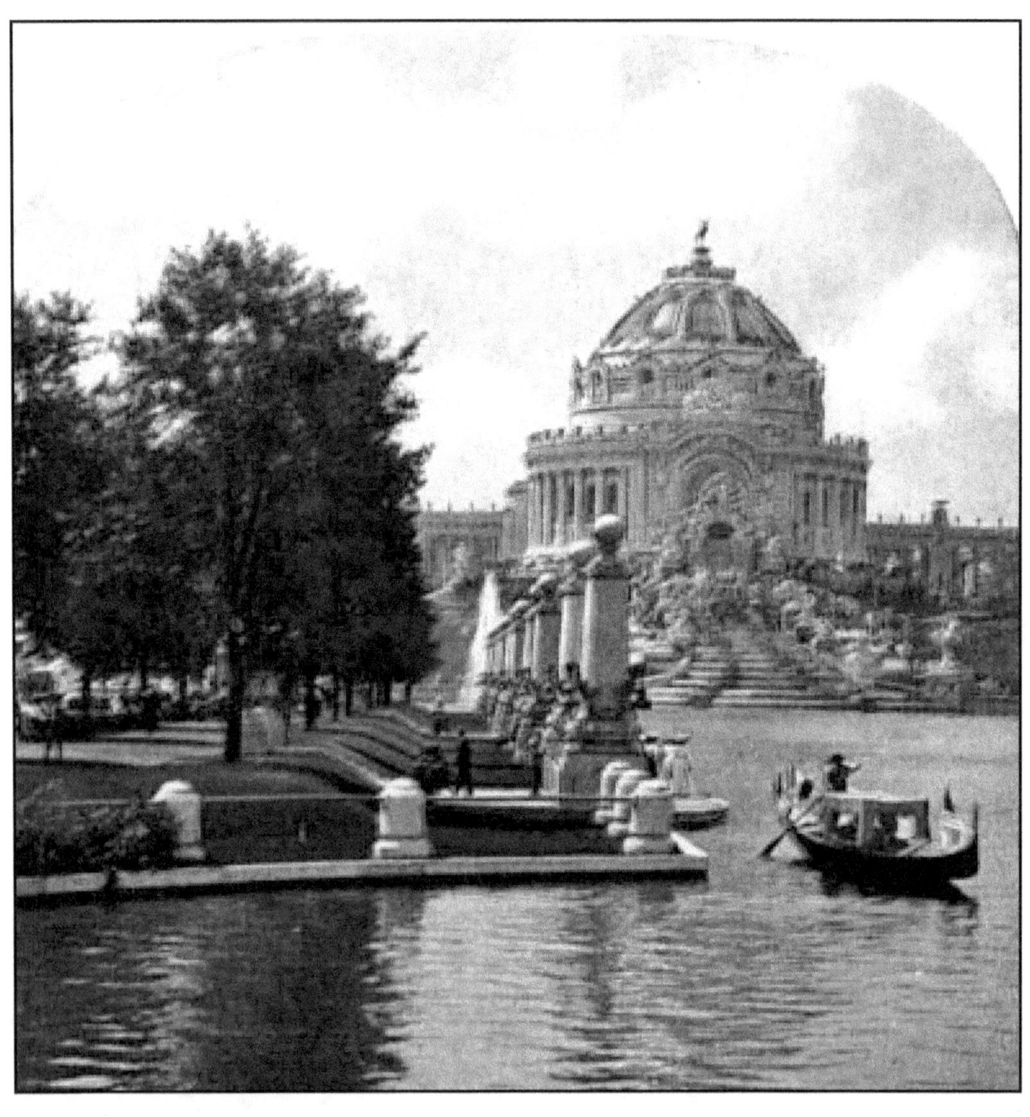

No. 81. Festival Hall from Across Grand Basin

The beautiful Venetian craft that ply the waters of the Exposition lagoons give just the needed touch of romance. A gondola anywhere is a luxurious and a useful boat, but it is never prosaic. Many of these long, dark, graceful boats are in constant use at the Fair... These are real gondoliers from Venice, many of them gifted singers. (*Universal Exposition*)

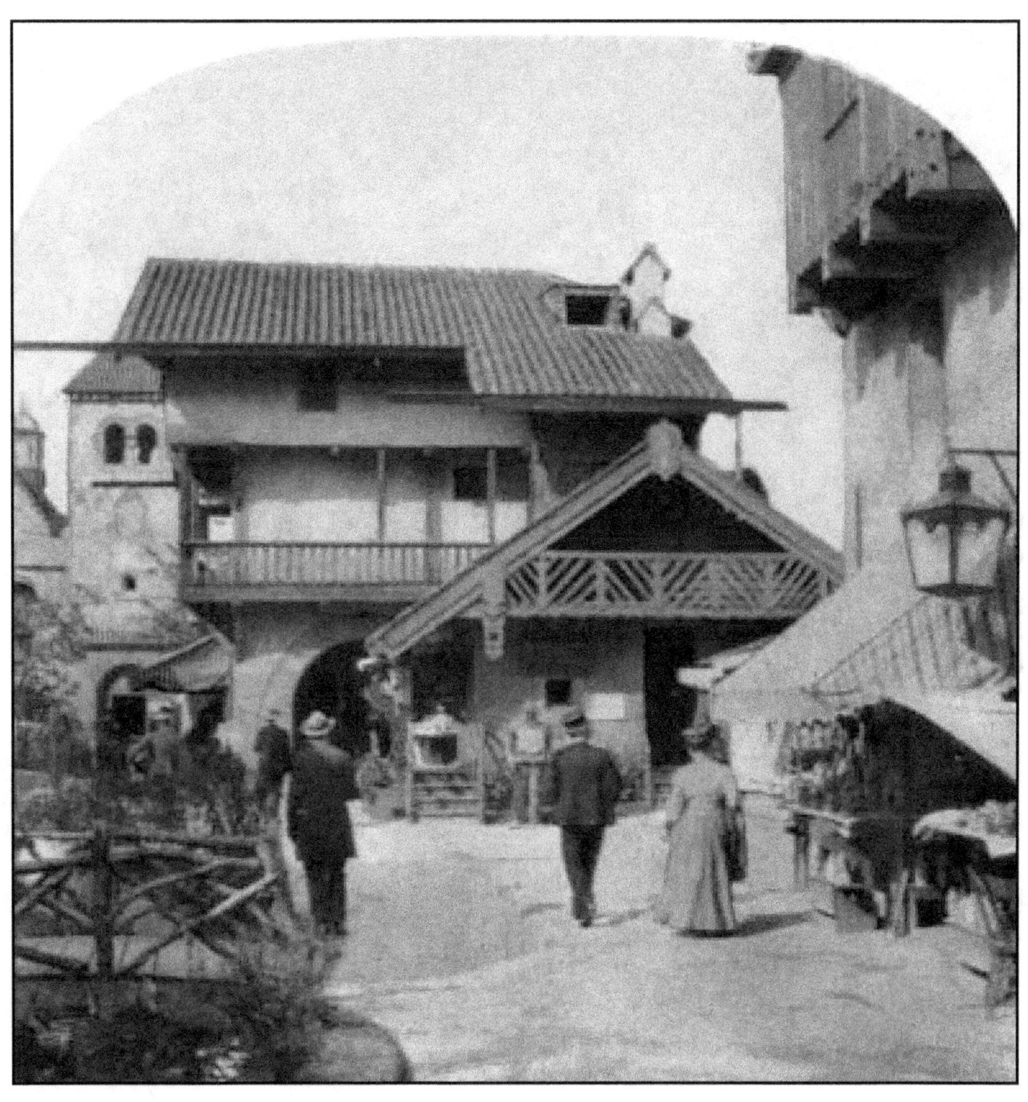

No. 82. Inner Court of the Tyrolean Alps Village

The Tyrolean Alps Village covers a quarter-million square feet and featured restaurants, shops, and beer gardens, along with performances by native singers. The choruses, twelve or fourteen voices strong, have existed many years, and their leaders possess large chains of medals and jewelry presented to them and to former leaders by all the crowned heads of Europe during the last fifty years. *(St. Louis World's Fair)*

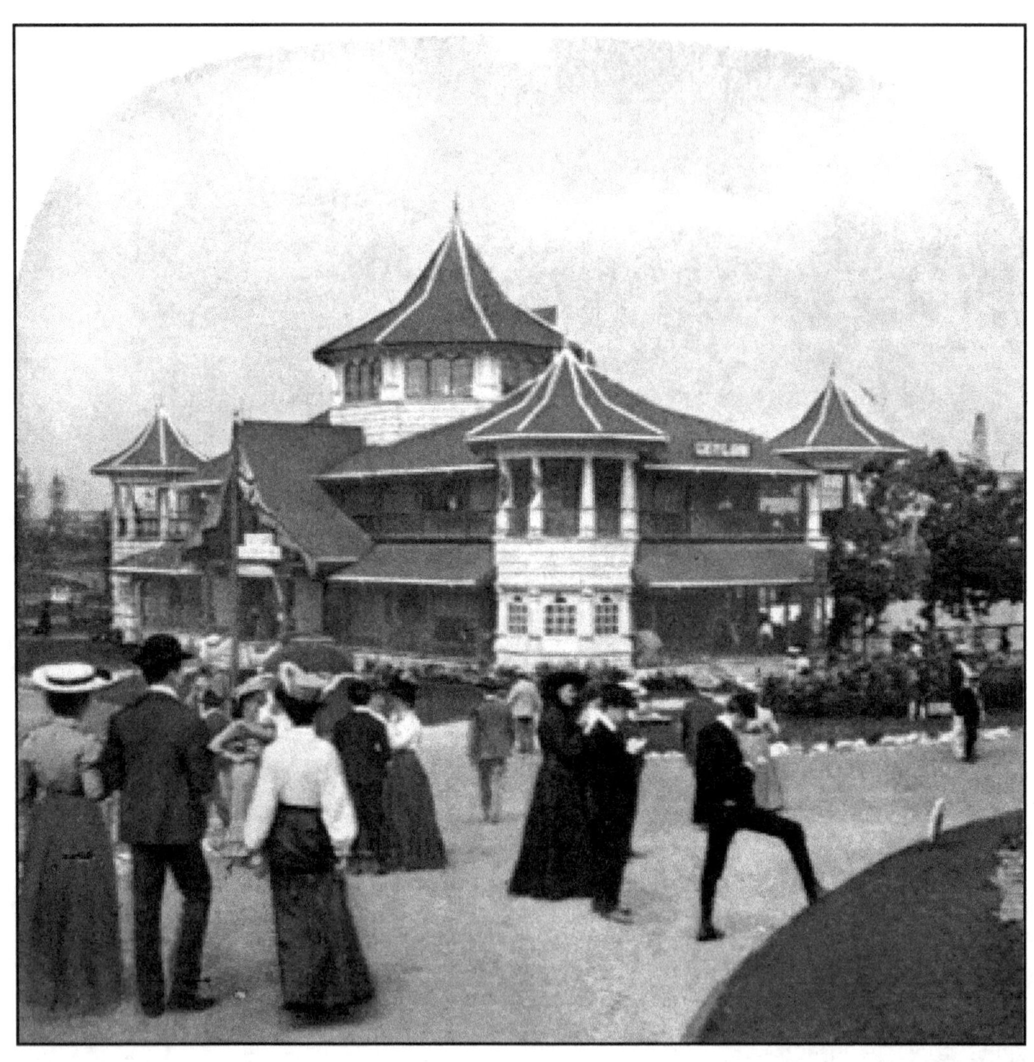

No. 83. Ceylon's National Pavilion

Ceylon's national pavilion recreated the Temple of the Tooth, at Kandy, one of the famous Buddhist temples. There is a full set of furniture made from porcupine quills. Dainty tables, inlaid, and showing the wealth of Ceylon's timber resources are plentifully scattered about. There are relics recovered from ruins that existed as long as 300 years B.C. *(St. Louis World's Fair)*

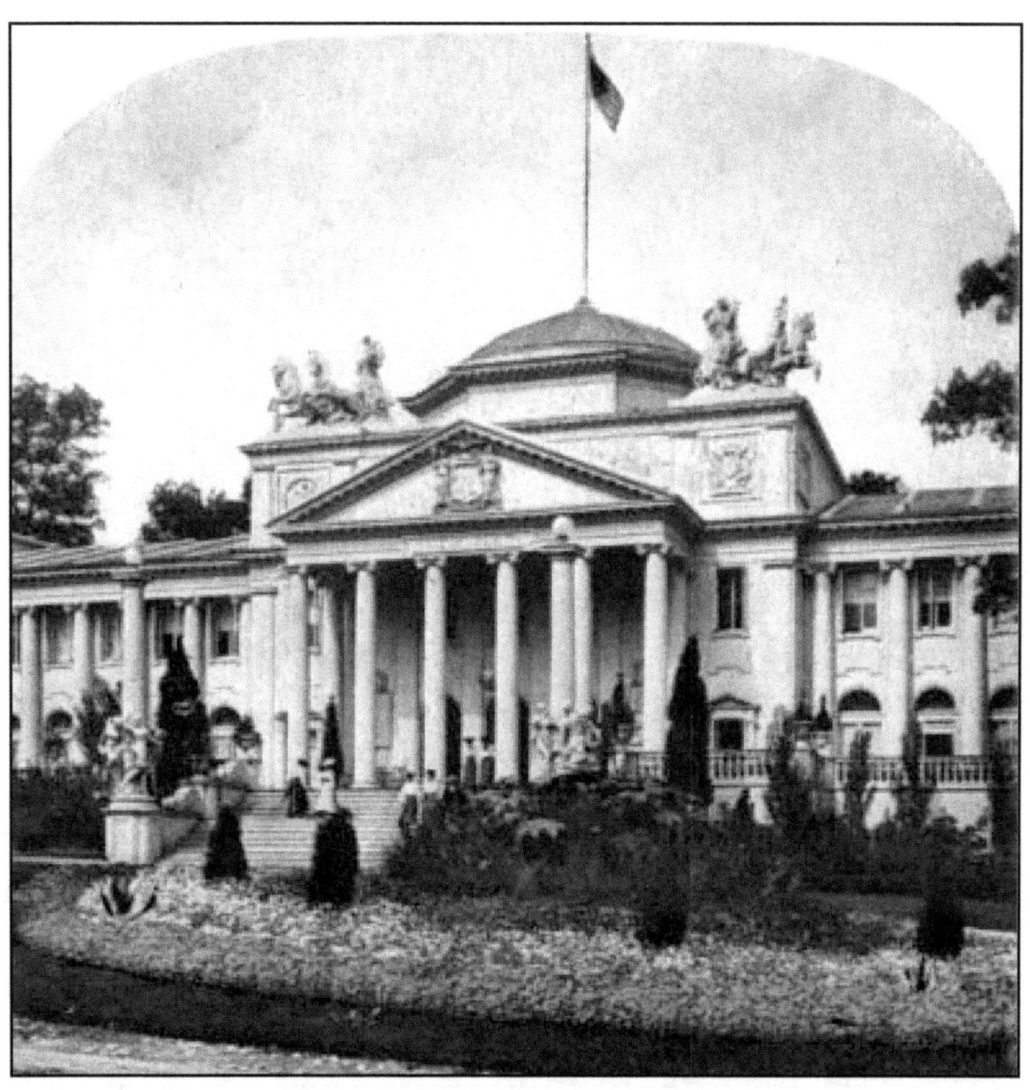

No. 84. The New York State Building

The Empire State had built for the use of its Commissioners a magnificent structure in the Colonial style. At the corners of the square central portion, surmounted by a flat dome, stood the colossal groups of Roman triumphal chariots, counterbalanced by the groups, "Progress of Art" and "Progress of Commerce," on pedestals flanking the broad flight of steps leading up to the portal. The building was 300 feet long and cost $85,000. One wing was used as a banquet hall. In the basement an electric kitchen was provided. *(original 1904 caption)*

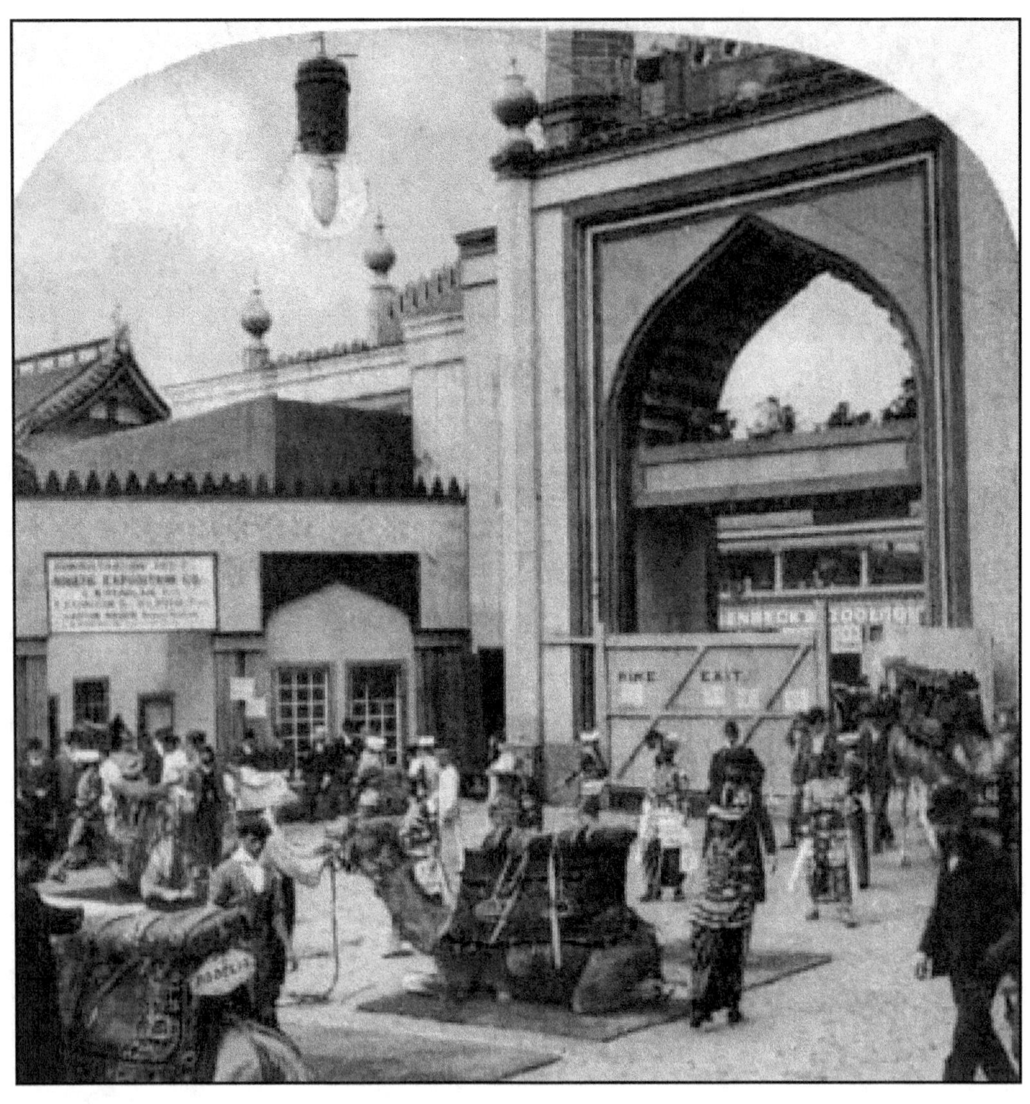

No. 85. In the Main Court of "Asia," on the Pike

The main court of "Mysterious Asia" invites the visitor into the intrigue of the Orient, with camel rides and exhibitions. The three men standing beyond the camel at the center of the photograph appear to be the three magicians from photo 17.

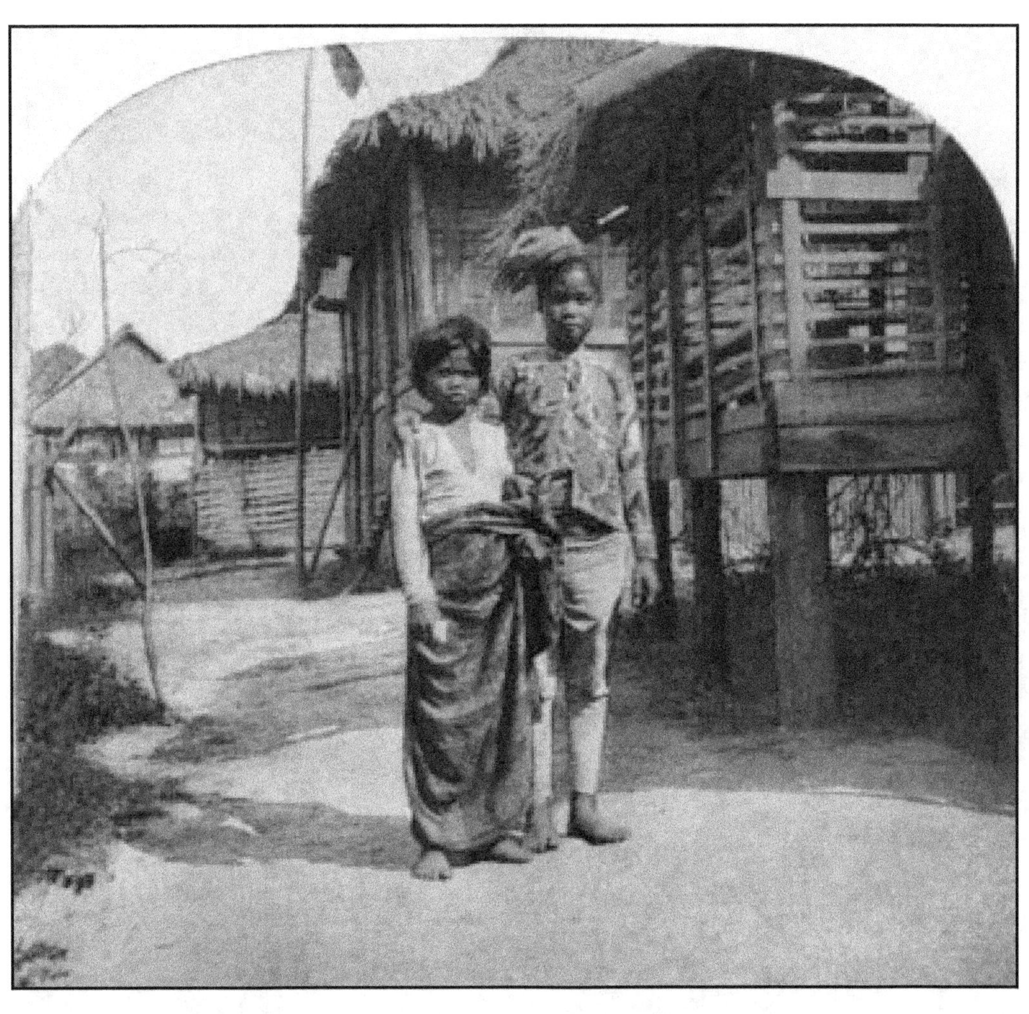

**No. 86. Bagobos Married Couple,
Bagobos, Philippine Village**

A Bagobos couple stands in front of one of the stilt houses built in the PhilippineVillage.

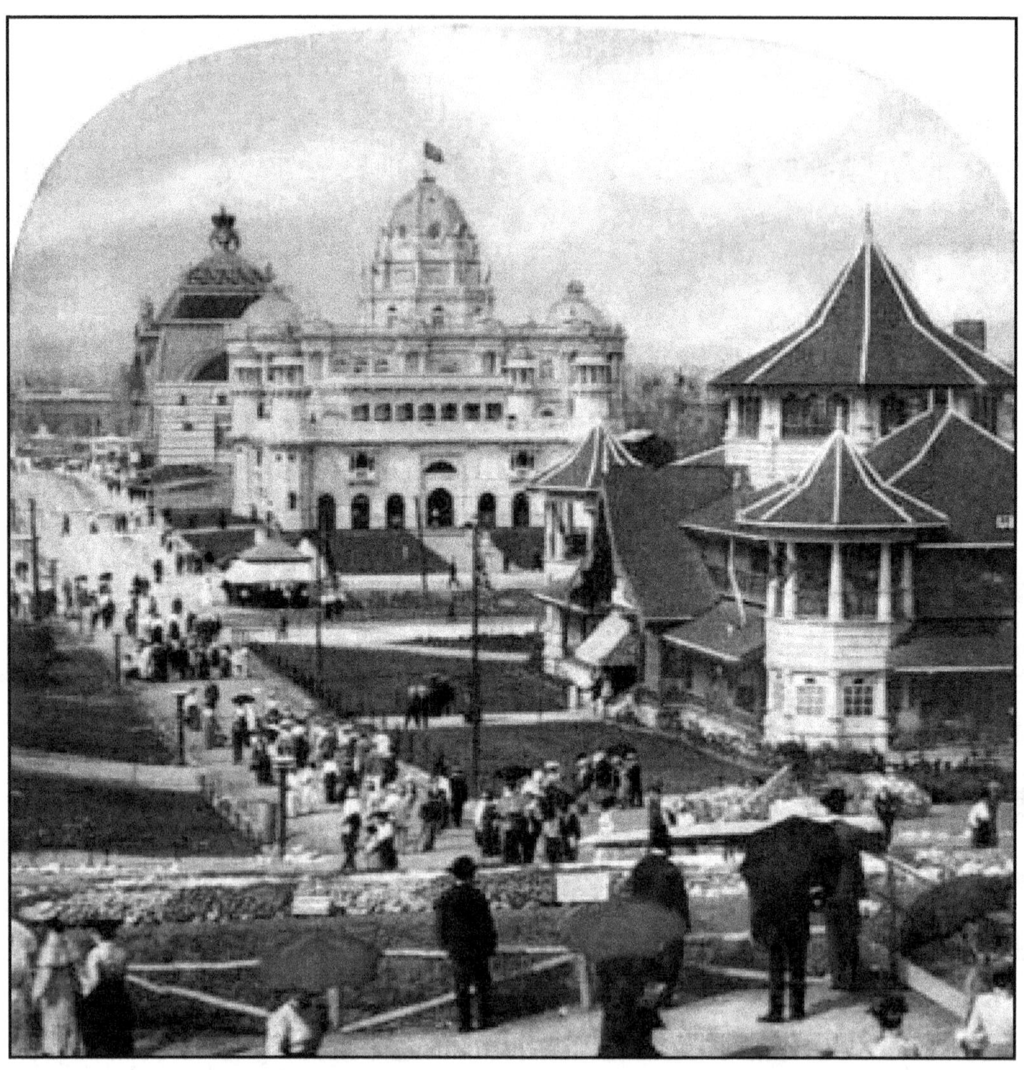

No. 87. Ceylon and Brazilian Buildings from Palace of Agriculture

At the right in the foreground is Ceylon's National Pavilion, beyond which looms the palatial Brazilian Building and further on that of Belgium, of old Flemish design. Great round arched wings met in a square dome 133 feet high and topped with the royal crown of Belgium. The construction was of steel, all prepared at home and shipped ready to be put together. Exhibitions in this building showed the two sides of Belgium life, the Flemish and the French. The furniture, draperies, rugs and laces were of Flemish character and gave a peculiar, highly attractive flavor to the whole. *(original 1904 caption)*

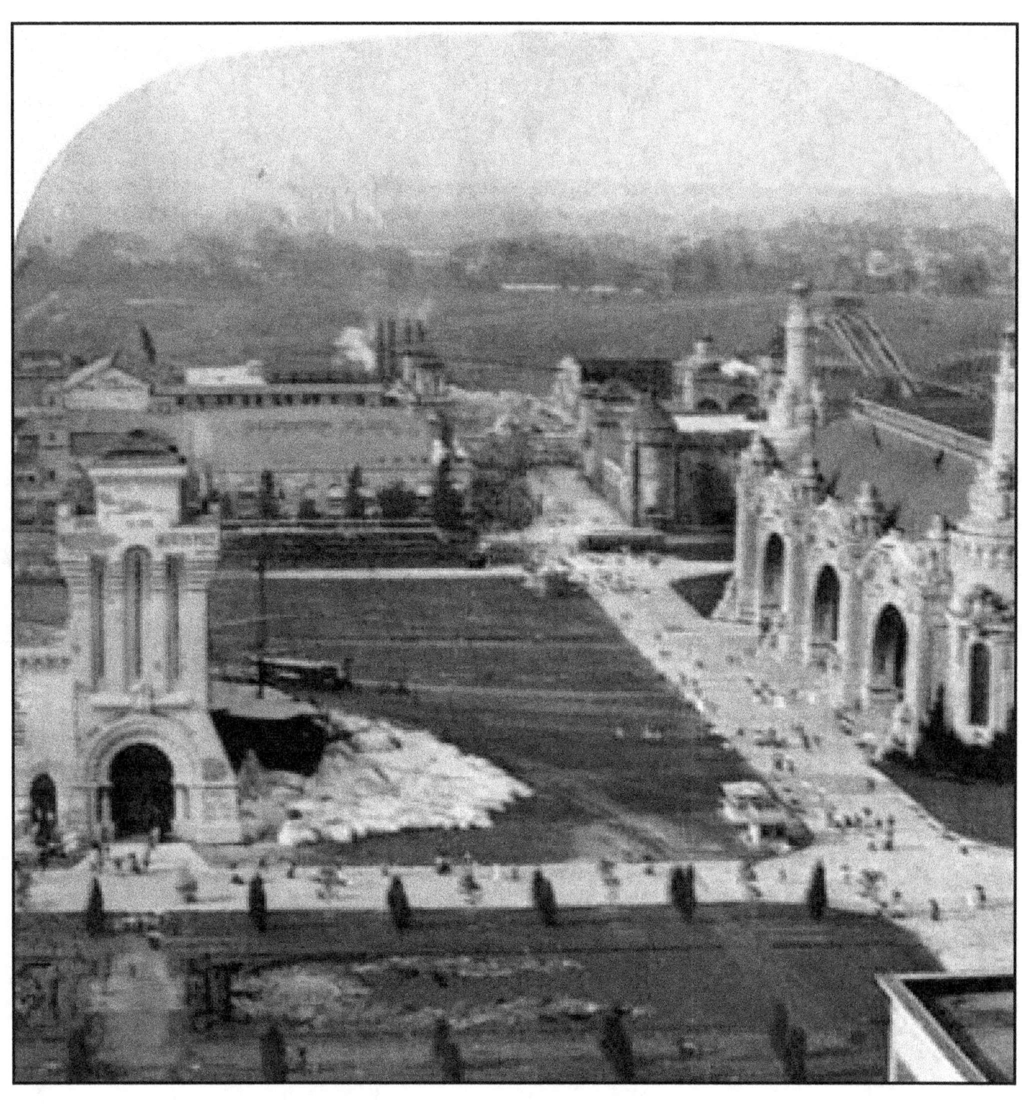

No. 88. Bird's-eye View from Observation Wheel

The Observation Wheel was first used at the World's Fair in Chicago in 1893, where it was called the Ferris Wheel for its builder. The wheel's 36 cars, each with an attendant on board, carried the sightseer 235 feet up in the air, making four revolutions each hour with a magnificent view over the entire exposition grounds. The wheel contained 4,200 tons of metal and the axle alone weighed 70 tons. *(St. Louis World's Fair)*

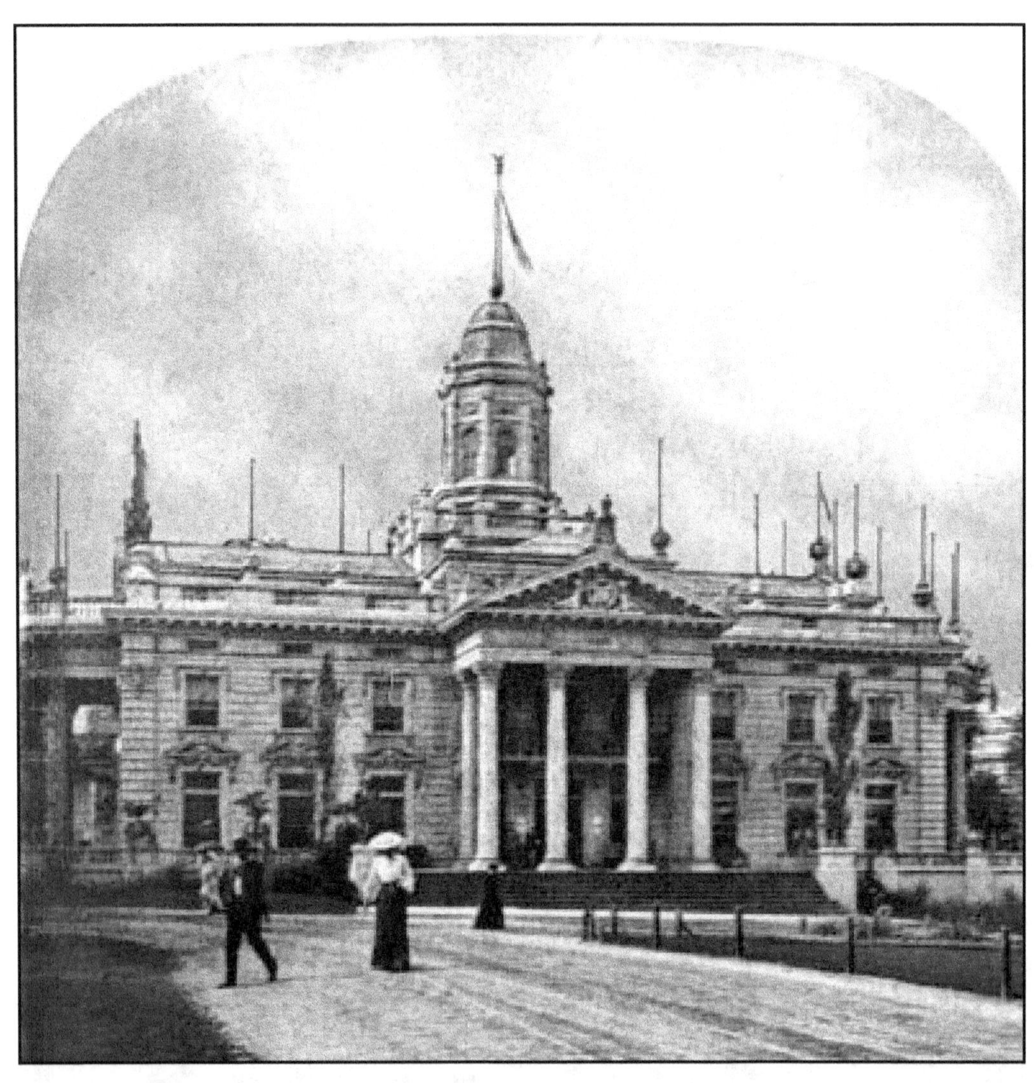

No. 89. The Iowa State Building

Iowa was the first state to erect a building at the World's Fair and chose one of the most commanding sites. It is a very large and commodious building, almost continually thronged with Iowa's people and their friends. A magnificent pipe organ is a feature of this building and well attended organ concerts are given daily. (*Universal Exposition*)

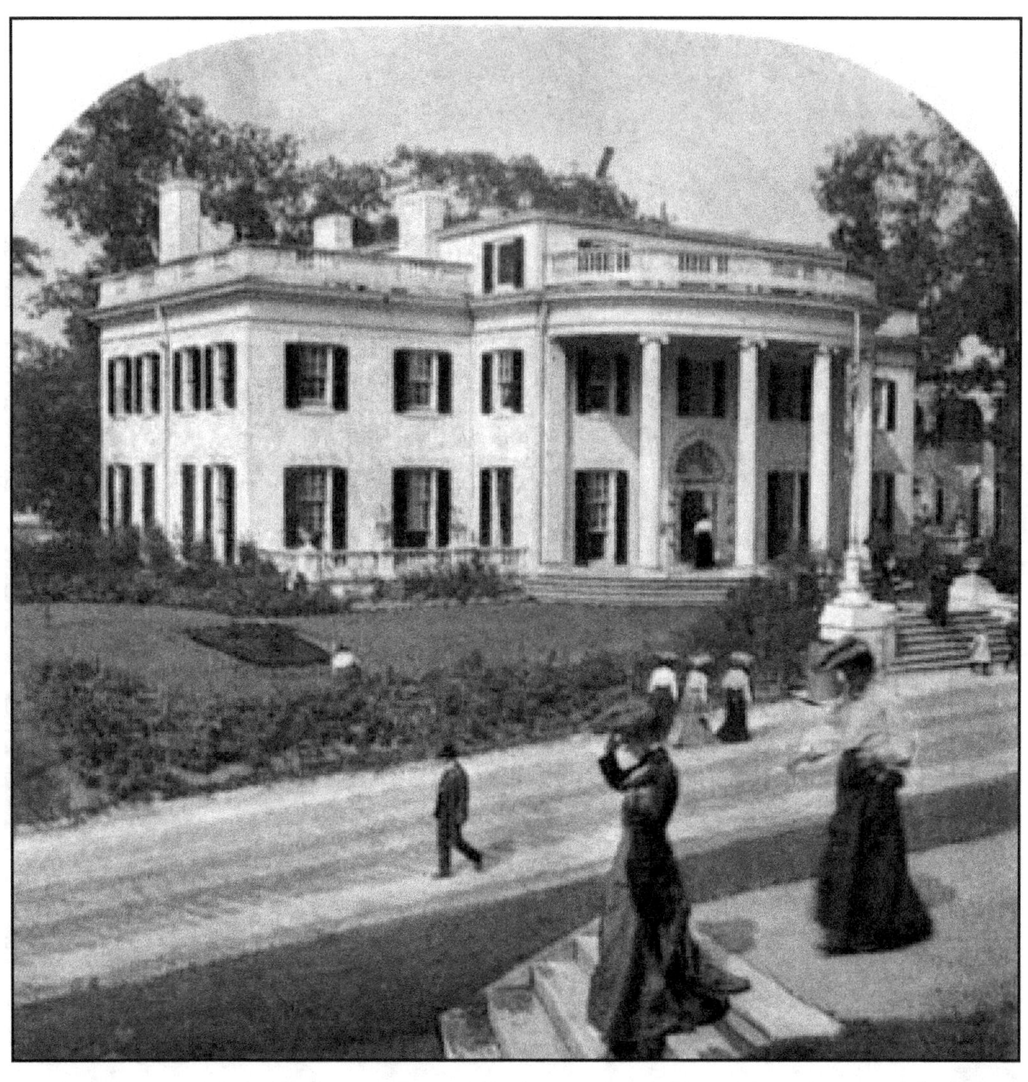

No. 90. The Connecticut State Building

The Connecticut Building represented an old-fashioned luxurious home of New England a century ago. Old wood work was taken from the home of the poet Mrs. Sigourney, at Hartford and the Slater house in Norwich, which were recently torn down, and the material used in the construction of this gilding, which cost $40,000. (*Universal Exposition*)

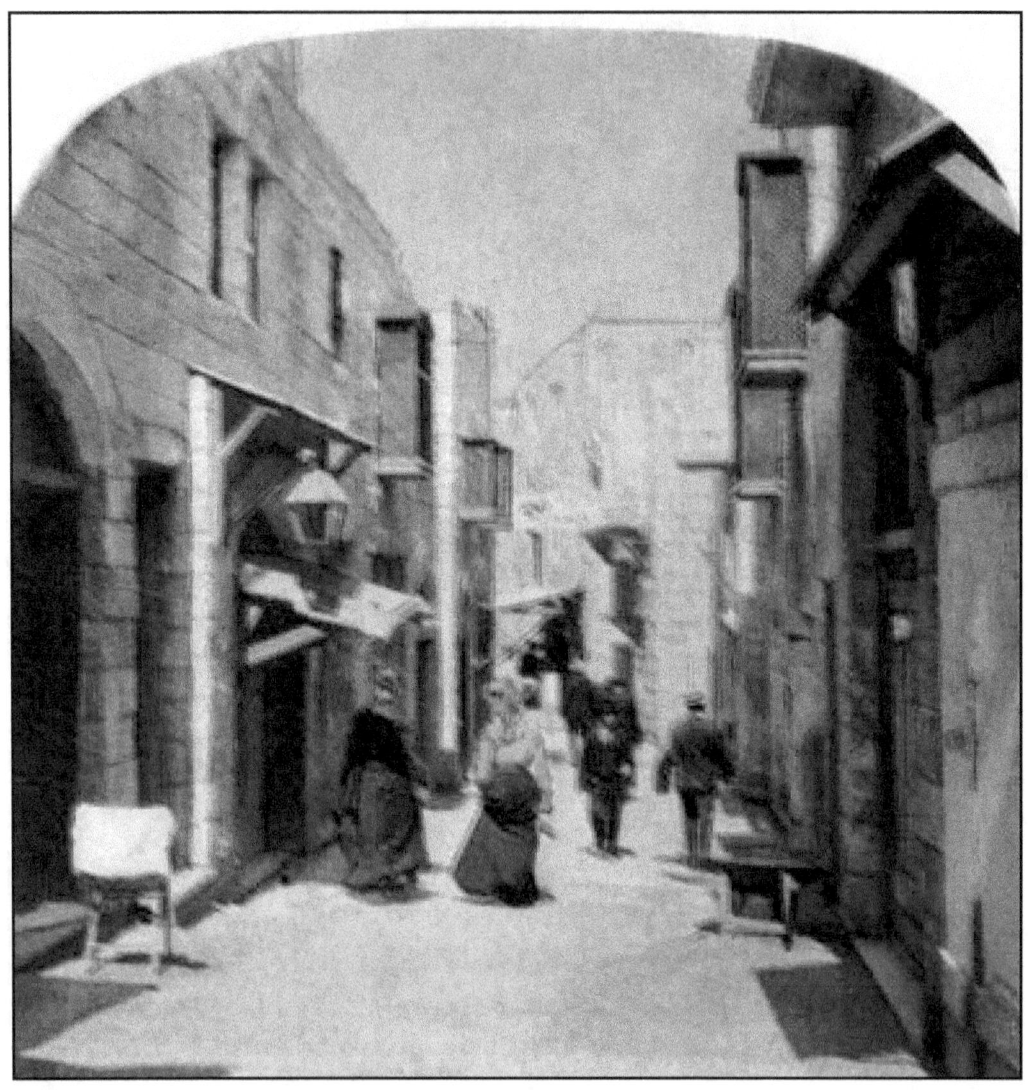

No. 91. Moorish Street in "City of Jerusalem"

When David became king over all Israel (II Sam. v. 1 sqq.), he discerned the advantages of Jerusalem and determined to make it his capital. The exact location of David's palace has not been determined. Solomon built his palace north of David's house, and still further north, on the highest elevation, the courts and buildings of the temple. The Jerusalem of the present day, with its commercial houses, modern hotels, stores and institutions, has little in common with the city of the past. The town is laid out irregularly, and the streets are narrow, tortuous and dirty. *(original 1904 caption)*

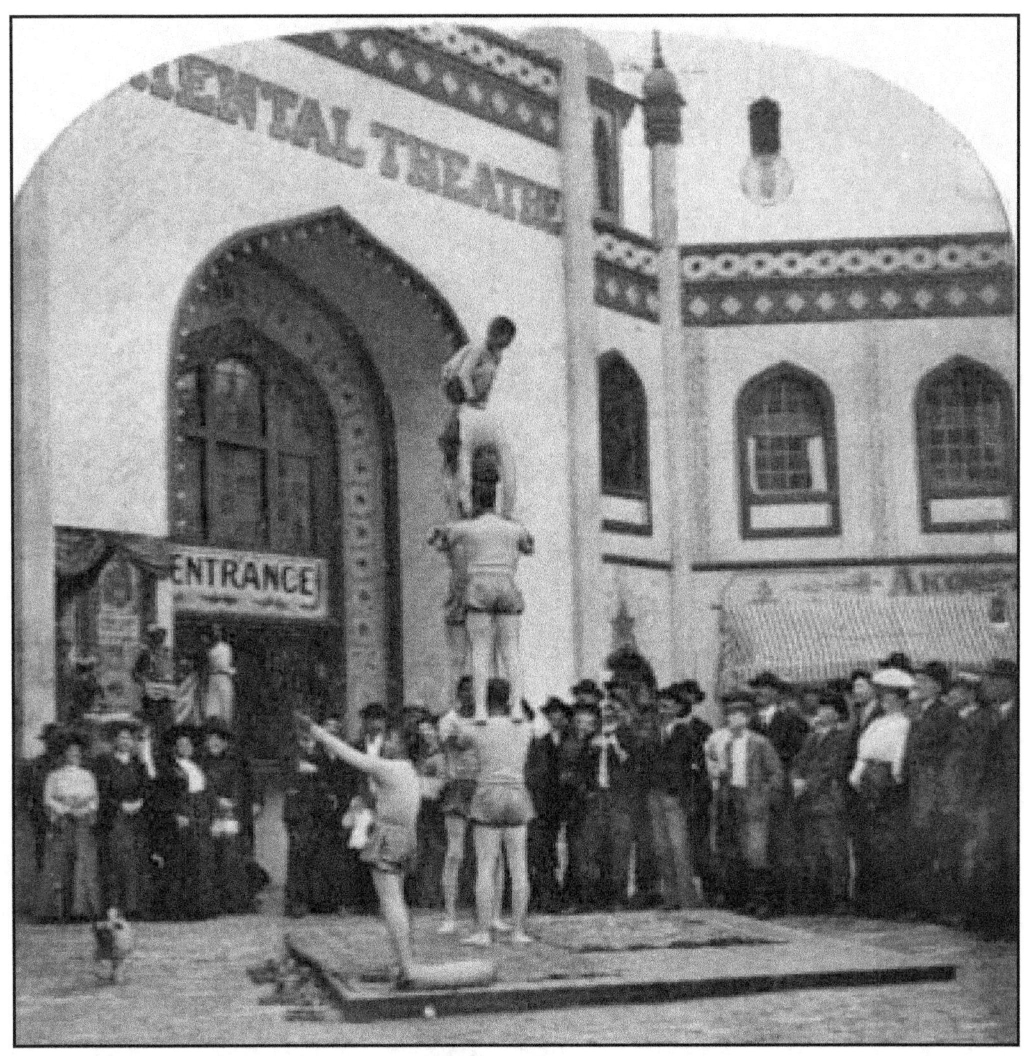

No. 92. Oriental Acrobats in the Streets of "Asia," on the Pike

While the performers build human pyramids with their agile frames, and tumble them down in thrilling maneuvers, an orchestra of queer-sounding instruments gives verve and rhythm to the movements of the actors. Tumbling and contorting are the chief features of the performance, and in those arts the Hindu people claim to have no superiors. As a climax for the display of strength and agility one of the giants mounts upon his shoulders all of the other acrobats and spins his human burden around in a dizzy whirl, dispersing the actors one by one, each alighting upon his feet. *(St. Louis World's Fair)*

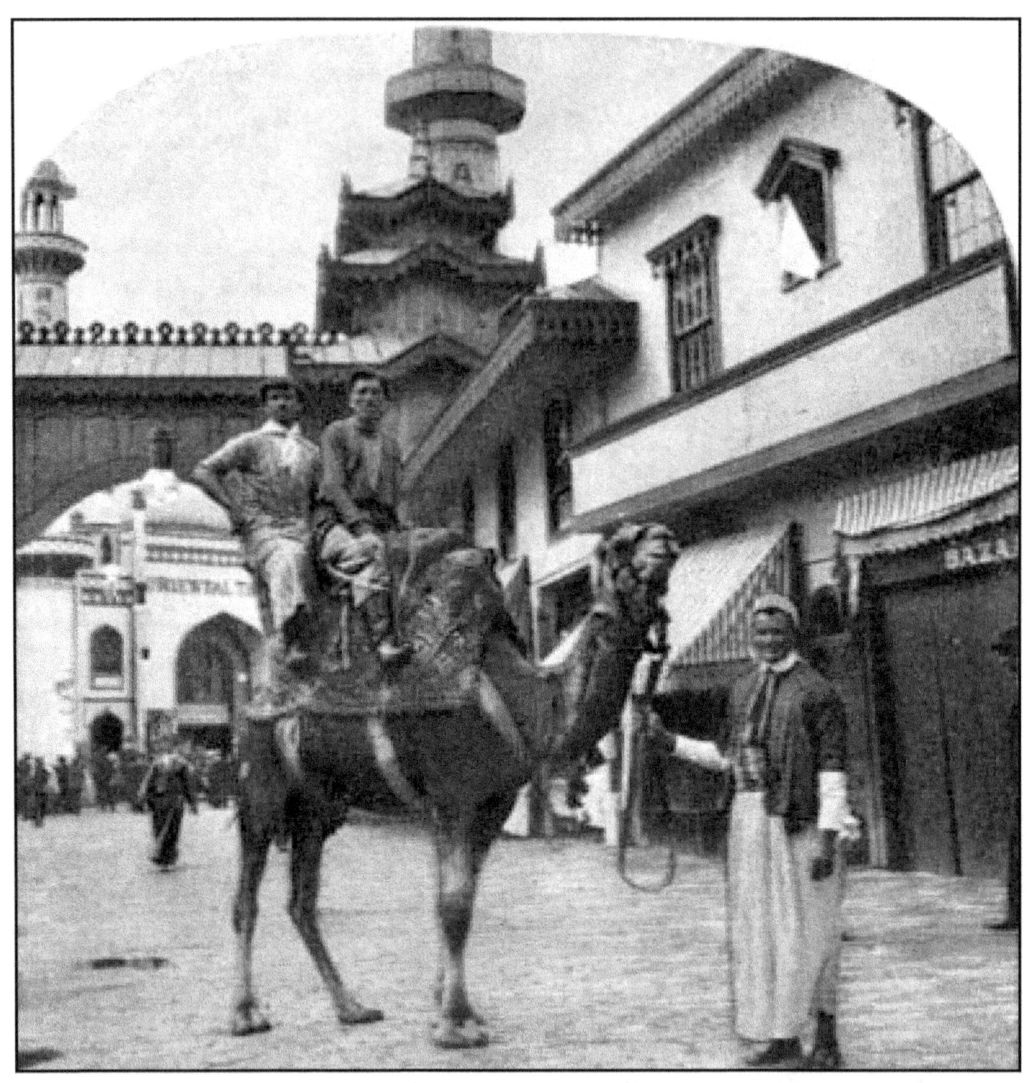

No. 93. Camel and Driver in "Asia," on the Pike

About the year 1857 the United States Government spent much money and energy to acclimatize the camel for the army transport service in the arid southwestern regions, hut the results were not satisfactory. The camel is singularly adapted to subsist in the desert by its structural peculiarities and by its ability to bite off and consume the tough, thorny vegetation, and to endure the burning heat and flying sand. The great wastes south and east of the Mediterranean, Caspian and Black Seas could never have been colonized but for the assistance of this ungainly creature. *(original 1904 caption)*

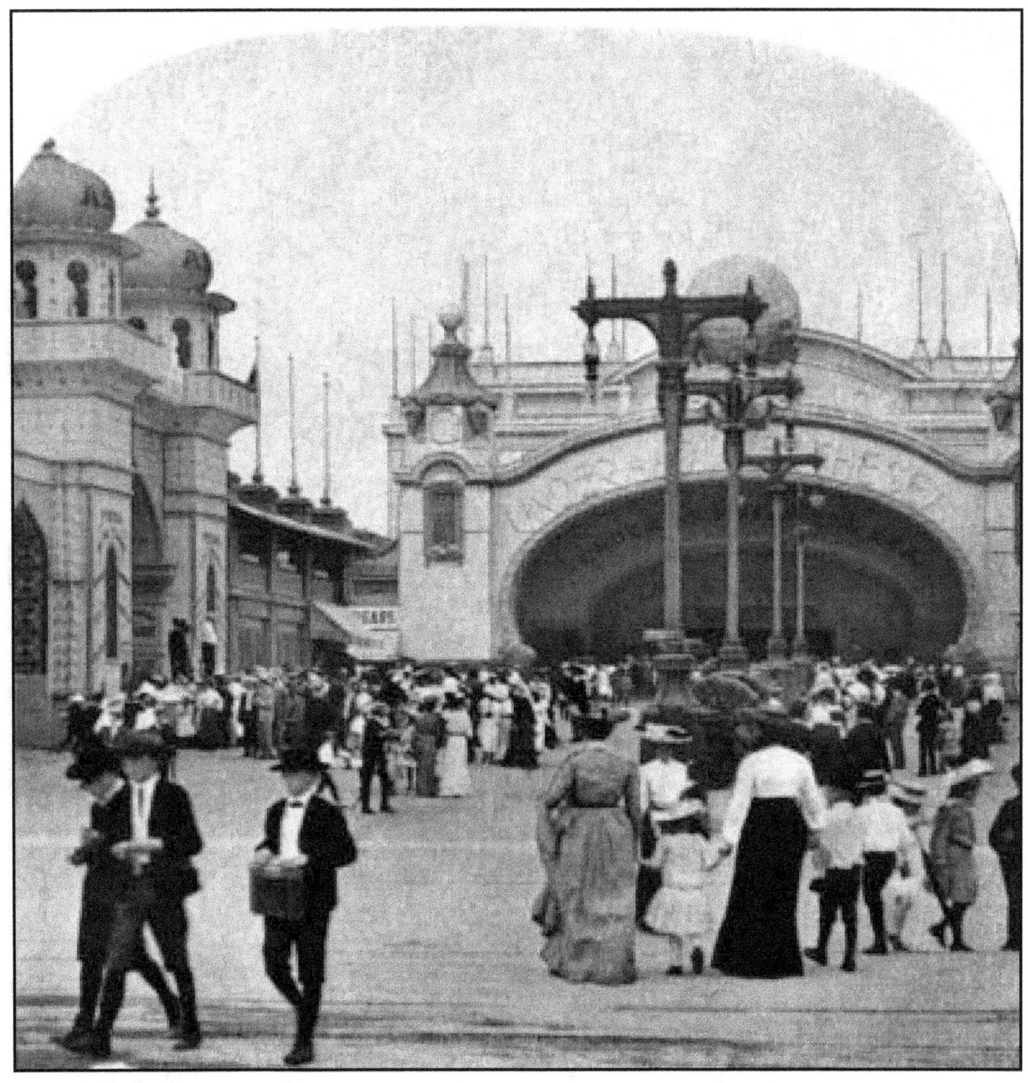

No. 94. Entrance to the "Pike" from Plaza St. Louis

"Under and Over the Sea", shown in the background here, is a Pike illusion that gives a vivid idea of two of our modern inventions, the submarine boat and the airship. One sees the hull of the boat, awash in real water... electric devices cause a constantly changing view of the deep sea and its denizens to glide past... at last Paris is reached, and everybody aboard steps out into the large basket of the airship... in mid-ocean a terrific storm is weathered. The city of St. Louis is seen, and finally the Exposition itself lies before the traveler who descends to the familiar Pike. *(St. Louis World's Fair)*

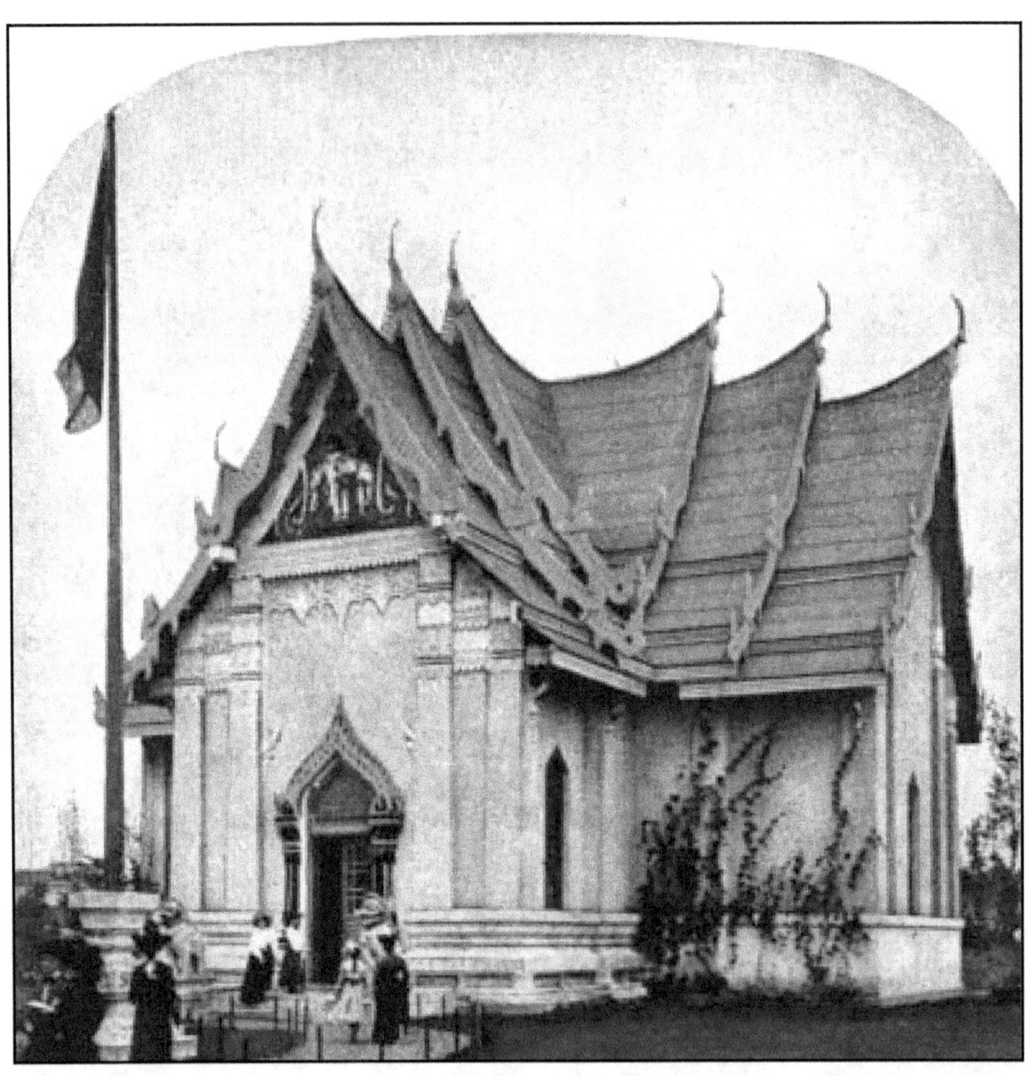

No. 95. Ben Chama Temple, the Siamese Pavilion

The Siamese Pavilion was a faithful representation of the new Ben Chama Temple at Bangkok. The ground plan, seventy feet each way, had the form of a cross, and the hall inside was sixty feet high. The symbols of Buddhism, the lotus flower and the flame, both emblematic of purity, were in evidence everywhere in the inner and outer decorations. Specimens of Siamese art industries, such as delicate work in hammered brass, embroideries, musical instruments, richly worked elephant saddles and boxes inlaid with mother-of-pearl, filled the hall, the windows of which consisted in handsome transparencies depicting Siamese temples. *(original 1904 caption)*

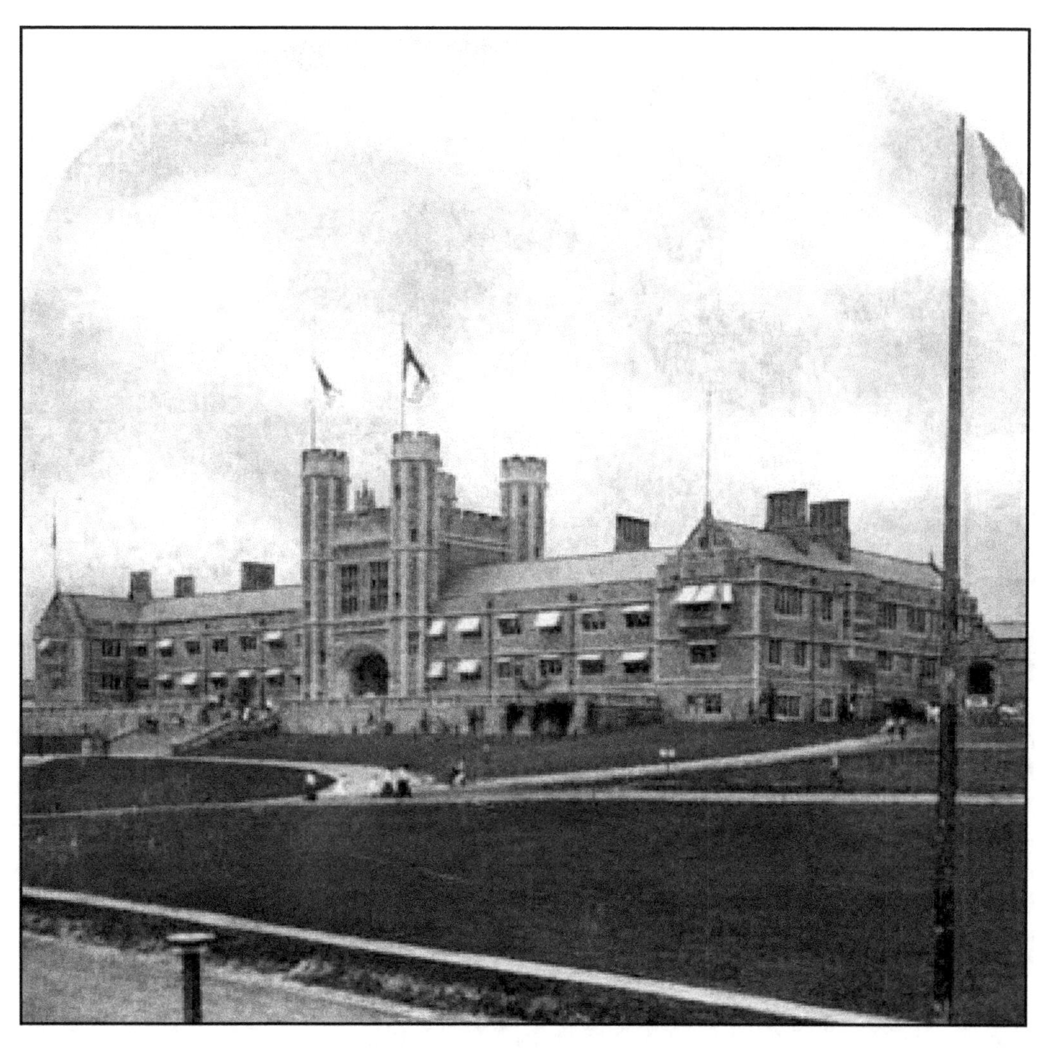

No. 96. The Administration Building

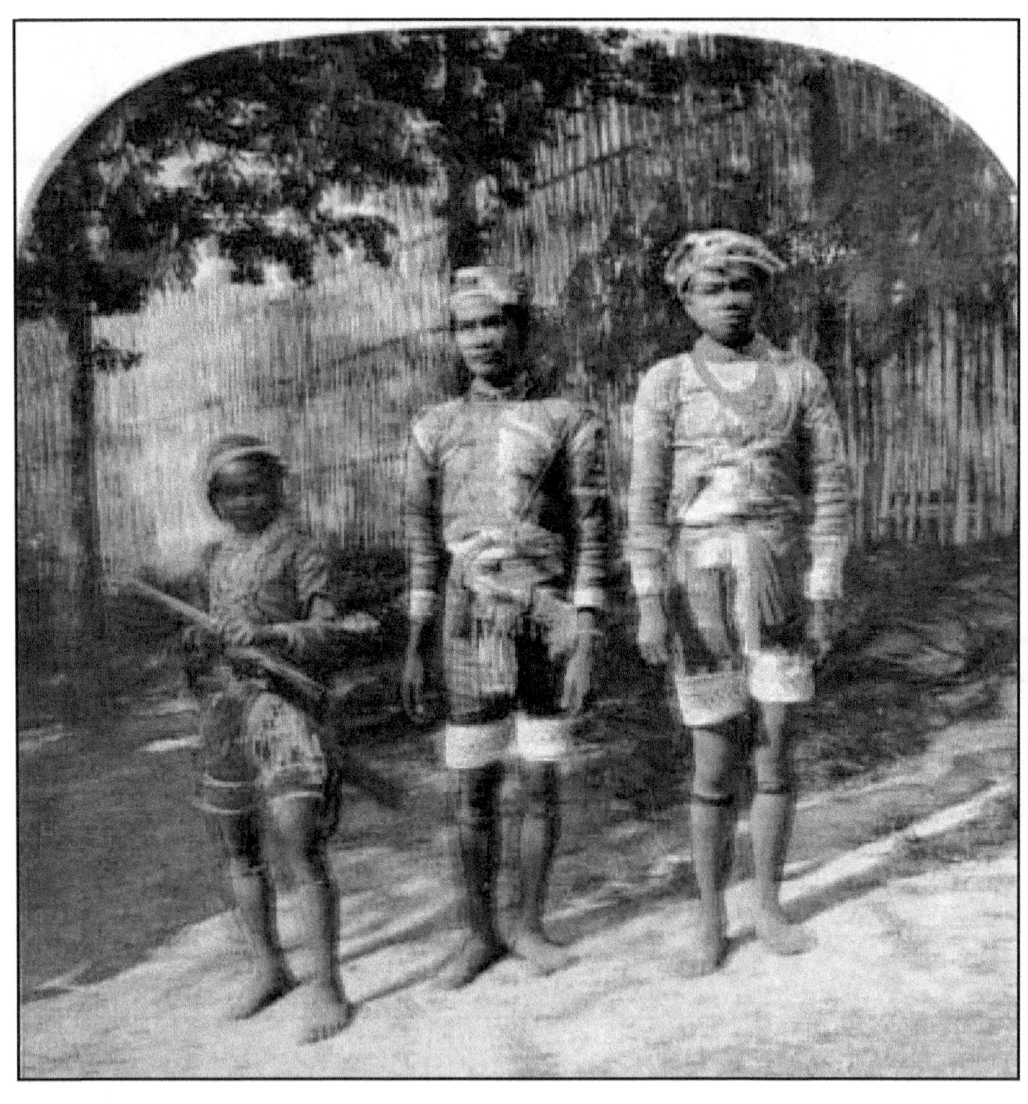

No. 97. Members Bagabos Tribe, Philippine Village

Bagabos musicians and dancers entertain visitors all during the day. *(St. Louis World's Fair)*

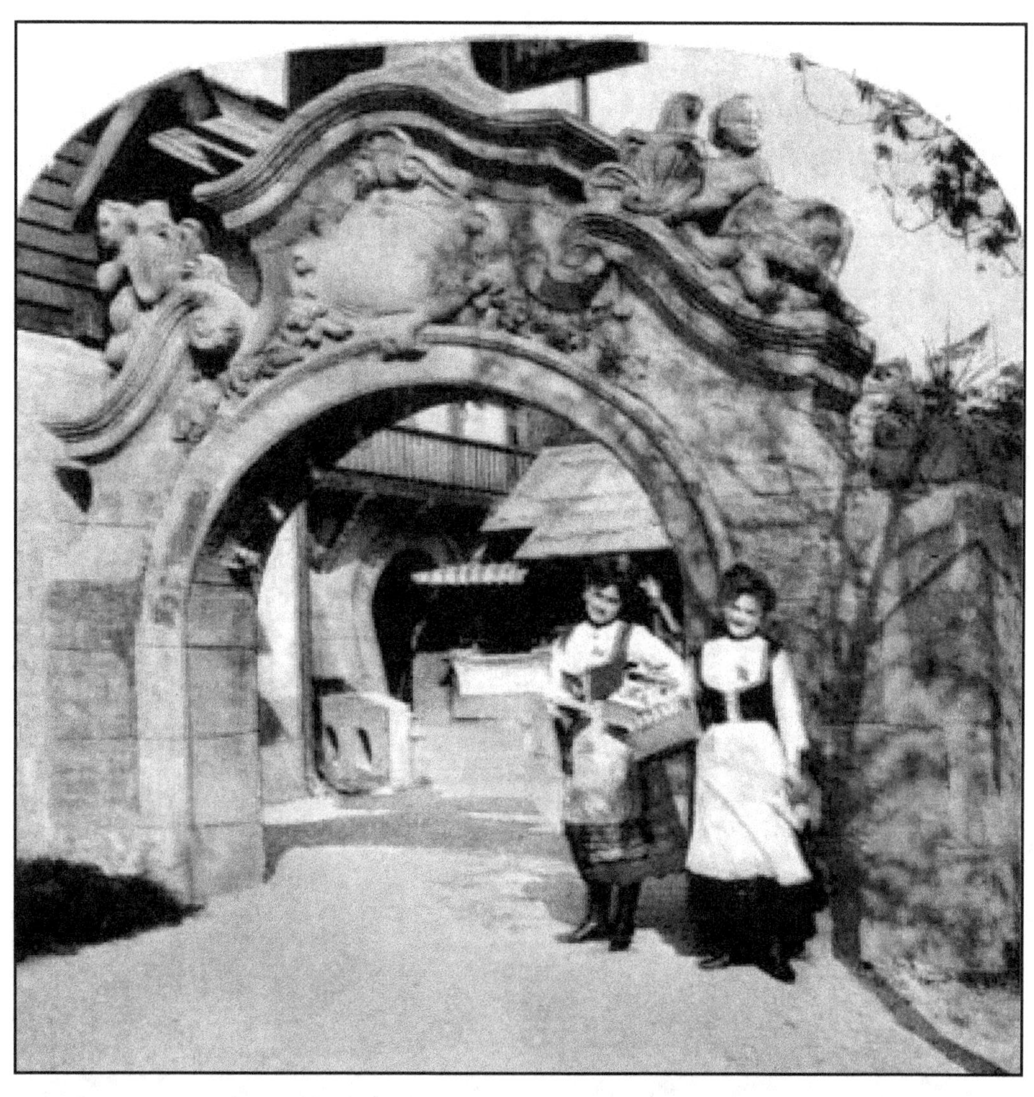

NO. 98. GATEWAY TO TYROLEAN ALPS VILLAGE

The western end of the Pike is dominated by the "Tyrolean Alps," a complex of German-style restaurants, shops, and outdoor beer gardens set against an immense painted backdrop of mountains. Beyond the gate is a village full of attractions. *(St. Louis World's Fair)*

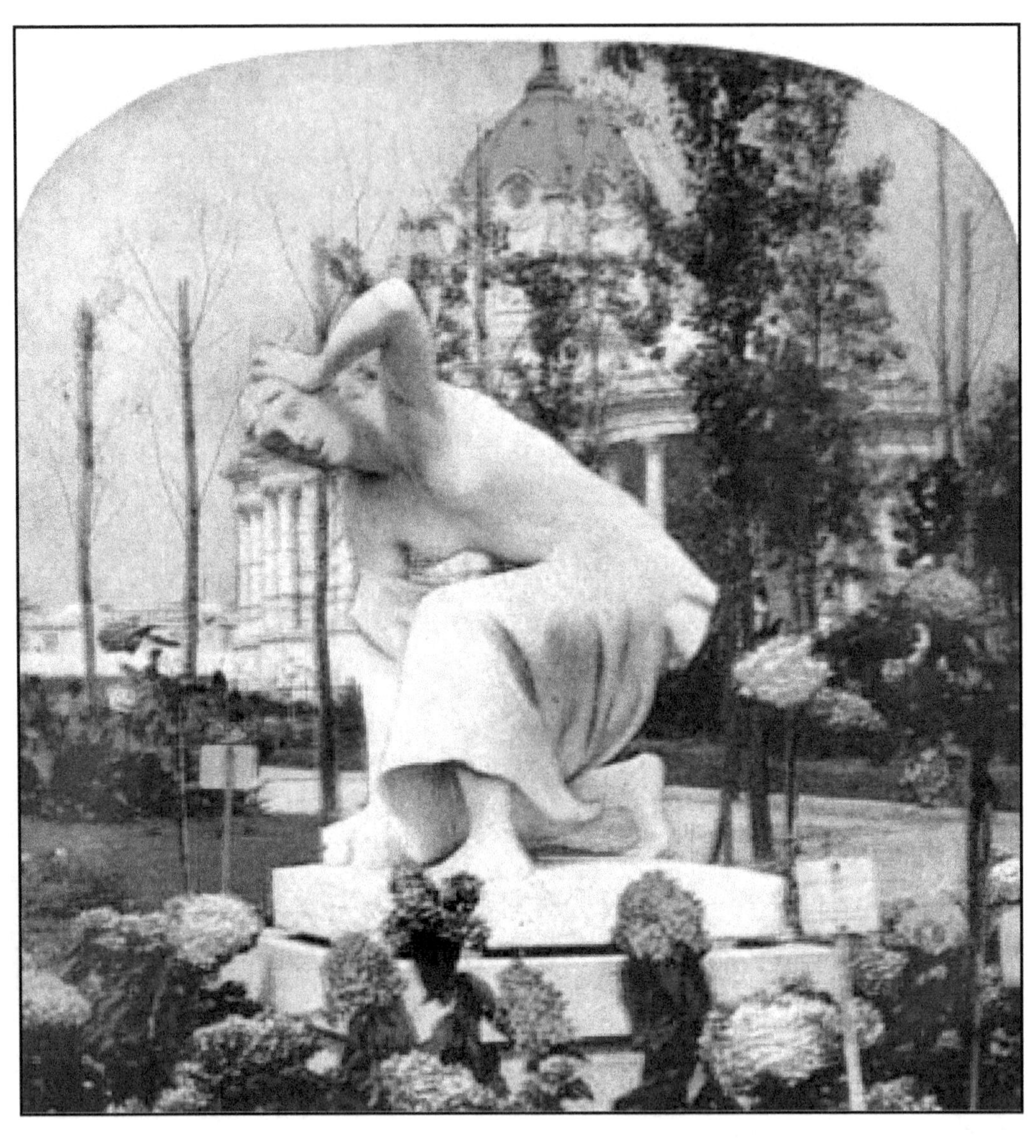

No. 99. Statue of Marguerite, in the French Gardens

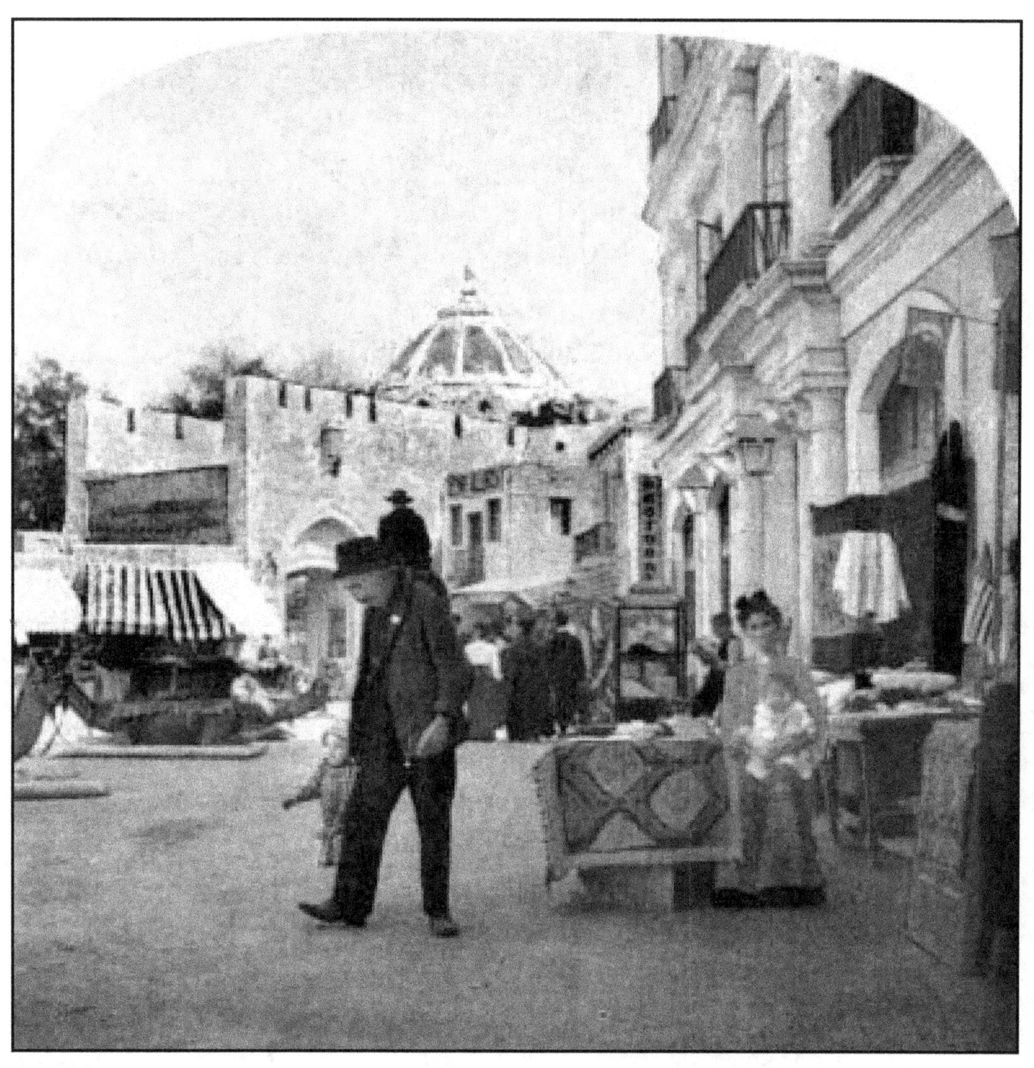

No. 100. David Street, in the "City of Jerusalem"

The south end of the Jerusalem concession presents a strange combination of the old and the new. At the west side of David Street are two hotels, reproductions of those that were built in the Holy City for the benefit of European and American tourists. In front of the Grand New Hotel is a camel stand. Here a long line of camels is always waiting for passengers who are looking for a novel sensation. Down a rather steep stairway from the street is the Courtyard of David, in front of the reproduction of the old synagogue. *(St. Louis World's Fair)*

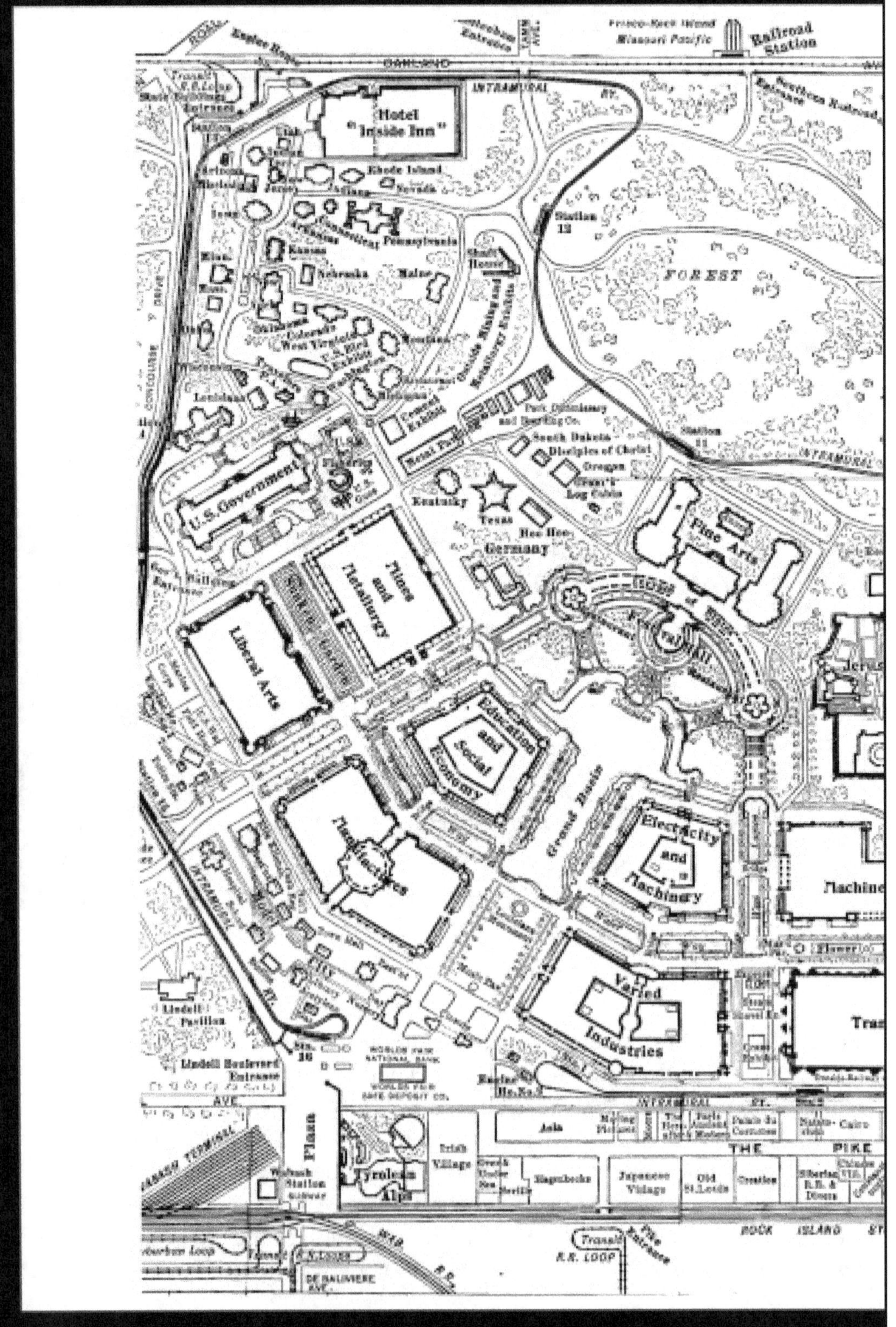

Missouri Pacific
Railroad Station
OAKLAND
INTRAMURAL RY.
Hotel "Inside Inn"
Rhode Island
Nevada
Indiana
Connecticut
Pennsylvania
Arkansas
Kansas
Nebraska
Maine
Colorado
West Virginia
Louisiana
Station 12
FOREST
Station 11
South Dakota
Disciples of Christ
Oregon
Grant's Log Cabin
U.S. Government
Fisheries
Kentucky
Texas
Hoo Hoo
Germany
Fine Arts
Festival Hall
Mines and Metallurgy
Liberal Arts
Education and Social Economy
Manufactures
Grand Basin
Electricity and Machinery
Machine
Varied Industries
Lindell Pavilion
Lindell Boulevard Entrance
WORLDS FAIR NATIONAL BANK
WORLDS FAIR SAFE DEPOSIT CO.
AVE
INTRAMURAL ST.
Plaza
Wabash Station
Tyrolean Alps
Irish Village
Asia
Cairo
THE PIKE
Hagenbecks
Japanese Village
Old St. Louis
Creation
ROCK ISLAND
R.R. LOOP
DE BALIVIERE AVE.

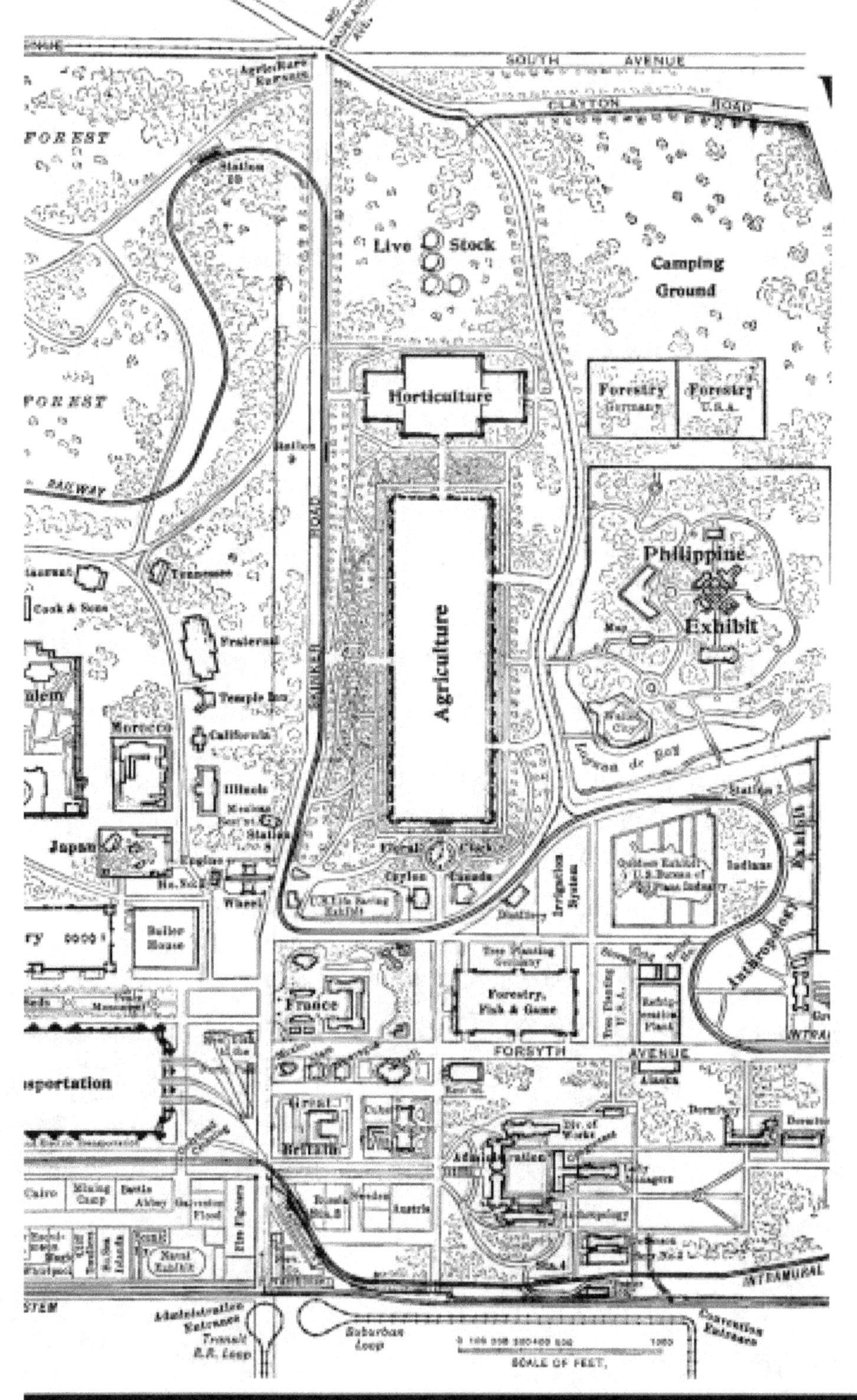

SOUTH AVENUE
CLAYTON ROAD
FOREST
FOREST
Station 10
Live Stock
Camping Ground
Horticulture
Forestry Germany
Forestry U.S.A.
Station 9
RAILWAY
Philippine Exhibit
Agriculture
Tennessee
Cook & Sons
Temple Inn
Morocco
California
Illinois
Japan
Station 8
Floral Clock
Ceylon
Canada
Distillery
Irrigation System
Station 2
Indians
Anthropology
Wheel
Boiler House
U.S. Life Saving Exhibit
Tree Planting Company
Forestry, Fish & Game
France
FORSYTH AVENUE
Alaska
Dormitory
Great Britain
Cuba
Div. of Works
Administration
Transportation
Cairo
Mining Camp
Battle Abbey
Galveston Flood
Fire Fighters
Sweden
Austria
Naval Exhibit
INTRAMURAL
Administration Entrance
Transit R.R. Loop
Suburban Loop
SCALE OF FEET.
Convention Entrance

Louisiana Purchase Exhibition Map

The map on the preceding two pages shows the fairgrounds in 1904. Unlike most maps, this one is laid out with north at the bottom of the page. Because the main entrances to the fair were on the northern or Lindell Boulevard side of the fairgrounds, this alignment made the map right side up for visitors as they entered the gates and got their first glimpses of the fair's wonders.

About the Authors

Michael W. Lemberger and Leigh Michaels have been fans of the St. Louis World's Fair since they honeymooned in Forest Park, the site of the fair. They are also the authors of a full color book about the fair, 1904 St. Louis World's Fair.

Michael W. Lemberger is a professional photographer, artist and historian. He received more than a hundred national, regional and state awards in photography, and creates intricate pen and ink drawings. His collection of historic photographs has been called the most extensive and best documented privately-held photo collection in existence. www.mlemberger.com.

Leigh Michaels is the author of more than 100 books, including historical romance novels, contemporary romance novels, local history, and non-fiction such as *On Writing Romance*. More than 35 million copies of her books have been printed in 25 languages and 120 countries. She teaches writing online at Gotham Writers Workshop. www.leighmichaels.com.

For more information about these and other PBL Limited books, visit www.pbllimited.com.

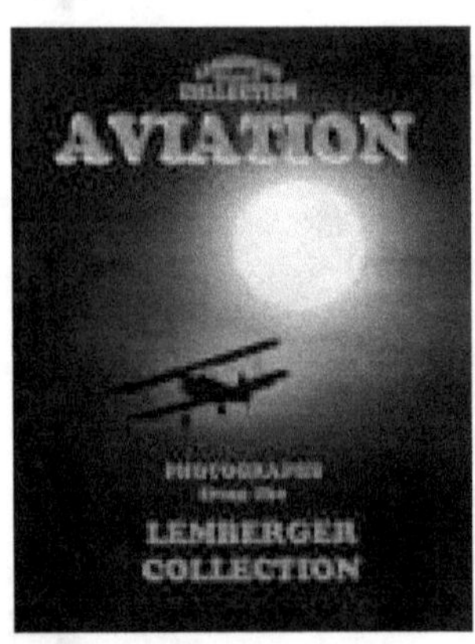

VISIT THE FAIR

IN FULL COLOR

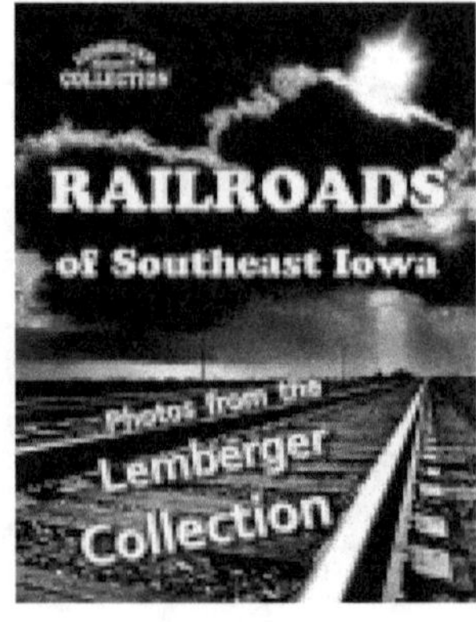

www.ingramcontent.com/pod-product-compliance
Lightning Source LLC
LaVergne TN
LVHW080311110826
845155LV00023B/115
* 9 7 8 1 8 9 2 6 8 9 1 6 0 *